That Time I Got Rèincarnated as a SLIME

The Ways of the Monster Nation

4

Sho Okagiri Original Story: **FUSE** Character Design: **Mitz Vah**

The Story So Far

After being asked to write a guidebook for Tempest, rabbitfolk girl Framea has spent every day taking in the food, sights, and events the land has to offer. What's more, at the suggestion of Tempest leader Rimuru, she's recently enrolled at the nation's main academy to get a taste of student life. But everything changes when a statue of Rimuru is stolen from the school workshop, leading the students to wonder...who could the culprit be? Crack detective Ramiris is on the case, and she won't quit until she finds out!

Contents

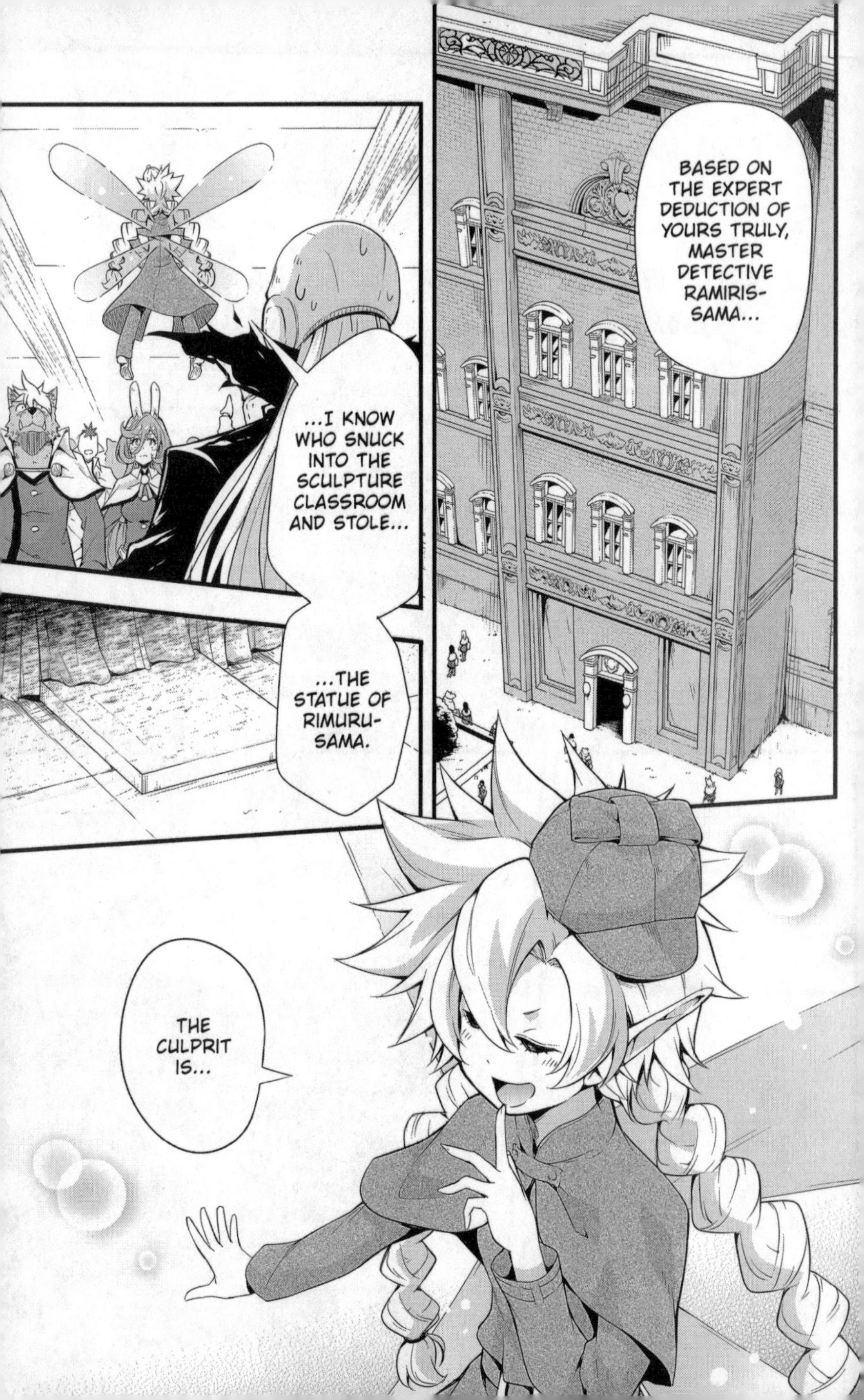
BASED ON THE EXPERT DEDUCTION OF YOURS TRULY, MASTER DETECTIVE RAMIRIS-SAMA...
...I KNOW WHO SNUCK INTO THE SCULPTURE CLASSROOM AND STOLE...
...THE STATUE OF RIMURU-SAMA.
THE CULPRIT IS...

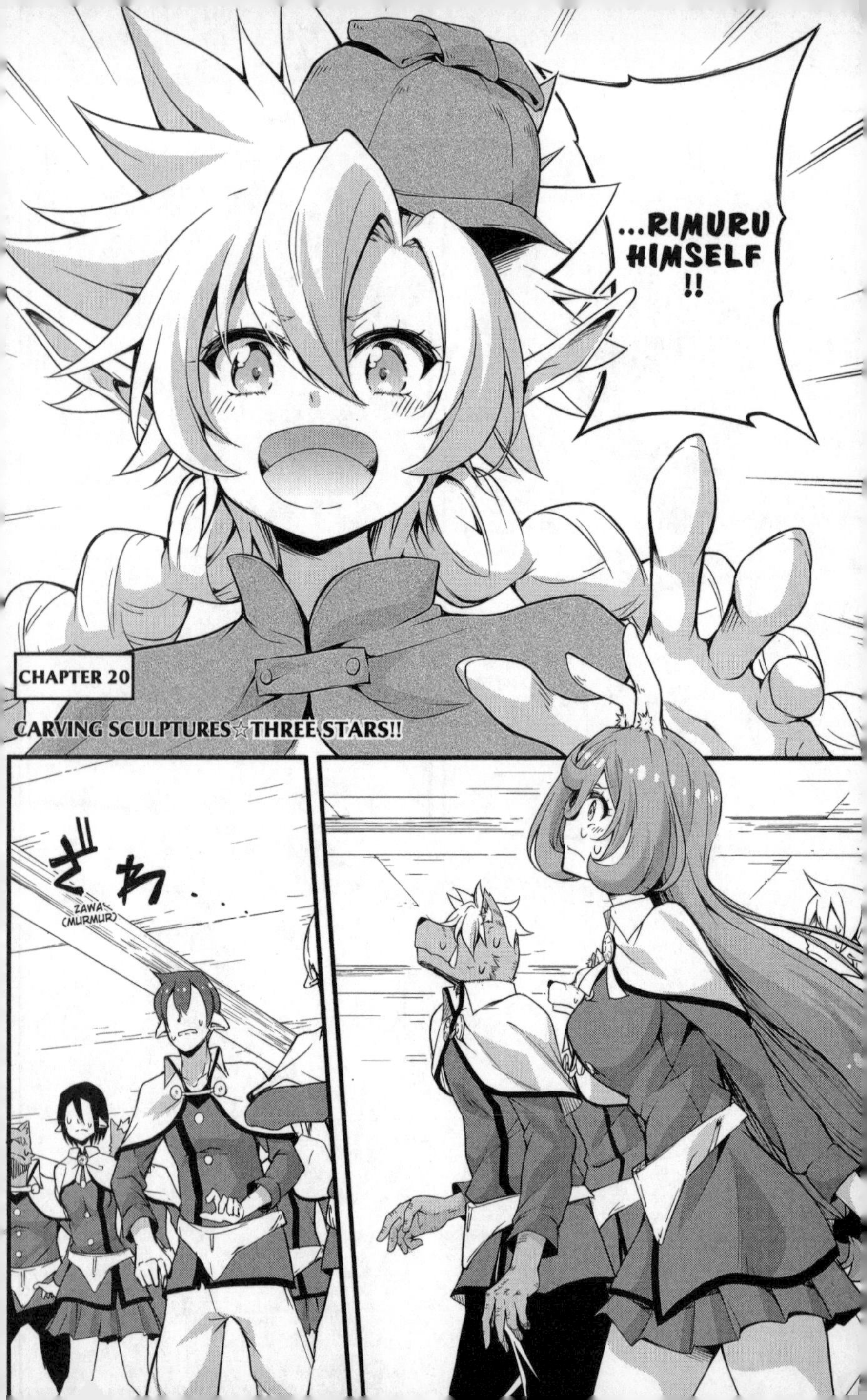
...RIMURU HIMSELF !!
CHAPTER 20
CARVING SCULPTURES☆THREE STARS!!
ざわ...
ZAWA (MURMUR)

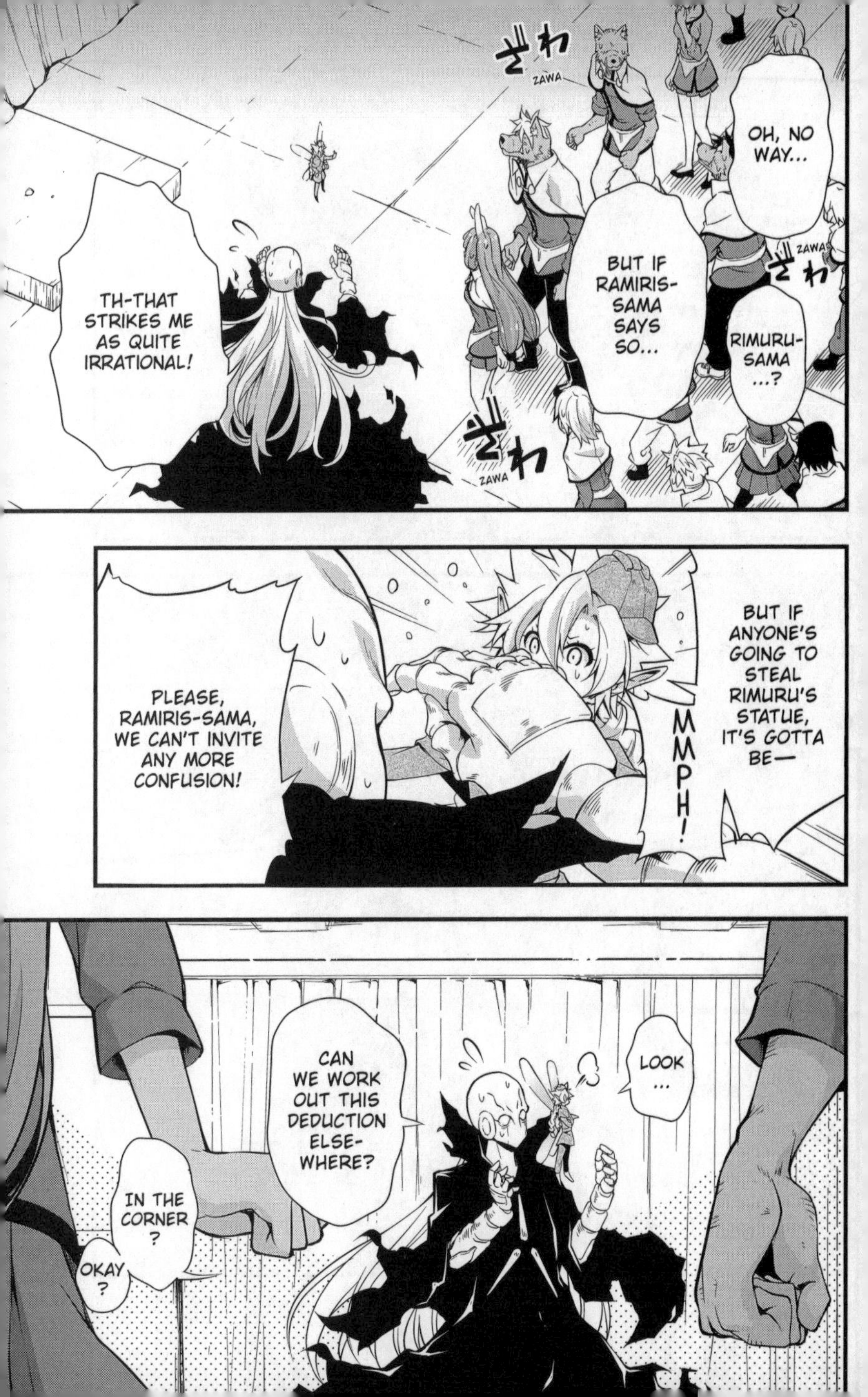
ざわ
ZAWA
OH, NO WAY...
ZAWA
ざわ
BUT IF RAMIRIS-SAMA SAYS SO...
RIMURU-SAMA ...?
ざわ
ZAWA
TH-THAT STRIKES ME AS QUITE IRRATIONAL!
BUT IF ANYONE'S GOING TO STEAL RIMURU'S STATUE, IT'S GOTTA BE—
MMPH!
PLEASE, RAMIRIS-SAMA, WE CAN'T INVITE ANY MORE CONFUSION!
LOOK ...
CAN WE WORK OUT THIS DEDUCTION ELSE-WHERE?
IN THE CORNER ?
OKAY ?

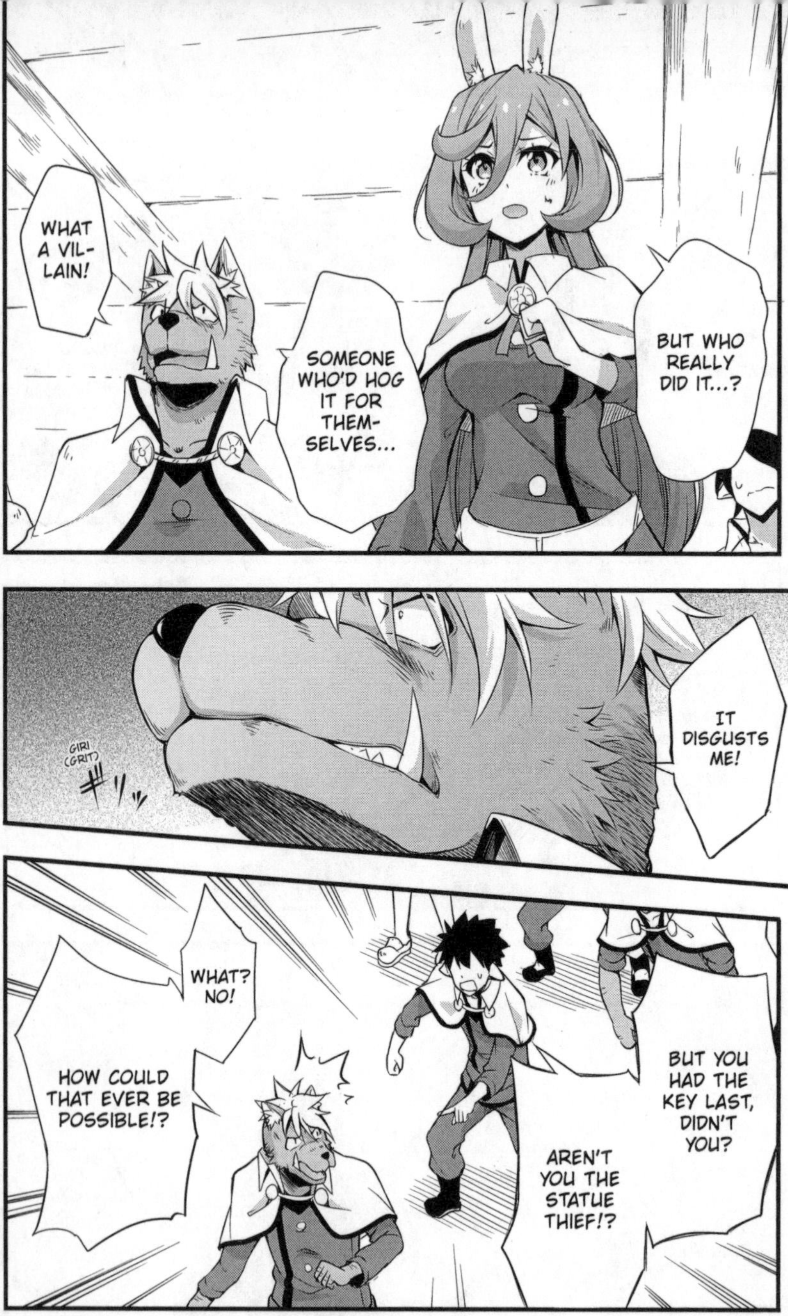
BUT WHO REALLY DID IT...?
SOMEONE WHO'D HOG IT FOR THEM-SELVES...
WHAT A VIL-LAIN!
IT DISGUSTS ME!
GIRI (GRIT)
BUT YOU HAD THE KEY LAST, DIDN'T YOU?
AREN'T YOU THE STATUE THIEF!?
WHAT? NO!
HOW COULD THAT EVER BE POSSIBLE!?

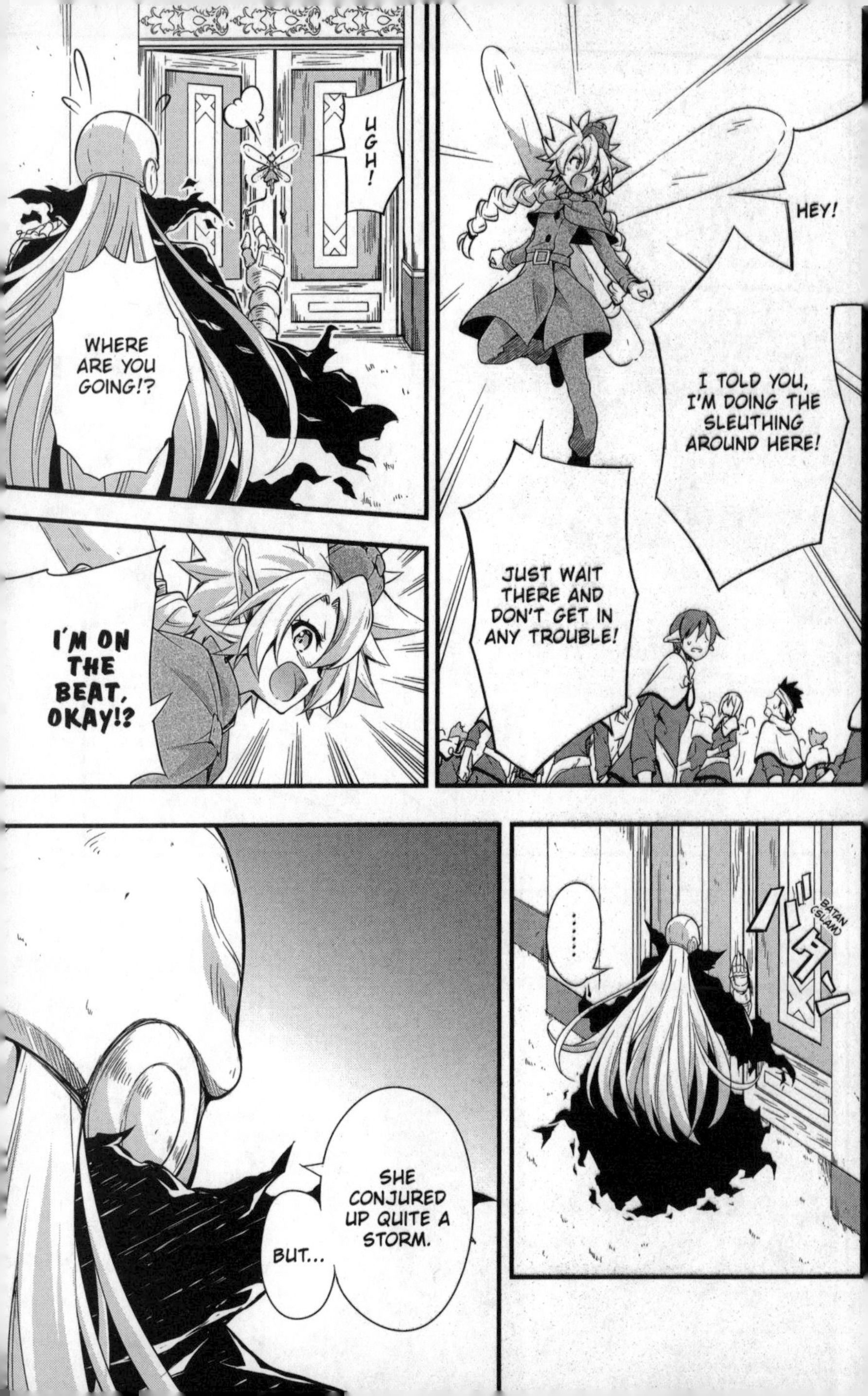
HEY!
I TOLD YOU, I'M DOING THE SLEUTHING AROUND HERE!
JUST WAIT THERE AND DON'T GET IN ANY TROUBLE!
UGH!
WHERE ARE YOU GOING!?
I'M ON THE BEAT, OKAY!?
......
BATAN (SLAM)
SHE CONJURED UP QUITE A STORM.
BUT...

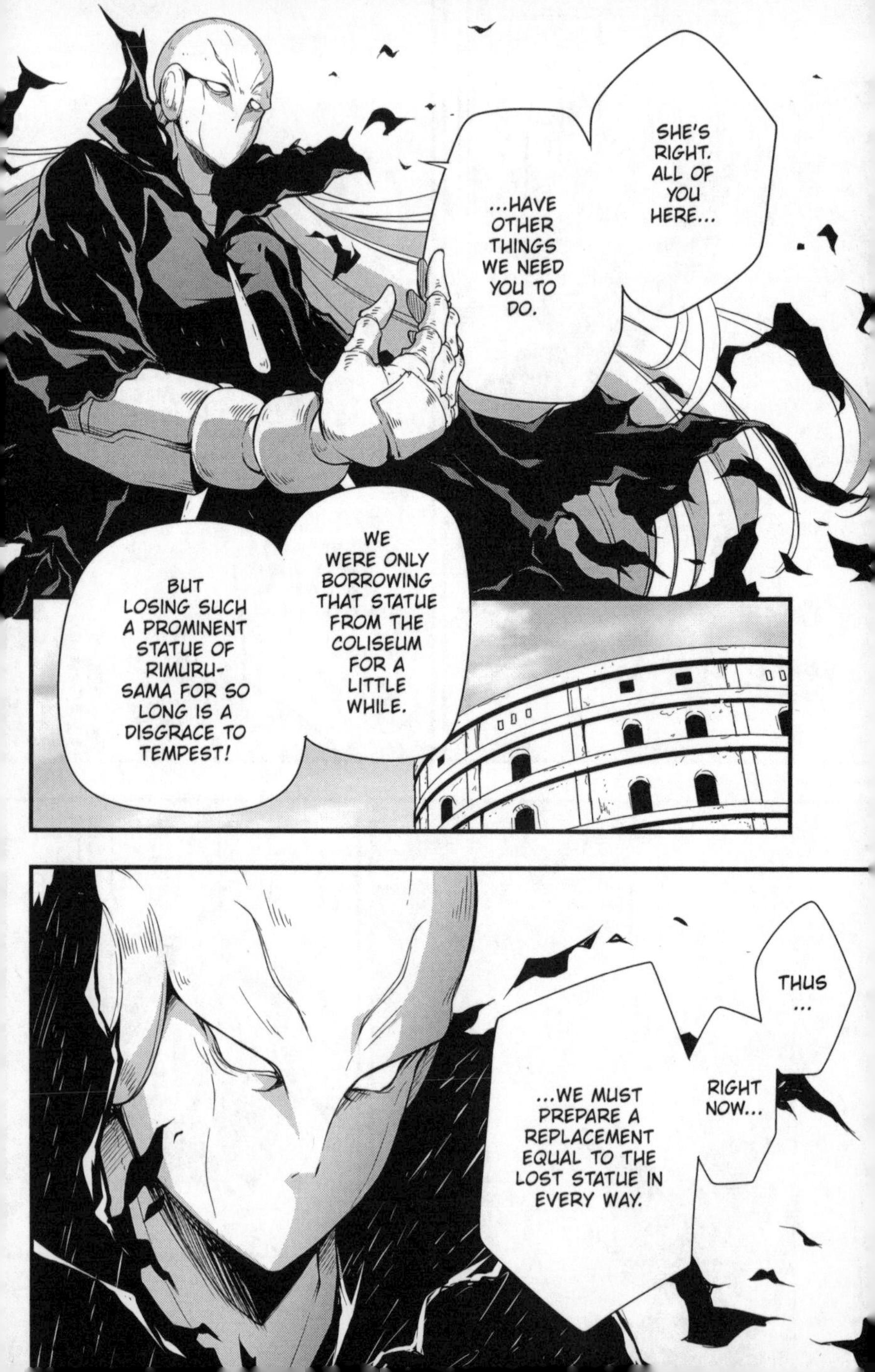
SHE'S RIGHT. ALL OF YOU HERE...
...HAVE OTHER THINGS WE NEED YOU TO DO.
WE WERE ONLY BORROWING THAT STATUE FROM THE COLISEUM FOR A LITTLE WHILE.
BUT LOSING SUCH A PROMINENT STATUE OF RIMURU-SAMA FOR SO LONG IS A DISGRACE TO TEMPEST!
THUS...
RIGHT NOW...
...WE MUST PREPARE A REPLACEMENT EQUAL TO THE LOST STATUE IN EVERY WAY.

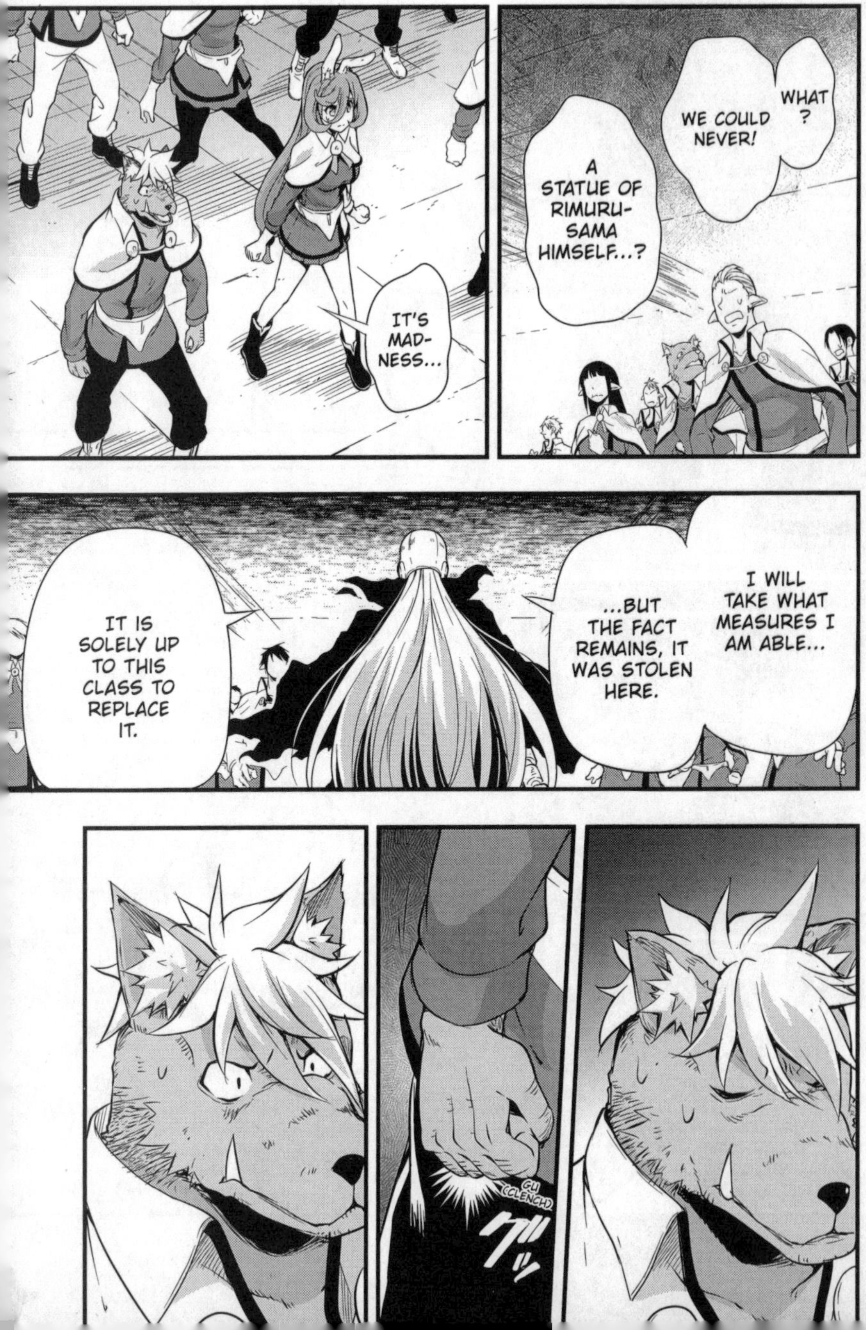
WHAT?
WE COULD NEVER!
A STATUE OF RIMURU-SAMA HIMSELF...?
IT'S MADNESS...
I WILL TAKE WHAT MEASURES I AM ABLE...
...BUT THE FACT REMAINS, IT WAS STOLEN HERE.
IT IS SOLELY UP TO THIS CLASS TO REPLACE IT.
GU (CLENCH)
グッ

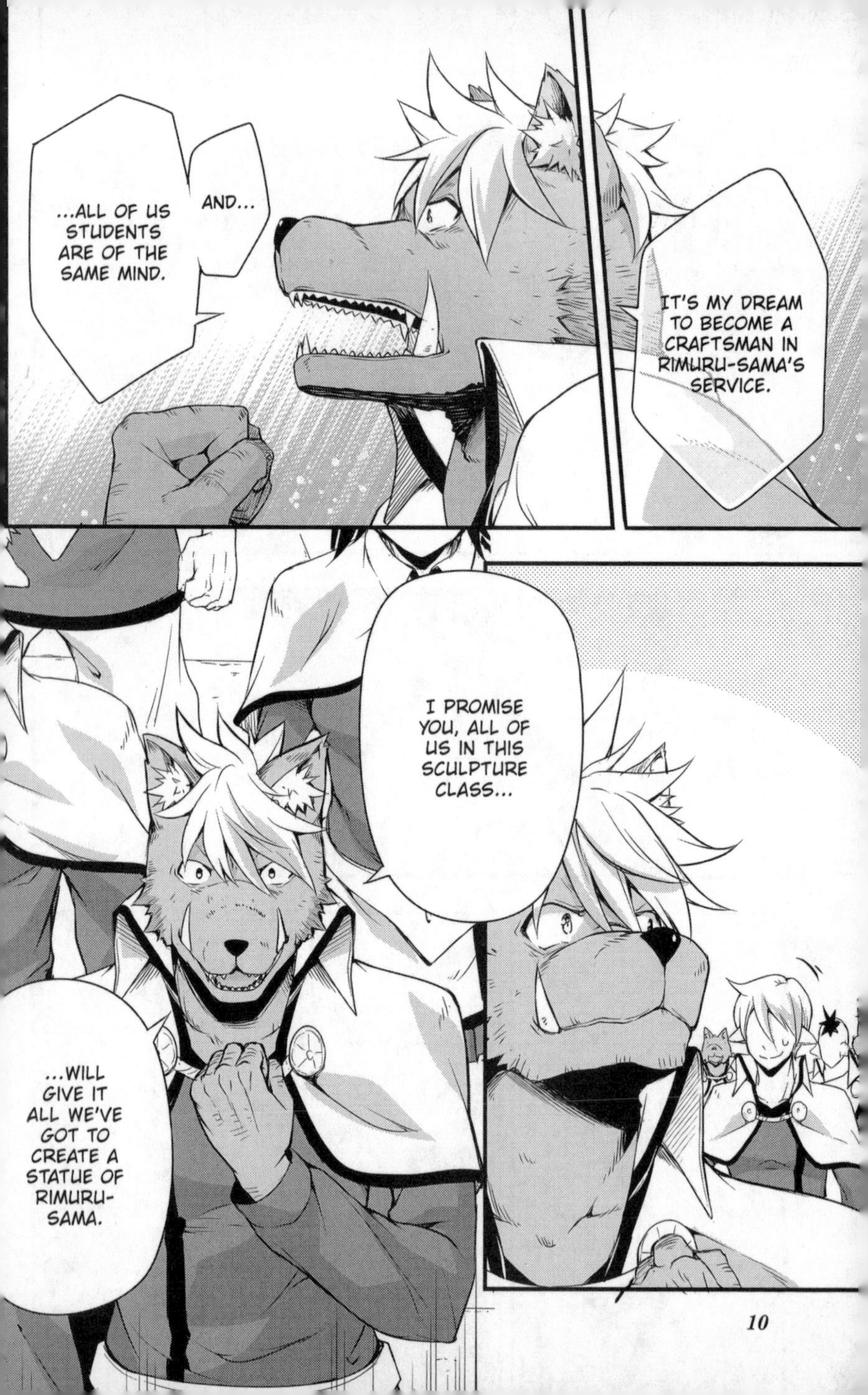
IT'S MY DREAM TO BECOME A CRAFTSMAN IN RIMURU-SAMA'S SERVICE.
AND...
...ALL OF US STUDENTS ARE OF THE SAME MIND.
I PROMISE YOU, ALL OF US IN THIS SCULPTURE CLASS...
...WILL GIVE IT ALL WE'VE GOT TO CREATE A STATUE OF RIMURU-SAMA.

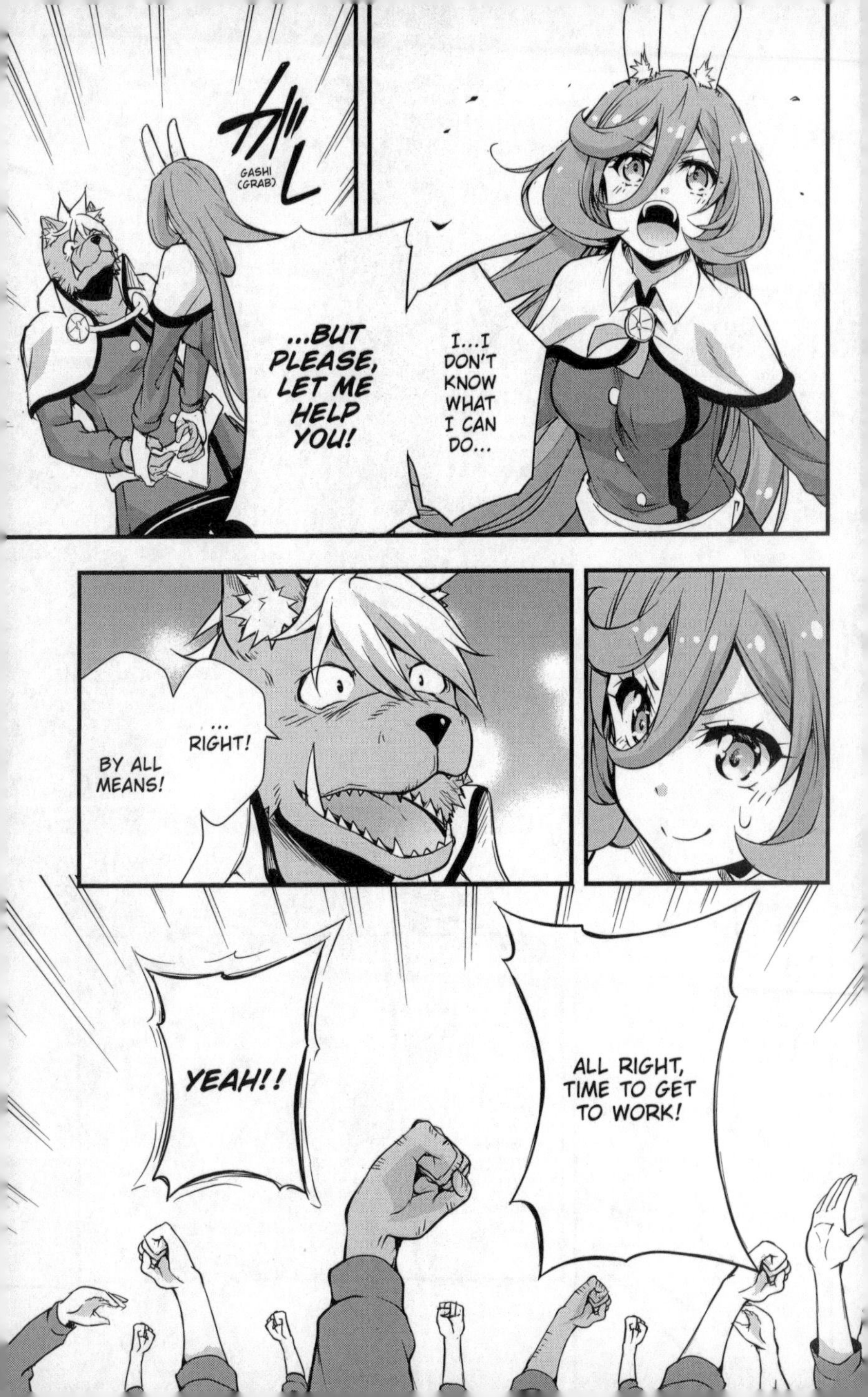
I...I DON'T KNOW WHAT I CAN DO...
...BUT PLEASE, LET ME HELP YOU!
GASHI (GRAB)
... RIGHT!
BY ALL MEANS!
ALL RIGHT, TIME TO GET TO WORK!
YEAH!!

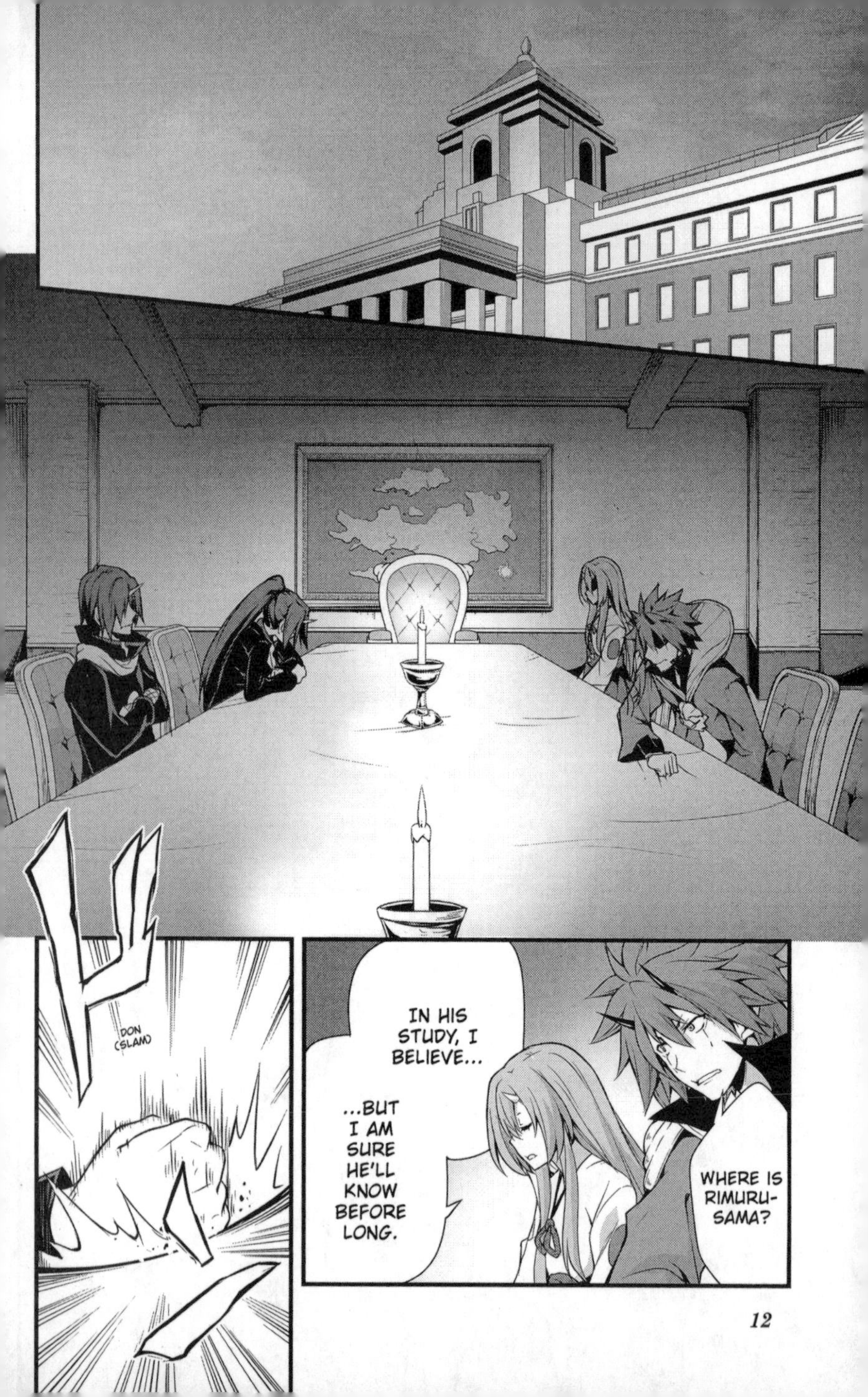
WHERE IS RIMURU-SAMA?
IN HIS STUDY, I BELIEVE...
...BUT I AM SURE HE'LL KNOW BEFORE LONG.
DON (SLAM)

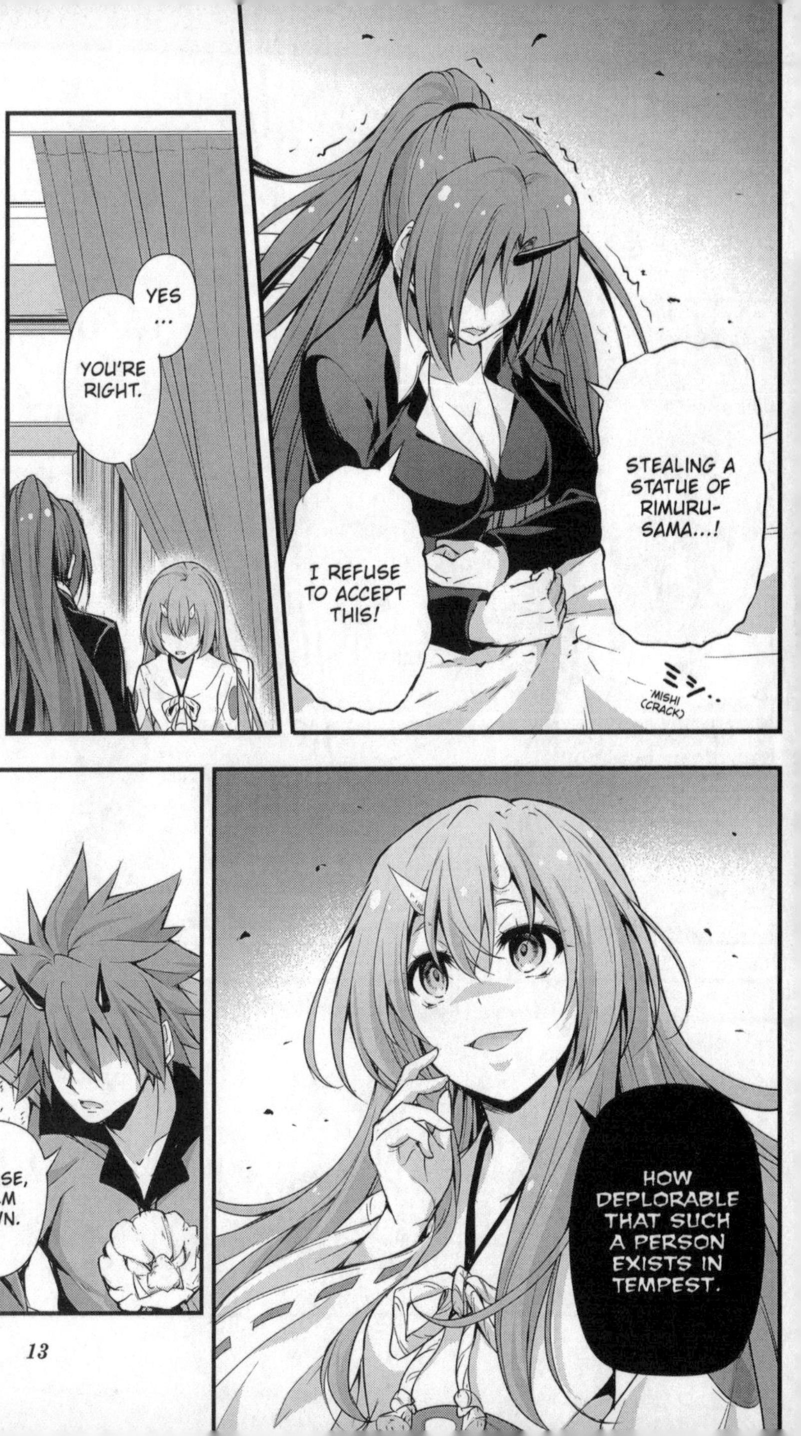
STEALING A STATUE OF RIMURU-SAMA...!
I REFUSE TO ACCEPT THIS!
ミシ…
MISHI (CRACK)
YES ... YOU'RE RIGHT.
HOW DEPLORABLE THAT SUCH A PERSON EXISTS IN TEMPEST.
PLEASE, CALM DOWN.

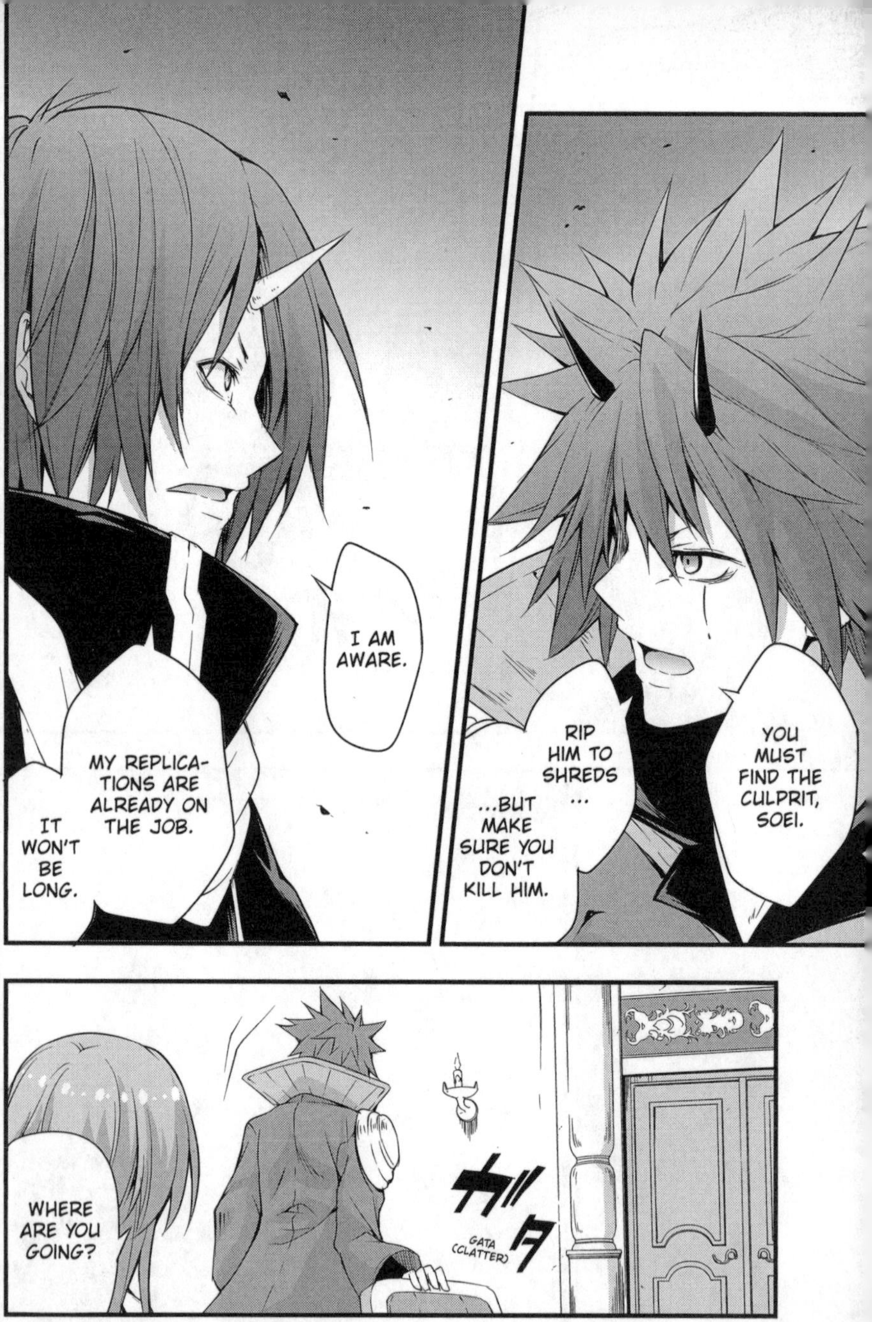
YOU MUST FIND THE CULPRIT, SOEI.
RIP HIM TO SHREDS ...
...BUT MAKE SURE YOU DON'T KILL HIM.
I AM AWARE.
MY REPLICATIONS ARE ALREADY ON THE JOB.
IT WON'T BE LONG.
GATA (CLATTER)
WHERE ARE YOU GOING?

OFF TO DEPLOY MY FORCE, "TEAM KURENAI."

HE'S NOT GETTING AWAY.

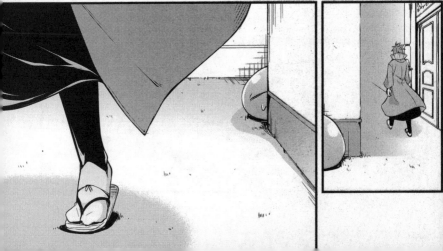

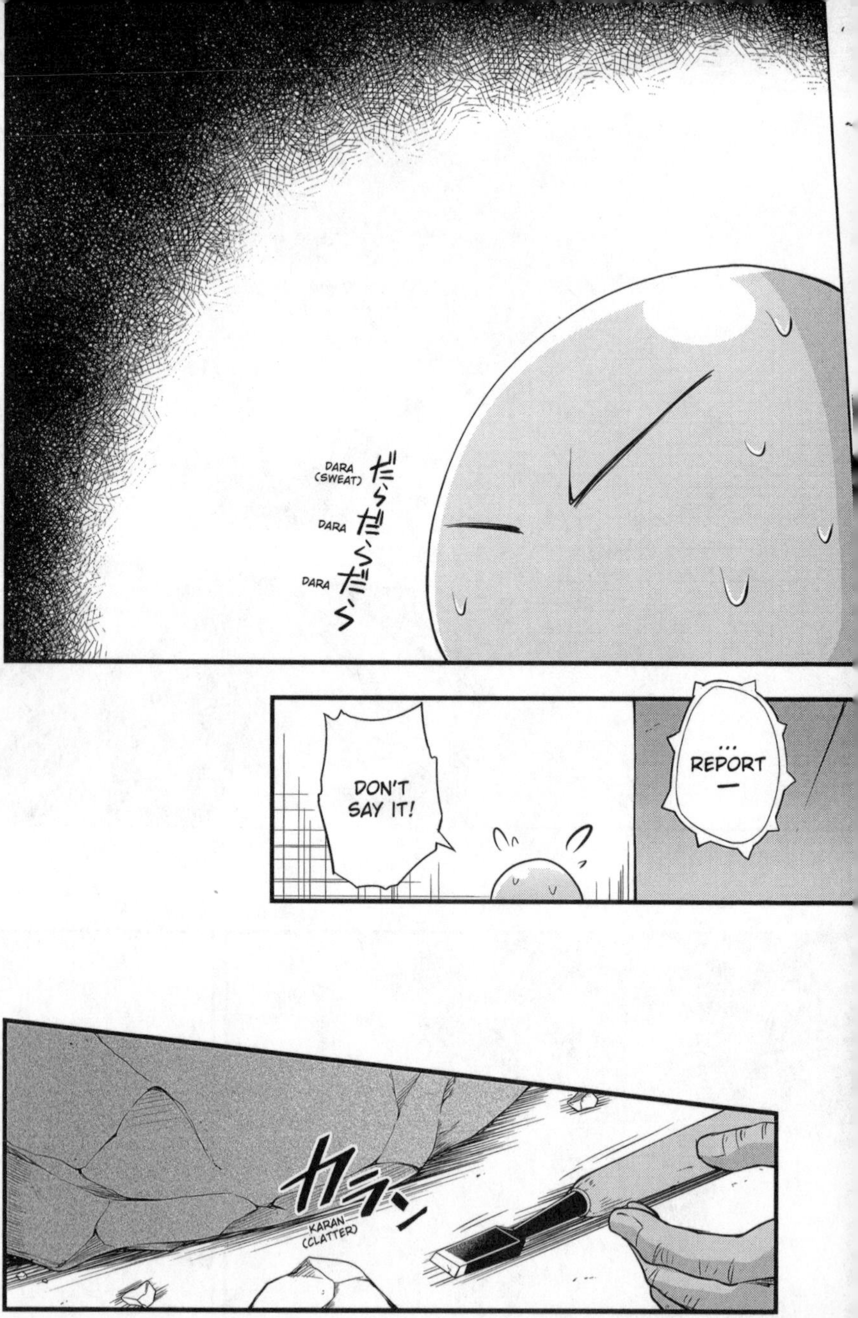
だらだらだら
DARA (SWEAT) DARA DARA
... REPORT —
DON'T SAY IT!
カラン
KARAN (CLATTER)

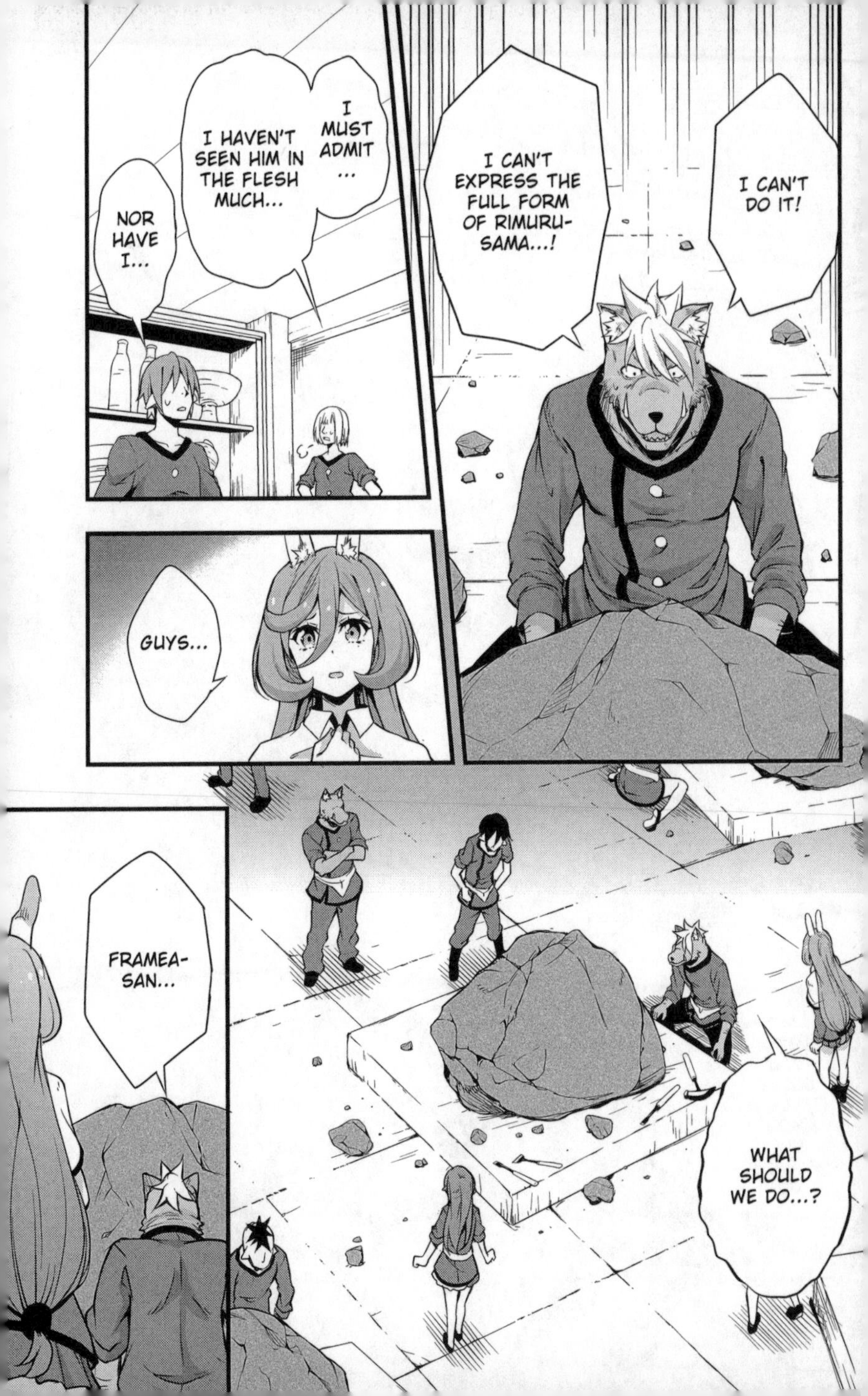
I CAN'T DO IT!
I CAN'T EXPRESS THE FULL FORM OF RIMURU-SAMA...!
I MUST ADMIT...
I HAVEN'T SEEN HIM IN THE FLESH MUCH...
NOR HAVE I...
GUYS...
WHAT SHOULD WE DO...?
FRAMEA-SAN...

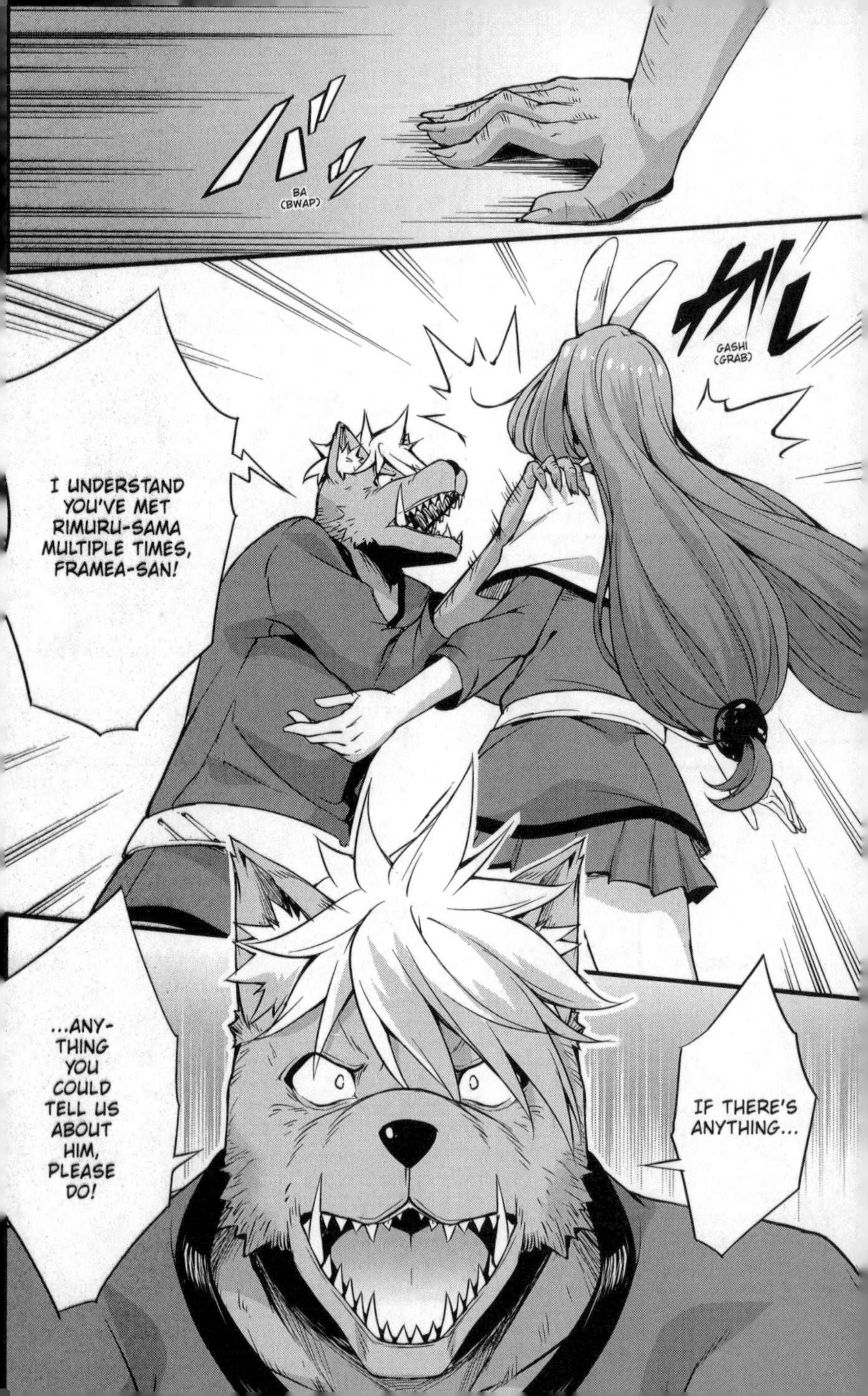
バ
BA (BWAP)
ガシ
GASHI (GRAB)
I UNDERSTAND YOU'VE MET RIMURU-SAMA MULTIPLE TIMES, FRAMEA-SAN!
IF THERE'S ANYTHING...
...ANY-THING YOU COULD TELL US ABOUT HIM, PLEASE DO!

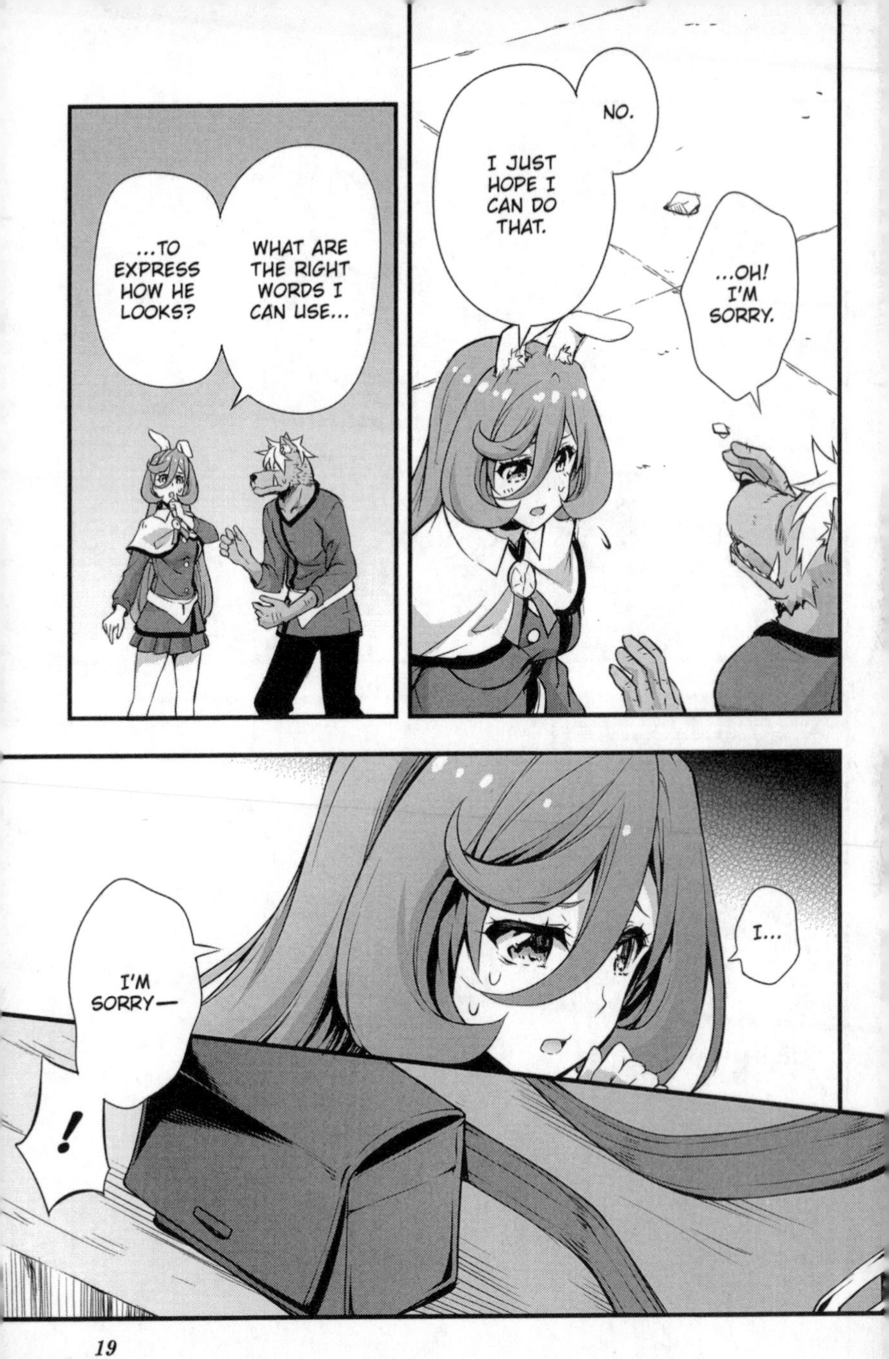
NO.
I JUST HOPE I CAN DO THAT.
...OH! I'M SORRY.
WHAT ARE THE RIGHT WORDS I CAN USE...
...TO EXPRESS HOW HE LOOKS?
I...
I'M SORRY—
!

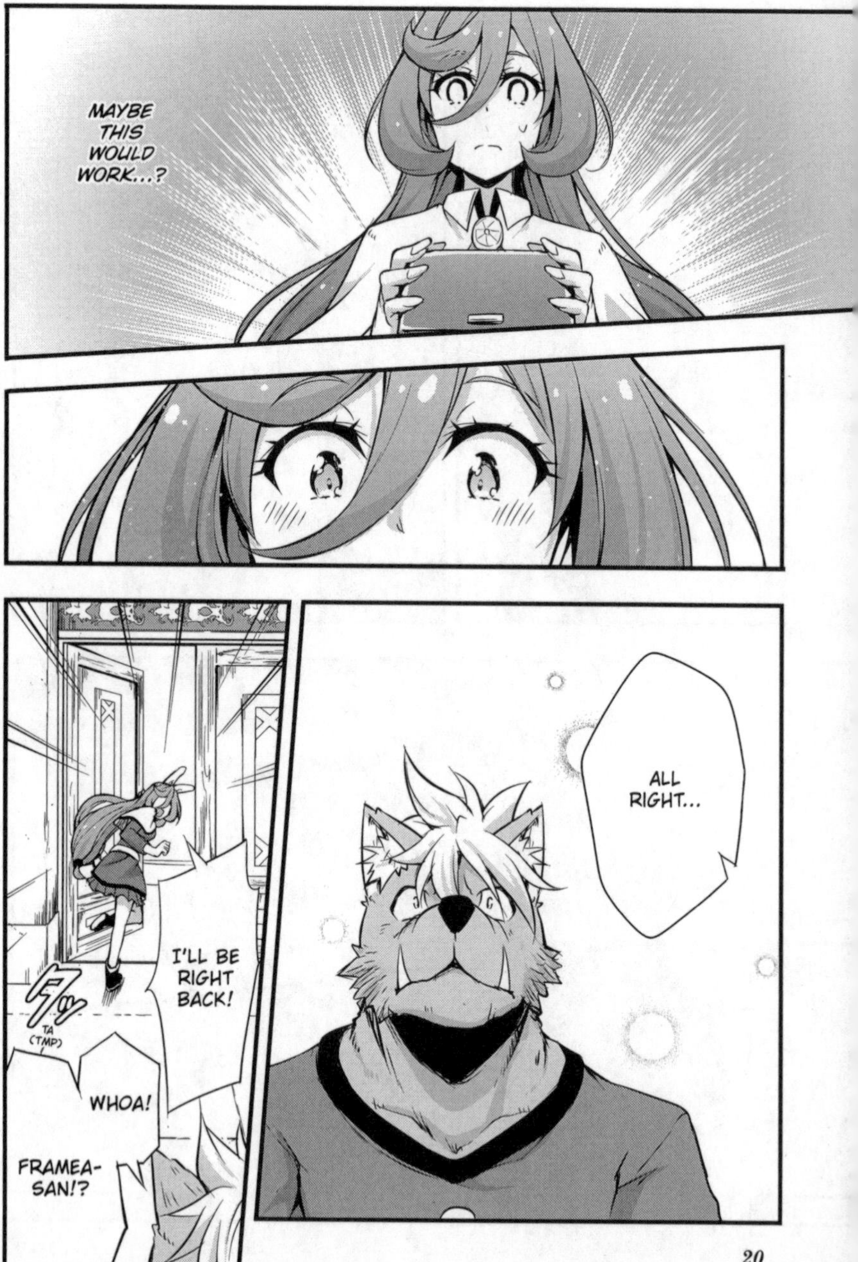
MAYBE THIS WOULD WORK...?
ALL RIGHT...
I'LL BE RIGHT BACK!
TA (TMP)
WHOA!
FRAMEA-SAN!?

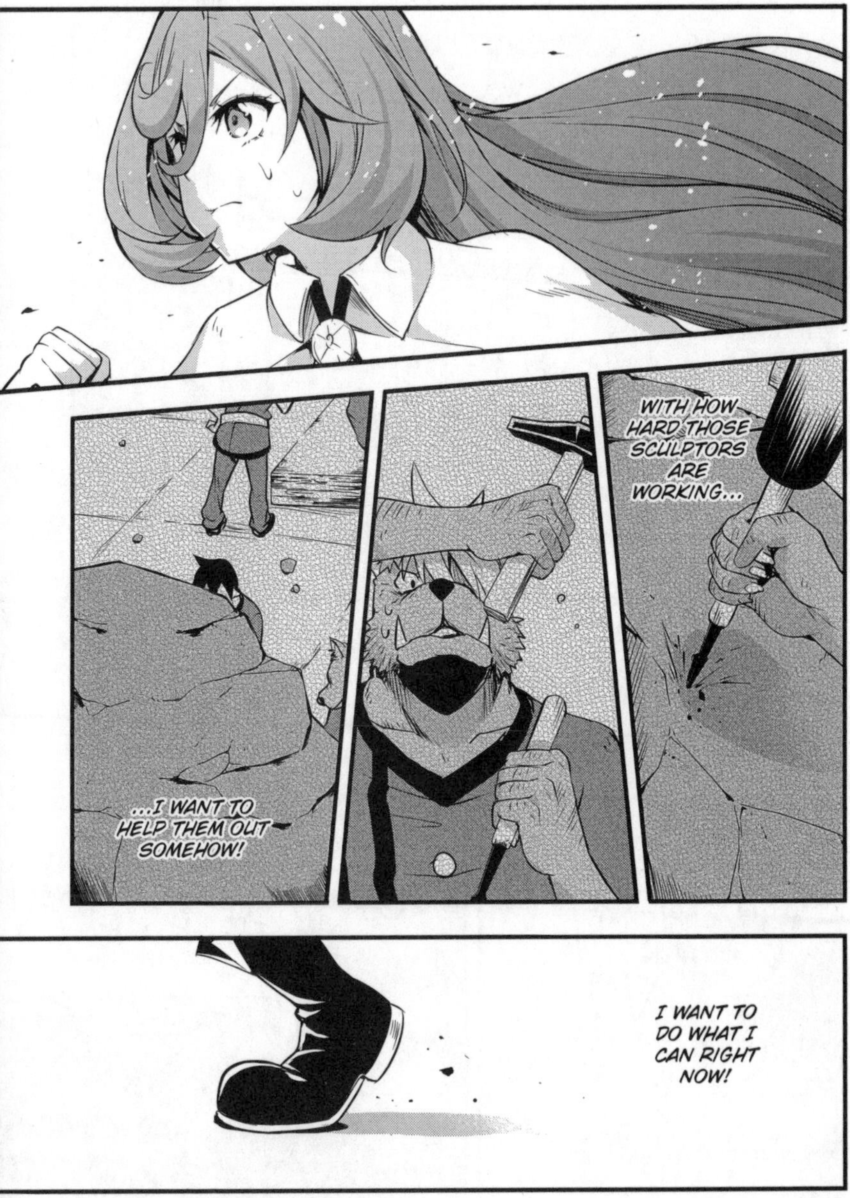
WITH HOW HARD THOSE SCULPTORS ARE WORKING...
...I WANT TO HELP THEM OUT SOMEHOW!
I WANT TO DO WHAT I CAN RIGHT NOW!

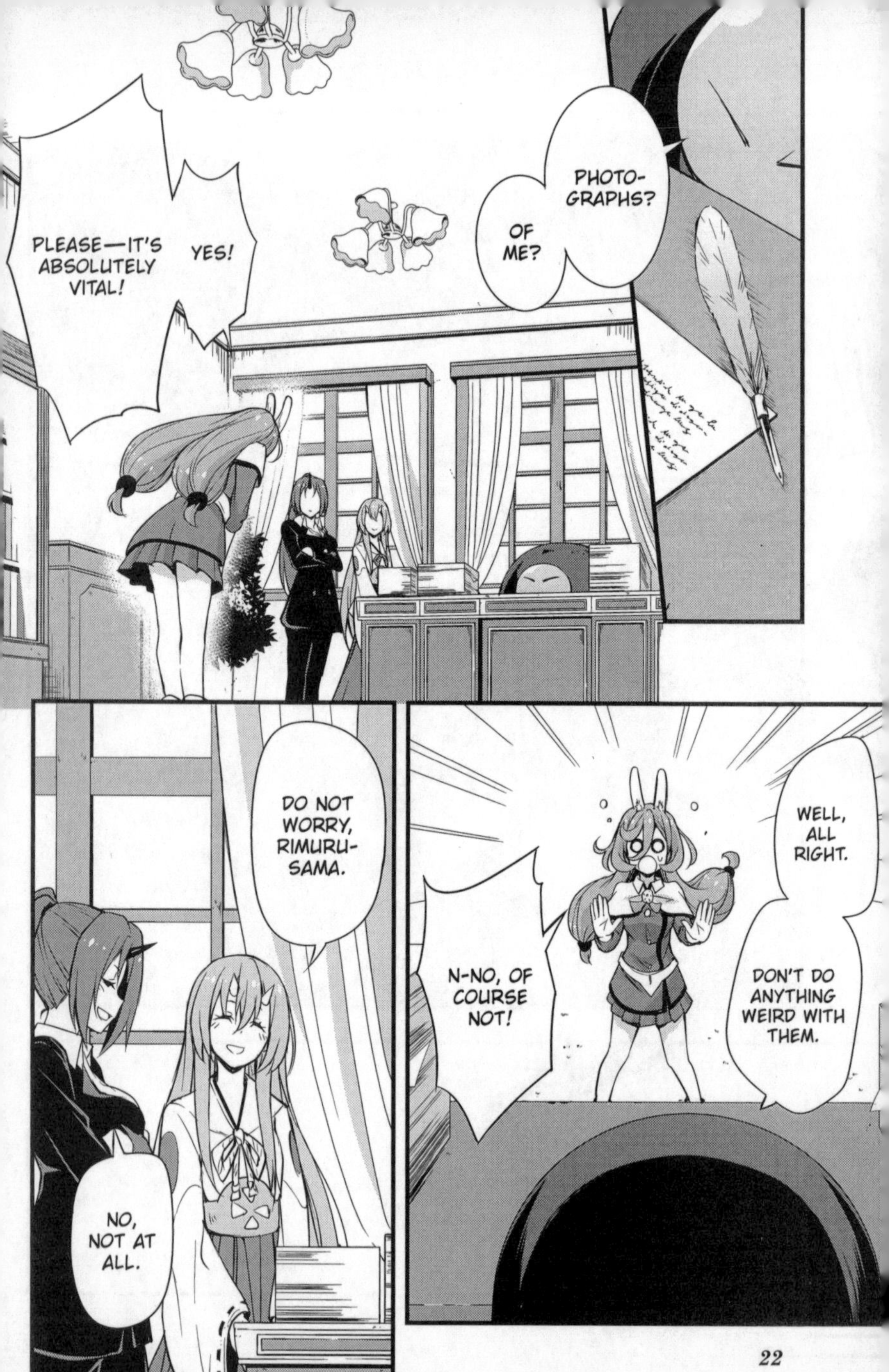
PHOTO-GRAPHS?
OF ME?
YES!
PLEASE—IT'S ABSOLUTELY VITAL!
WELL, ALL RIGHT.
DON'T DO ANYTHING WEIRD WITH THEM.
N-NO, OF COURSE NOT!
DO NOT WORRY, RIMURU-SAMA.
NO, NOT AT ALL.

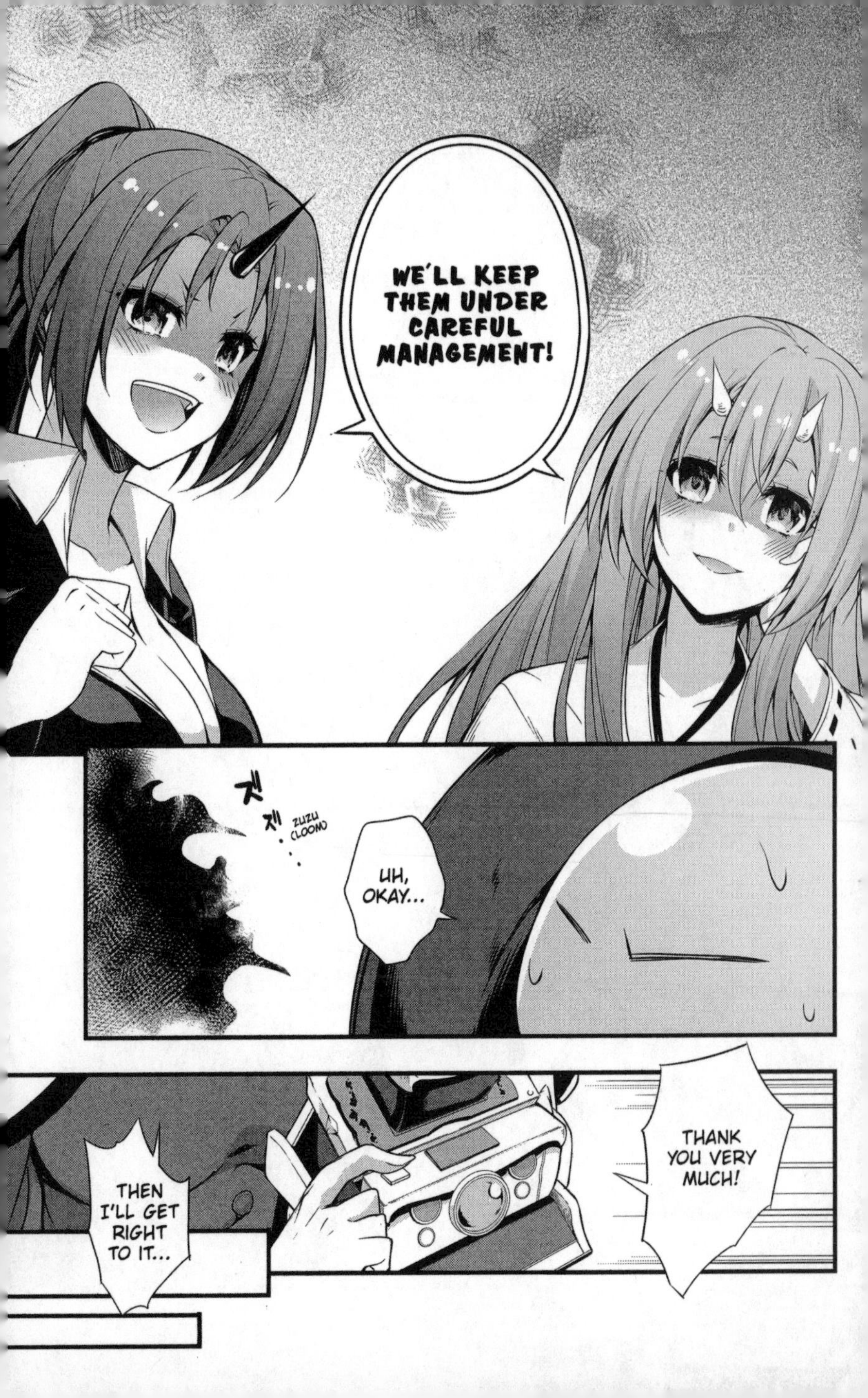
WE'LL KEEP THEM UNDER CAREFUL MANAGEMENT!
UH, OKAY...
ズ! ズ!
ZUZU (LOOM)
THANK YOU VERY MUCH!
THEN I'LL GET RIGHT TO IT...

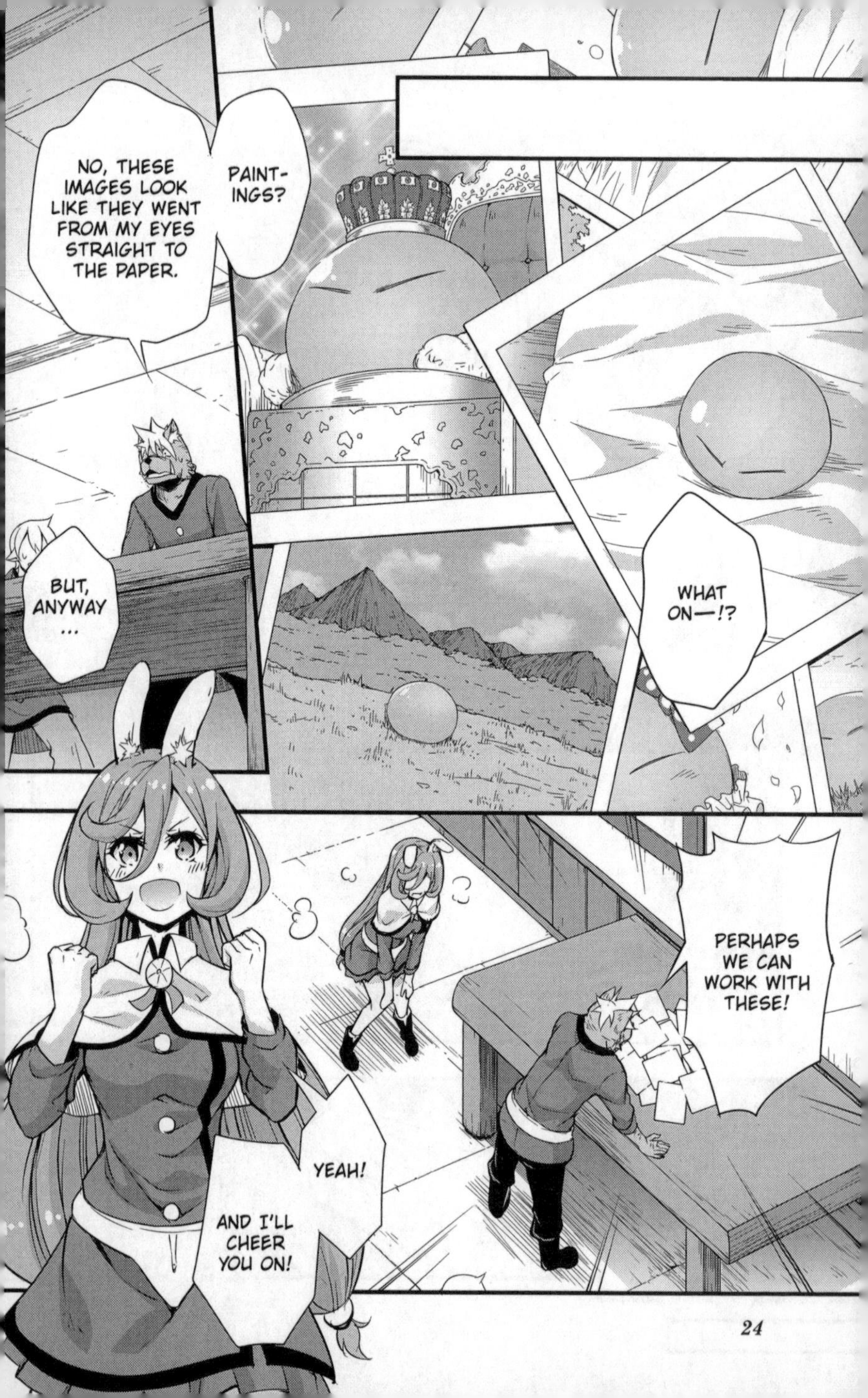
PAINT-INGS?
WHAT ON—!?
NO, THESE IMAGES LOOK LIKE THEY WENT FROM MY EYES STRAIGHT TO THE PAPER.
BUT, ANYWAY ...
PERHAPS WE CAN WORK WITH THESE!
YEAH!
AND I'LL CHEER YOU ON!

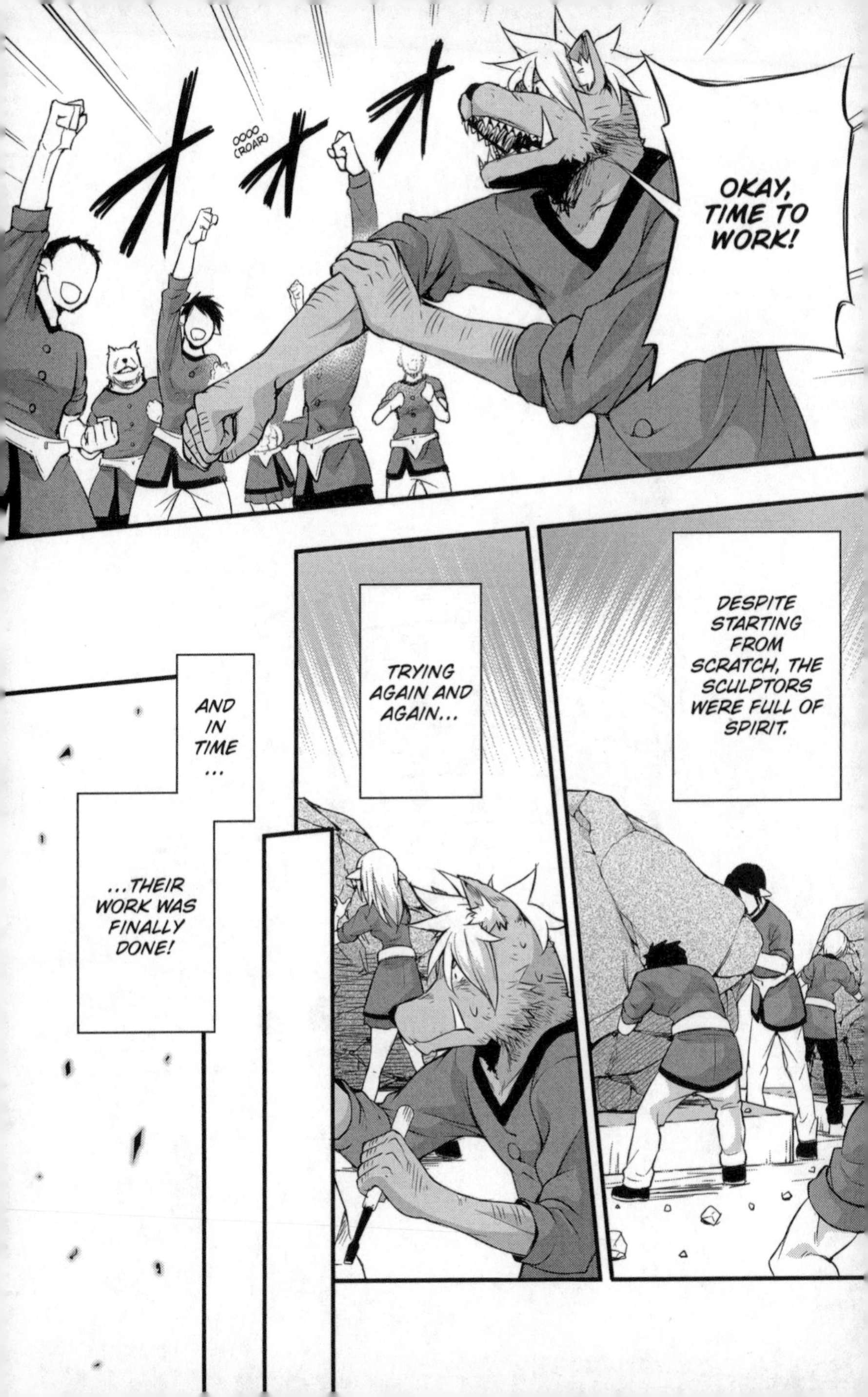
OKAY, TIME TO WORK!
OOOO (ROAR)
DESPITE STARTING FROM SCRATCH, THE SCULPTORS WERE FULL OF SPIRIT.
TRYING AGAIN AND AGAIN...
AND IN TIME...
...THEIR WORK WAS FINALLY DONE!

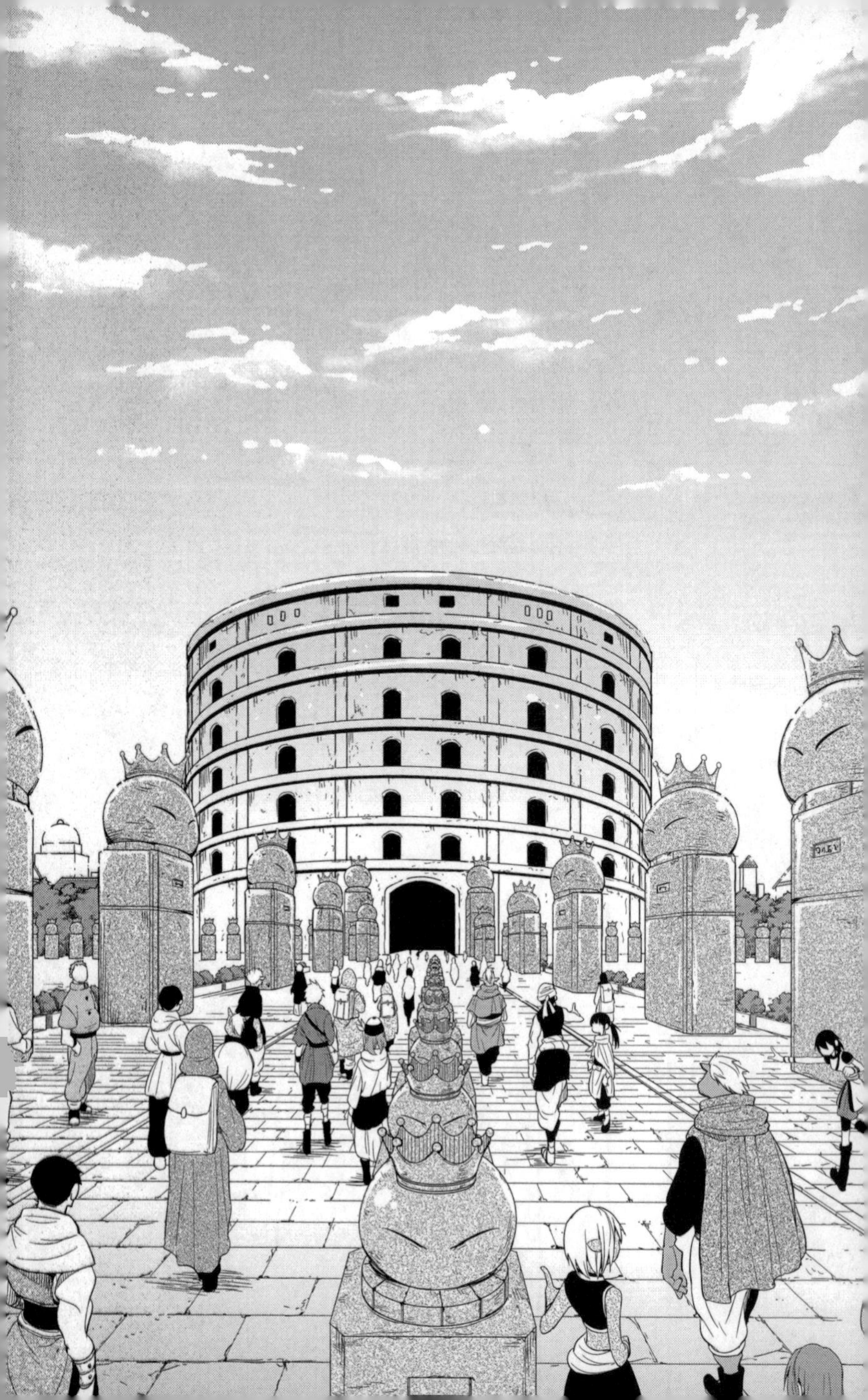

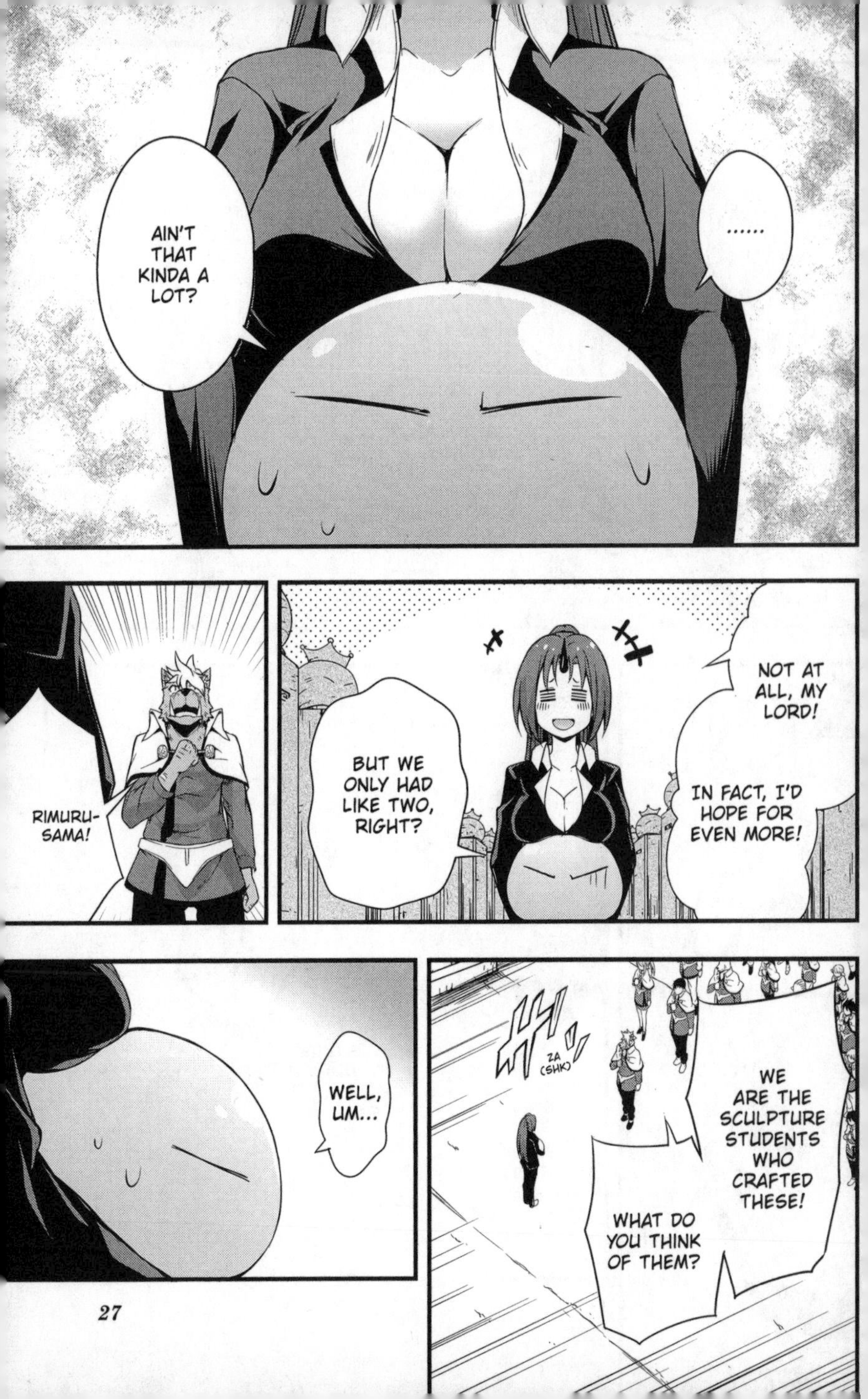
......
AIN'T THAT KINDA A LOT?
NOT AT ALL, MY LORD!
IN FACT, I'D HOPE FOR EVEN MORE!
BUT WE ONLY HAD LIKE TWO, RIGHT?
RIMURU-SAMA!
ZA (SHK)
WE ARE THE SCULPTURE STUDENTS WHO CRAFTED THESE!
WHAT DO YOU THINK OF THEM?
WELL, UM...

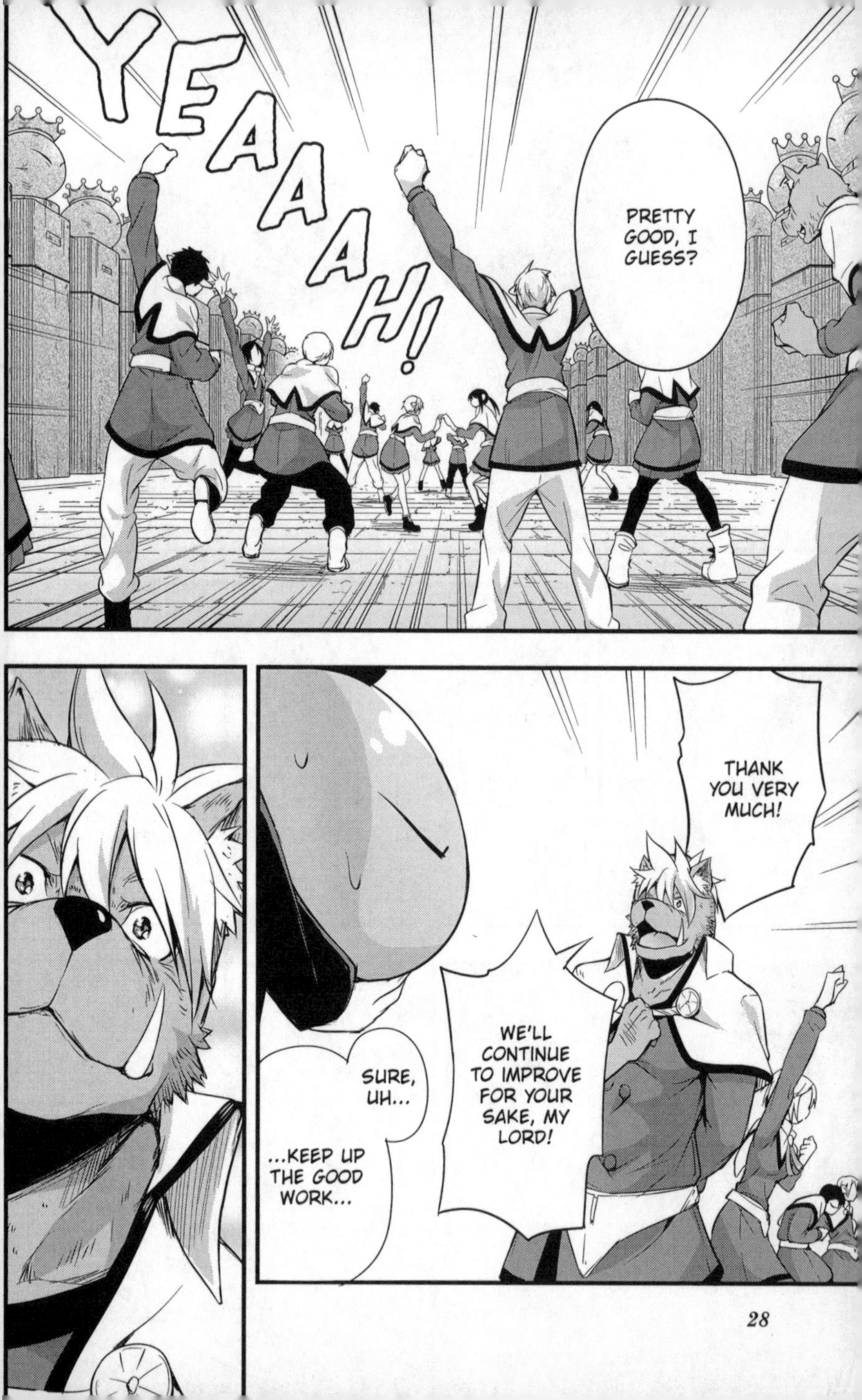
YEAAAAH!
PRETTY GOOD, I GUESS?
THANK YOU VERY MUCH!
WE'LL CONTINUE TO IMPROVE FOR YOUR SAKE, MY LORD!
SURE, UH...
...KEEP UP THE GOOD WORK...

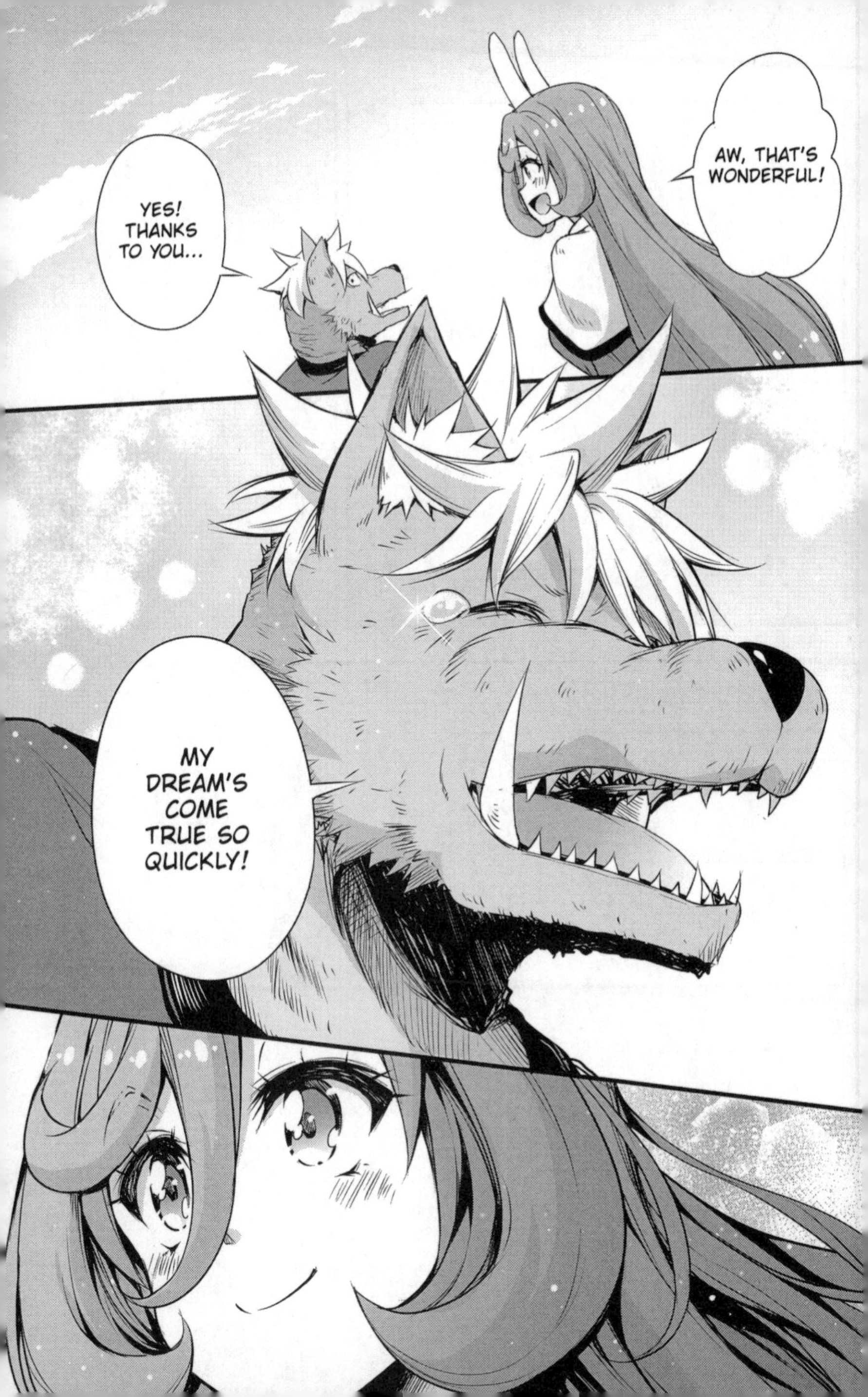
AW, THAT'S WONDERFUL!
YES! THANKS TO YOU...
MY DREAM'S COME TRUE SO QUICKLY!

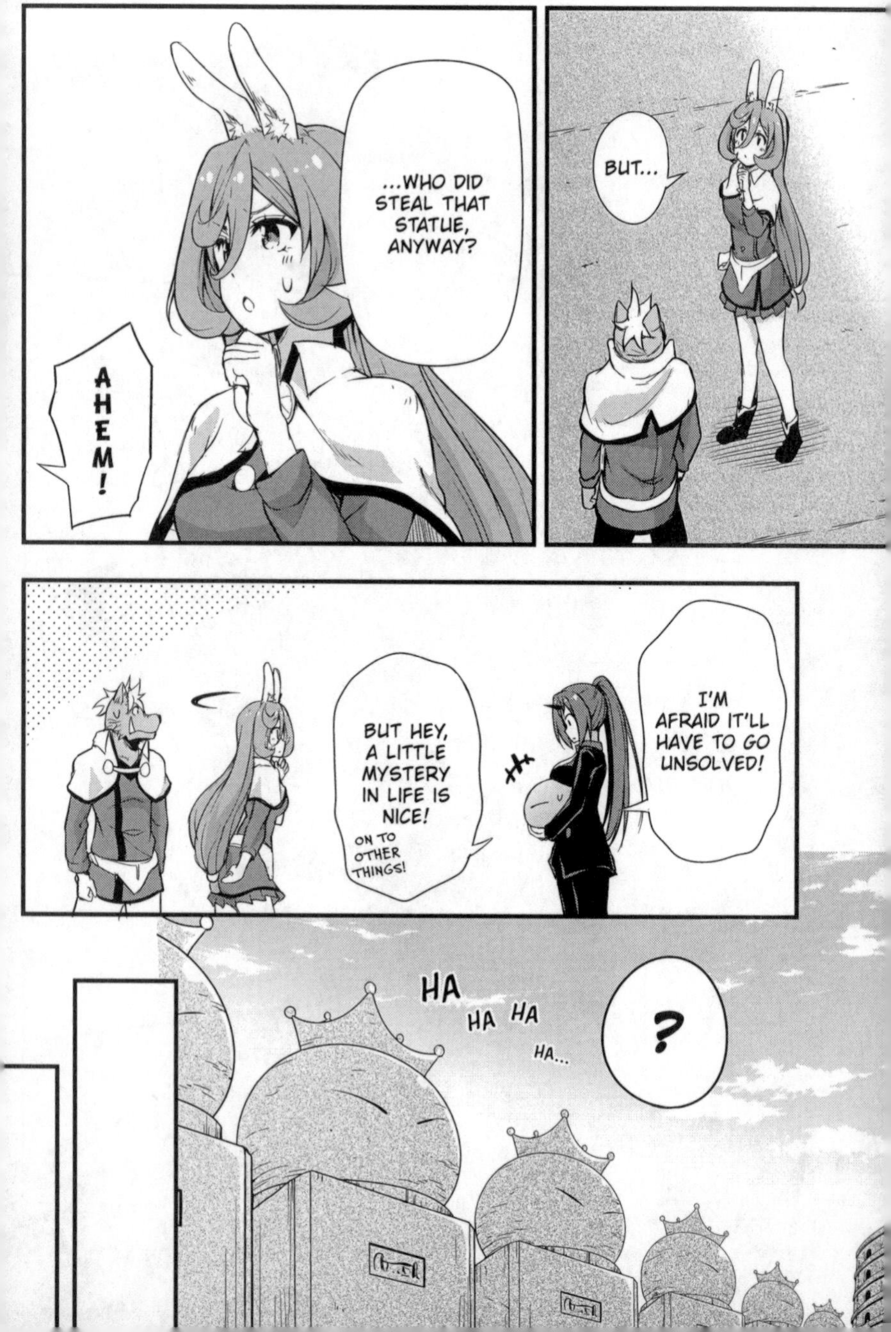
BUT...
...WHO DID STEAL THAT STATUE, ANYWAY?
AHEM!
I'M AFRAID IT'LL HAVE TO GO UNSOLVED!
BUT HEY, A LITTLE MYSTERY IN LIFE IS NICE!
ON TO OTHER THINGS!
?
HA HA HA HA...

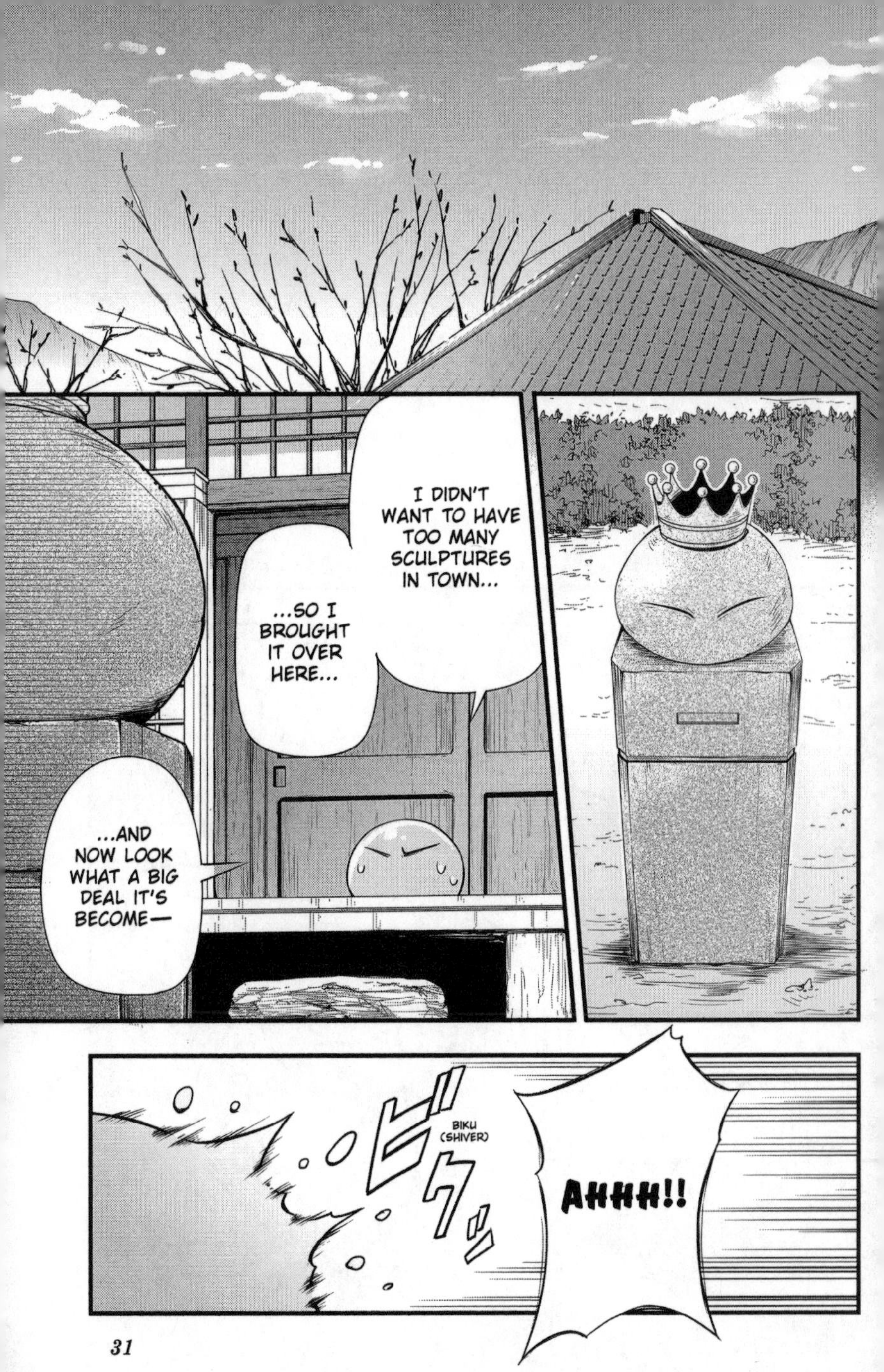
I DIDN'T WANT TO HAVE TOO MANY SCULPTURES IN TOWN...
...SO I BROUGHT IT OVER HERE...
...AND NOW LOOK WHAT A BIG DEAL IT'S BECOME—
AHHH!!
BIKU (SHIVER)

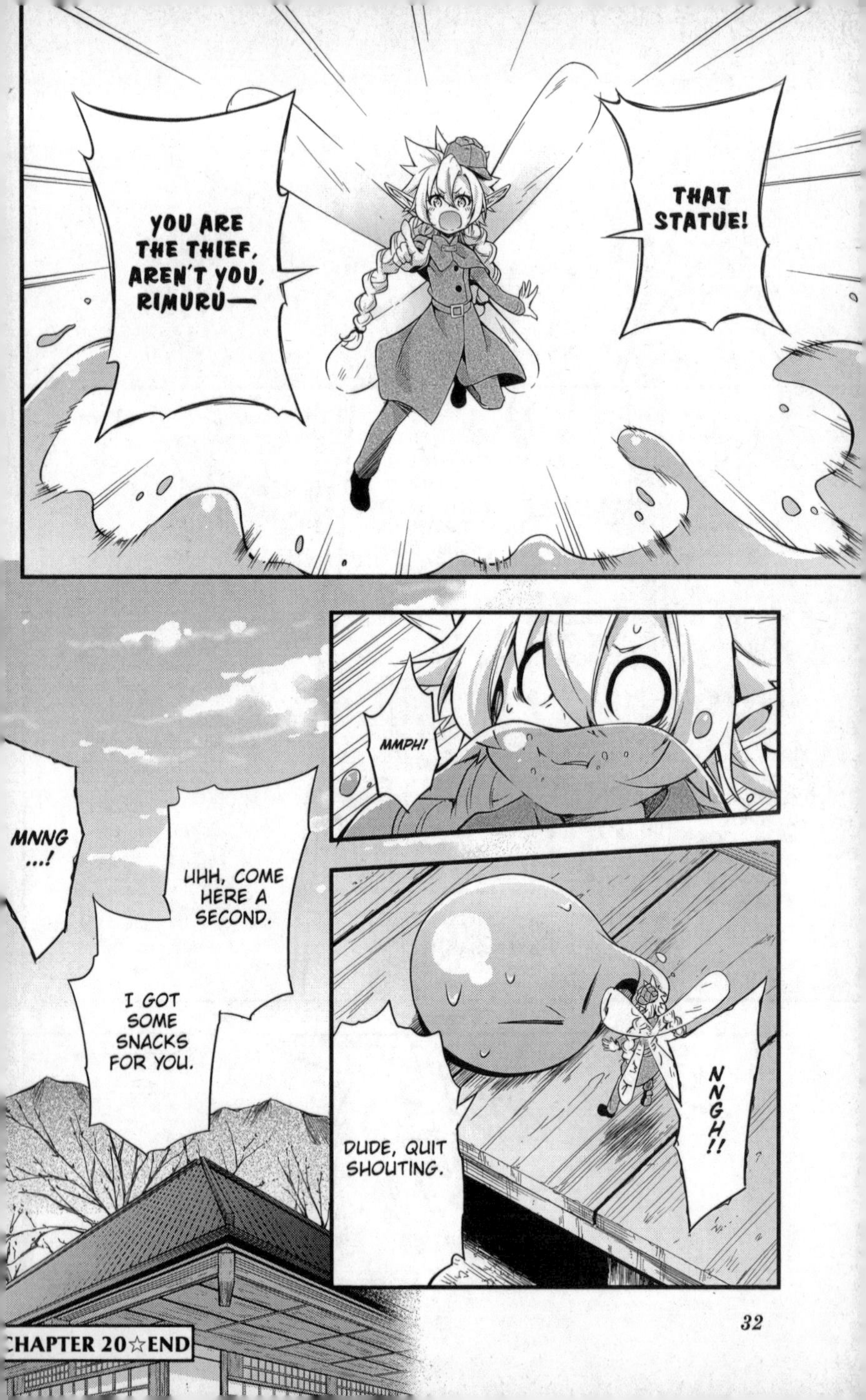
THAT STATUE!
YOU ARE THE THIEF, AREN'T YOU, RIMURU—
MMPH!
NNGH!!
DUDE, QUIT SHOUTING.
UHH, COME HERE A SECOND.
I GOT SOME SNACKS FOR YOU.
MNNG ...!
CHAPTER 20☆END

That Time I Got Reincarnated as a SLIME

The Ways of the Monster Nation

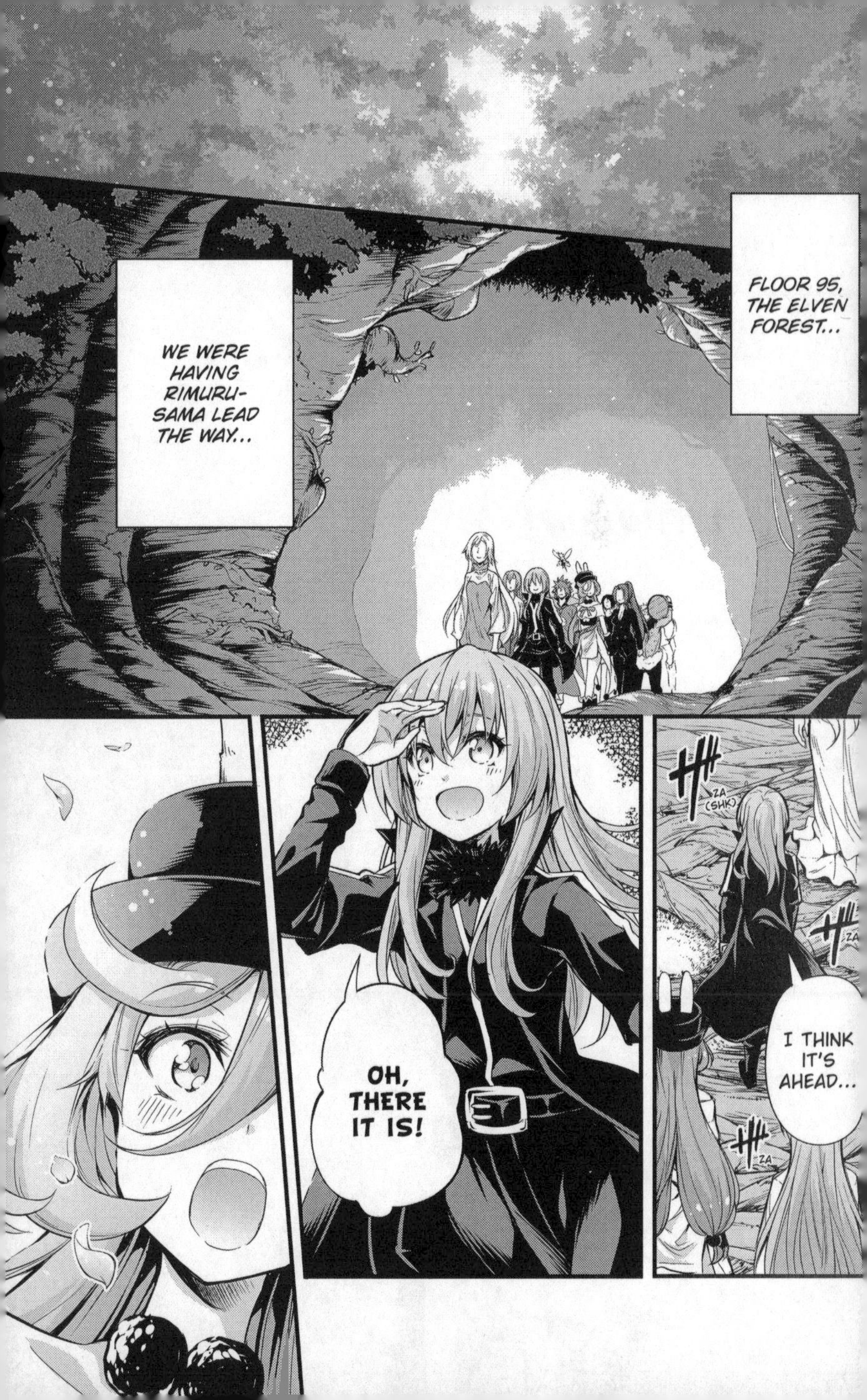
FLOOR 95, THE ELVEN FOREST...
WE WERE HAVING RIMURU-SAMA LEAD THE WAY...
ZA (SHK)
ZA
I THINK IT'S AHEAD...
ZA
OH, THERE IT IS!

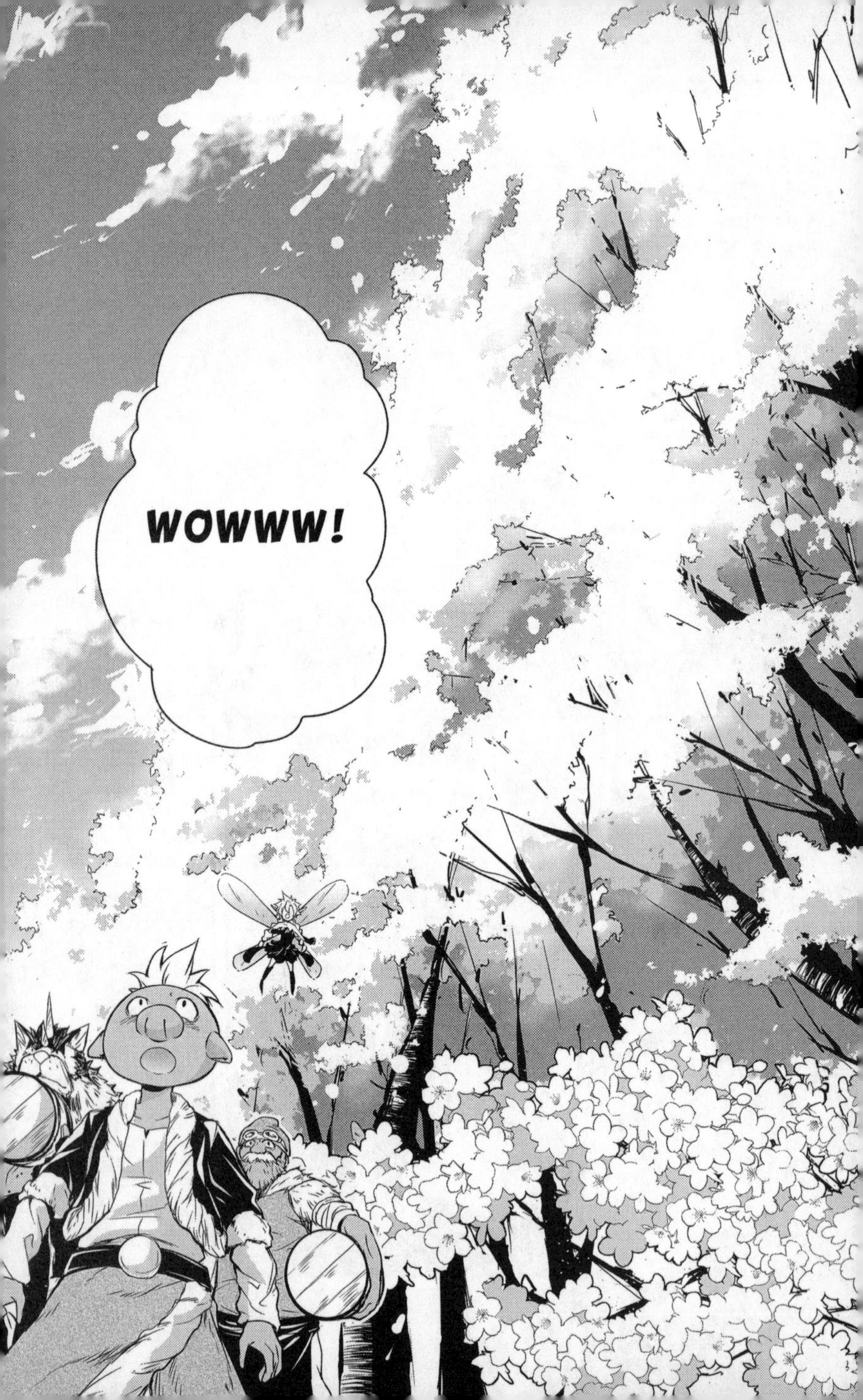
WOWWW!

CHAPTER 21

BLOSSOM VIEWING☆THREE STARS!!

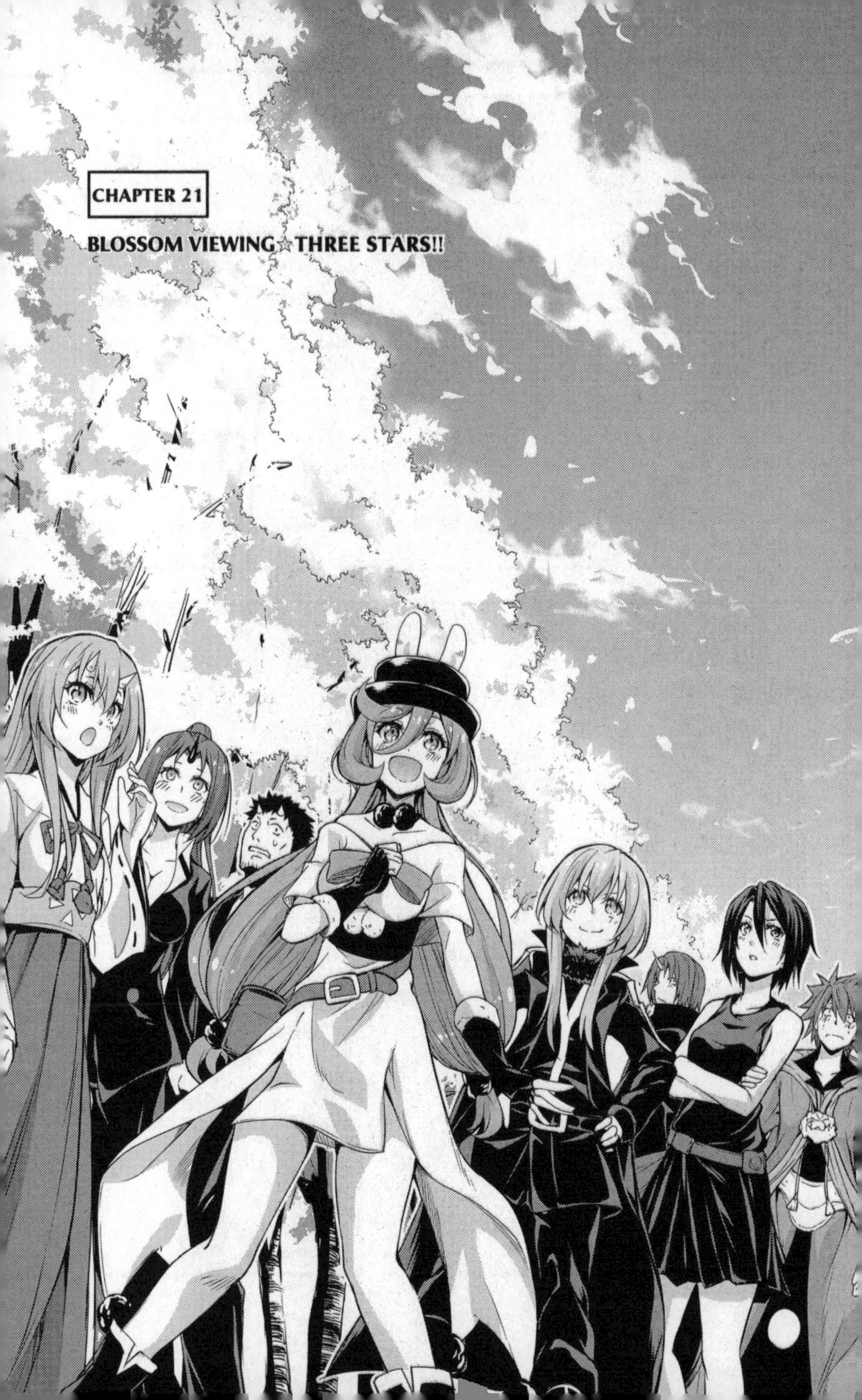

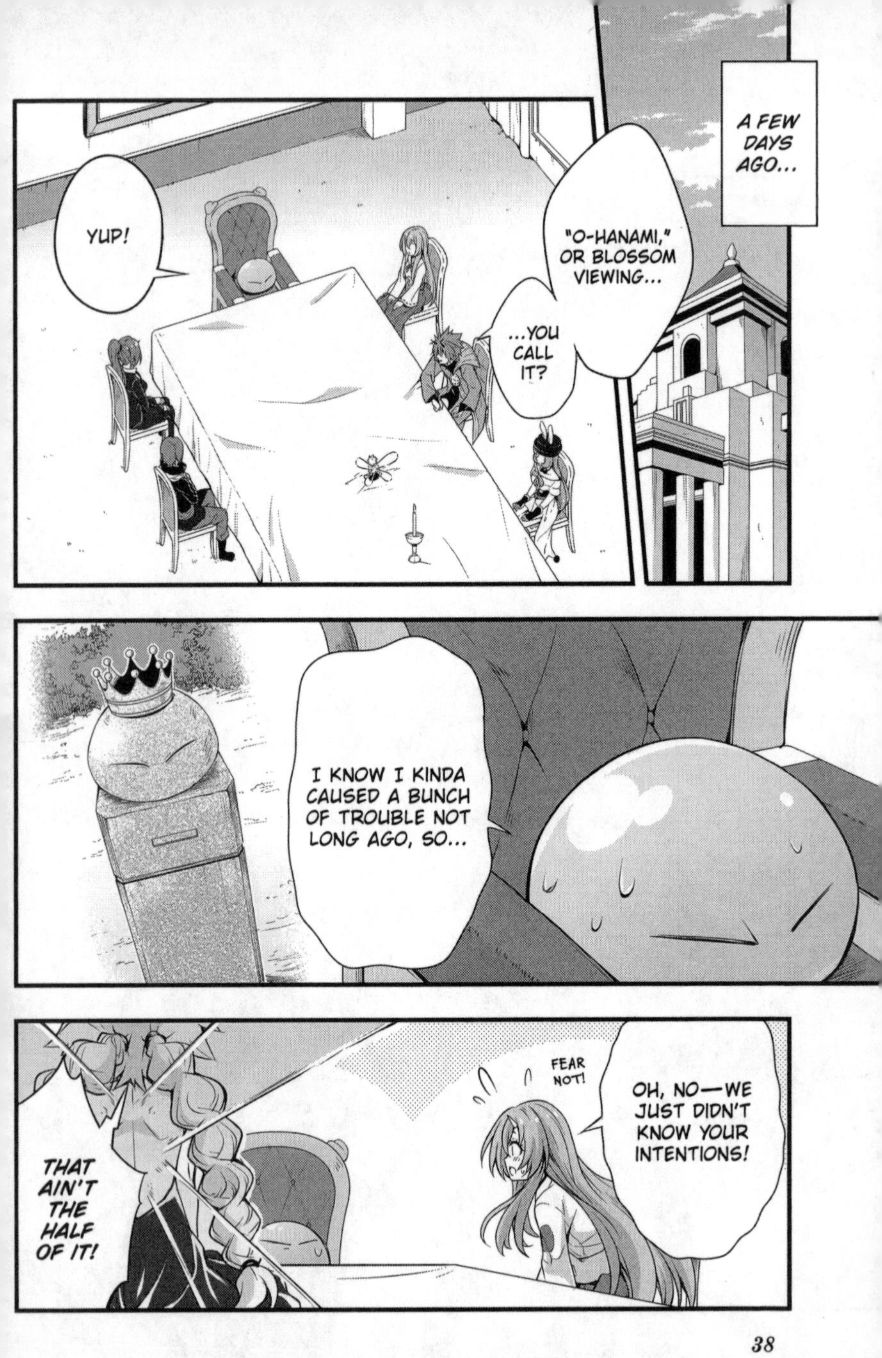

A FEW DAYS AGO...
"O-HANAMI," OR BLOSSOM VIEWING...
...YOU CALL IT?
YUP!
I KNOW I KINDA CAUSED A BUNCH OF TROUBLE NOT LONG AGO, SO...
OH, NO—WE JUST DIDN'T KNOW YOUR INTENTIONS!
FEAR NOT!
THAT AIN'T THE HALF OF IT!

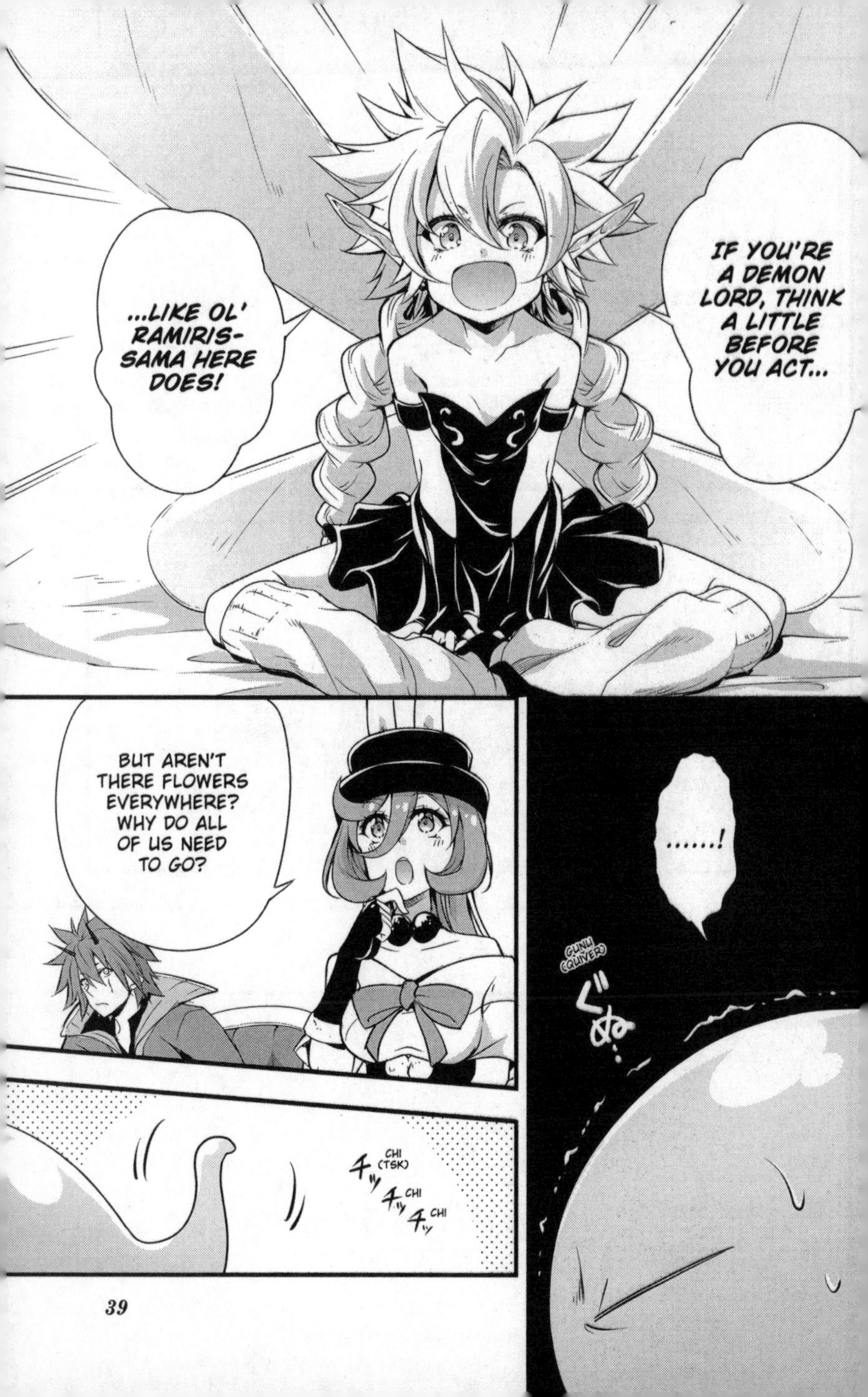
IF YOU'RE A DEMON LORD, THINK A LITTLE BEFORE YOU ACT...
...LIKE OL' RAMIRIS-SAMA HERE DOES!
......!
GUNU (QUIVER)
BUT AREN'T THERE FLOWERS EVERYWHERE? WHY DO ALL OF US NEED TO GO?
CHI (TSK)
CHI
CHI

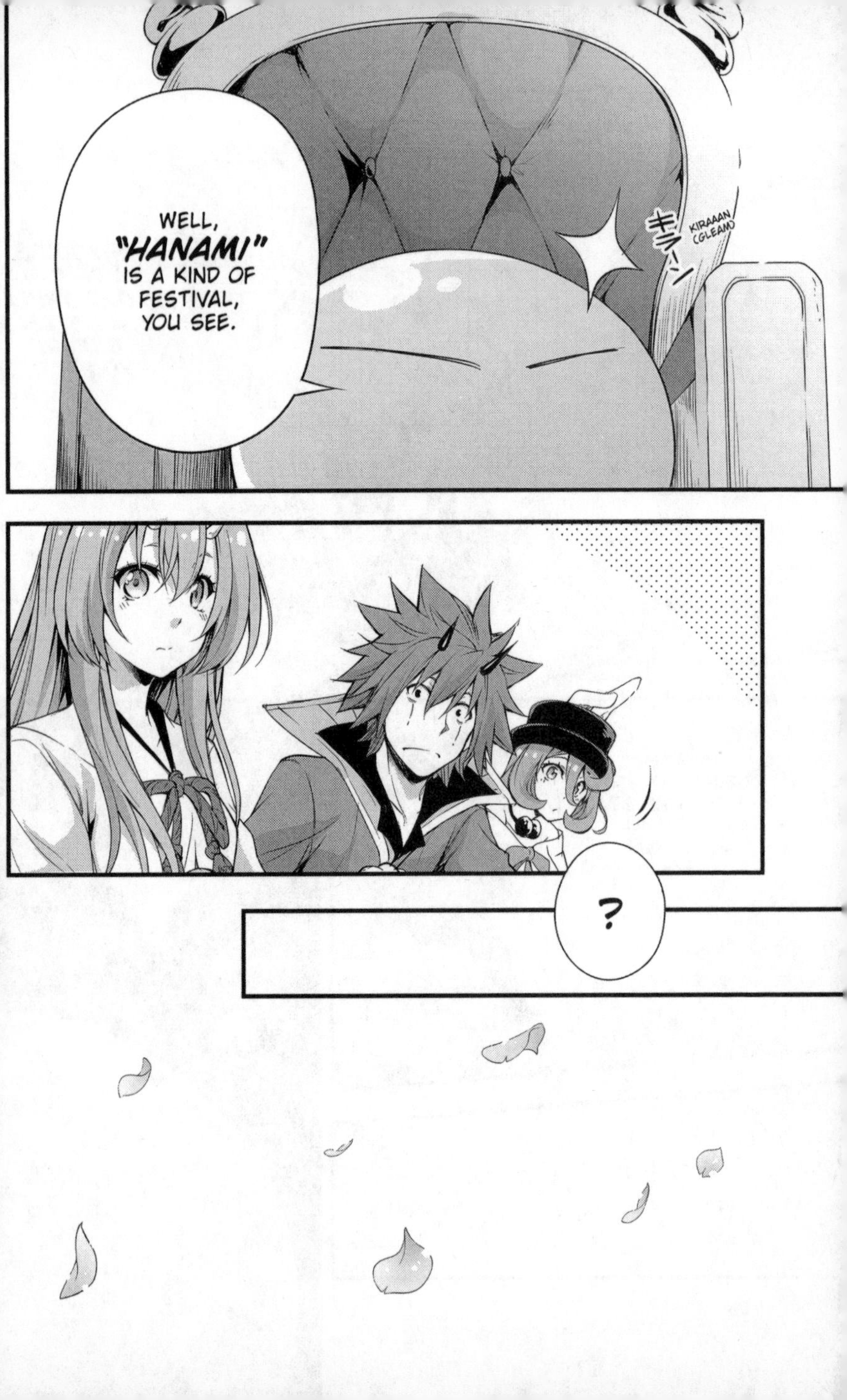
WELL, "HANAMI" IS A KIND OF FESTIVAL, YOU SEE.
キラーン
KIRAAAN (GLEAM)
?

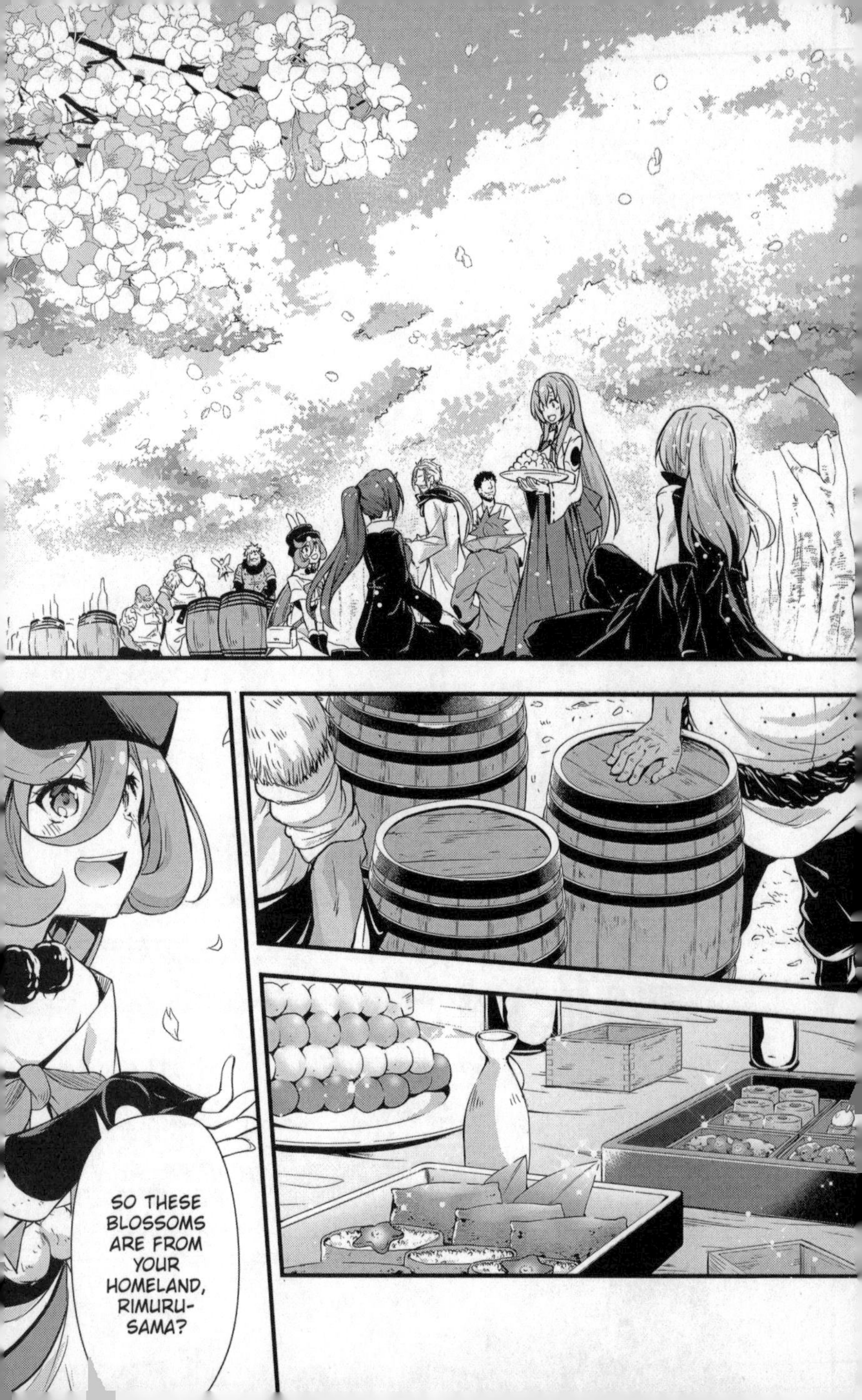
SO THESE BLOSSOMS ARE FROM YOUR HOMELAND, RIMURU-SAMA?

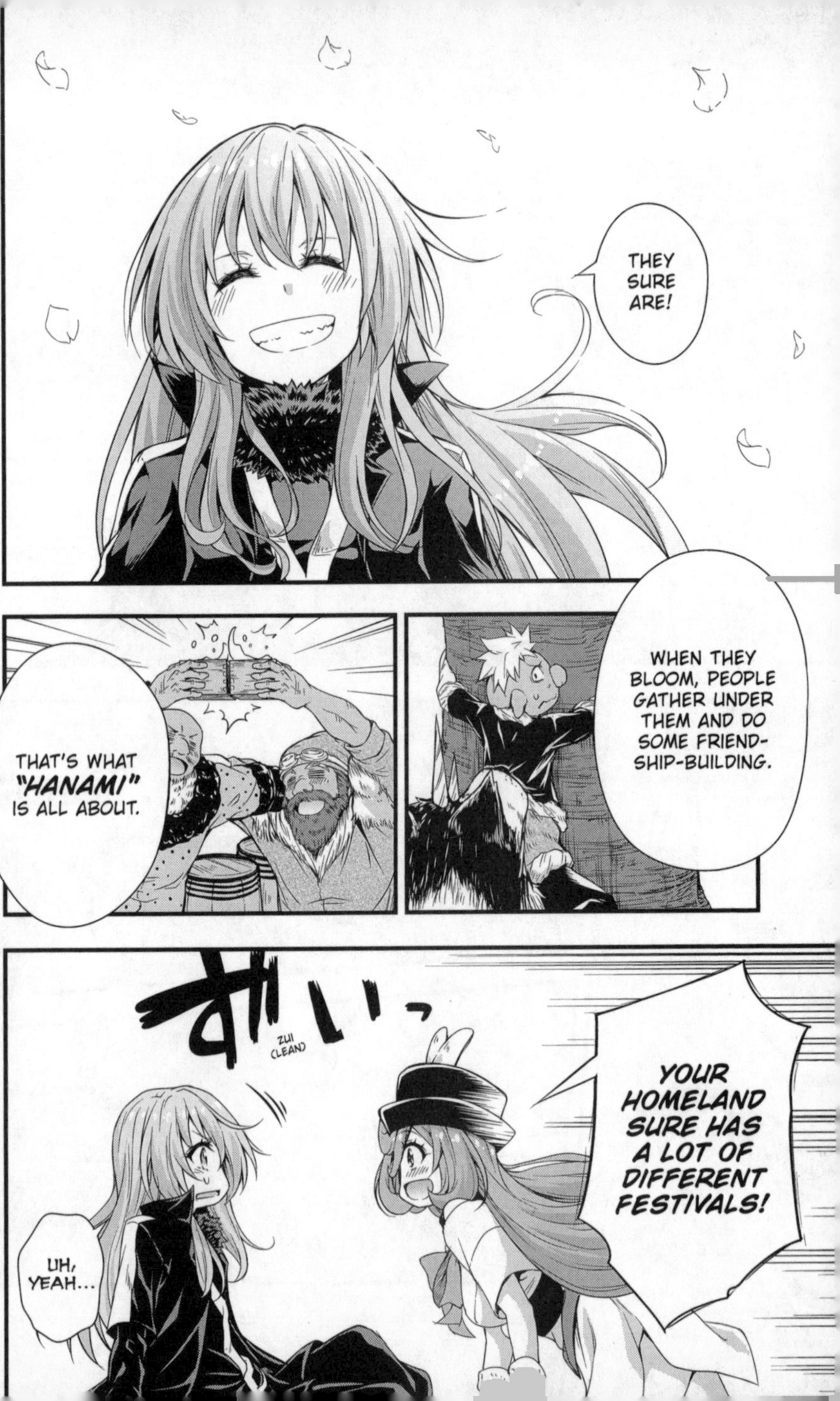
THEY SURE ARE!
WHEN THEY BLOOM, PEOPLE GATHER UNDER THEM AND DO SOME FRIEND-SHIP-BUILDING.
THAT'S WHAT "HANAMI" IS ALL ABOUT.
ZUI (LEAN)
YOUR HOMELAND SURE HAS A LOT OF DIFFERENT FESTIVALS!
UH, YEAH...

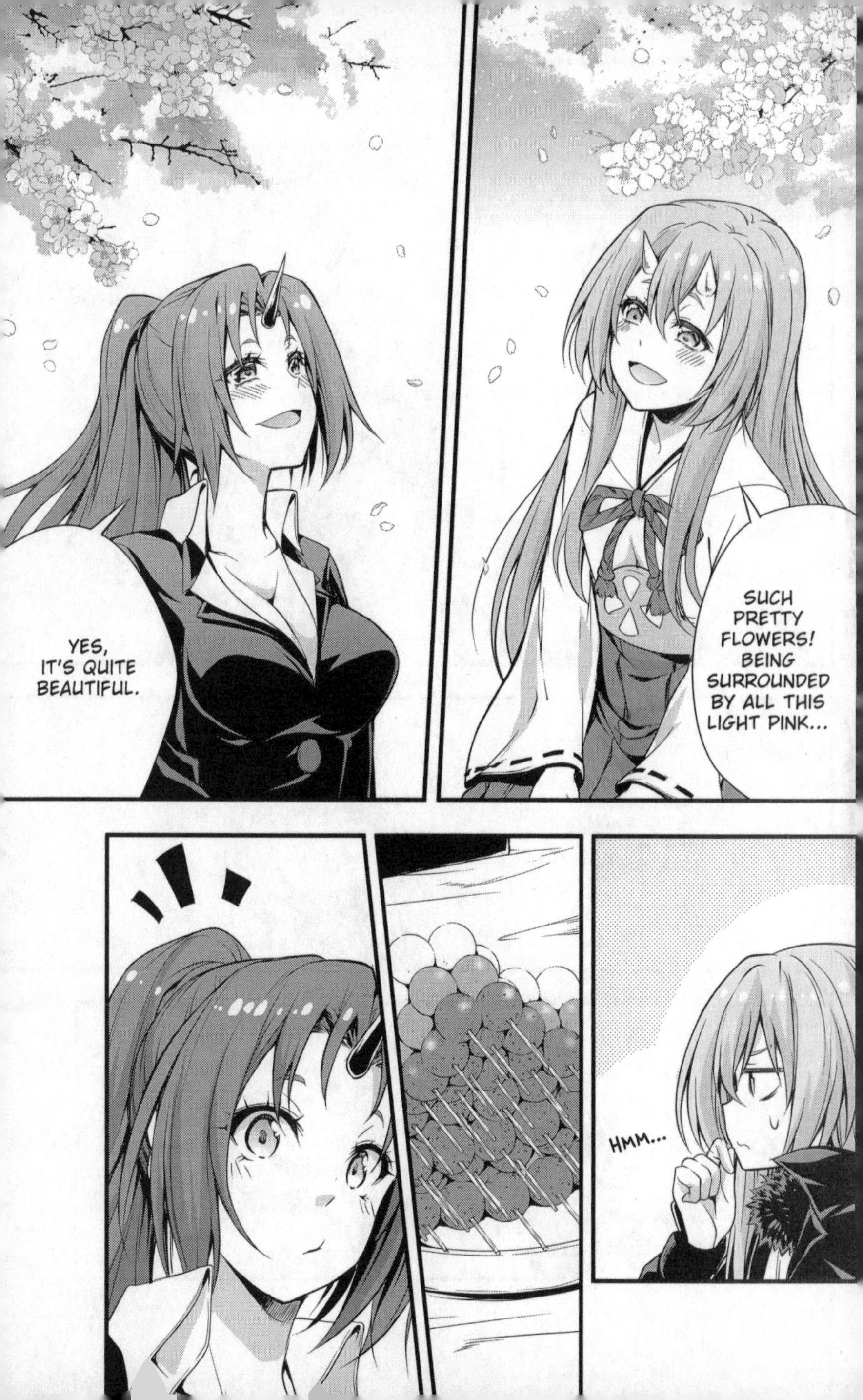
SUCH PRETTY FLOWERS! BEING SURROUNDED BY ALL THIS LIGHT PINK...
YES, IT'S QUITE BEAUTIFUL.
HMM...

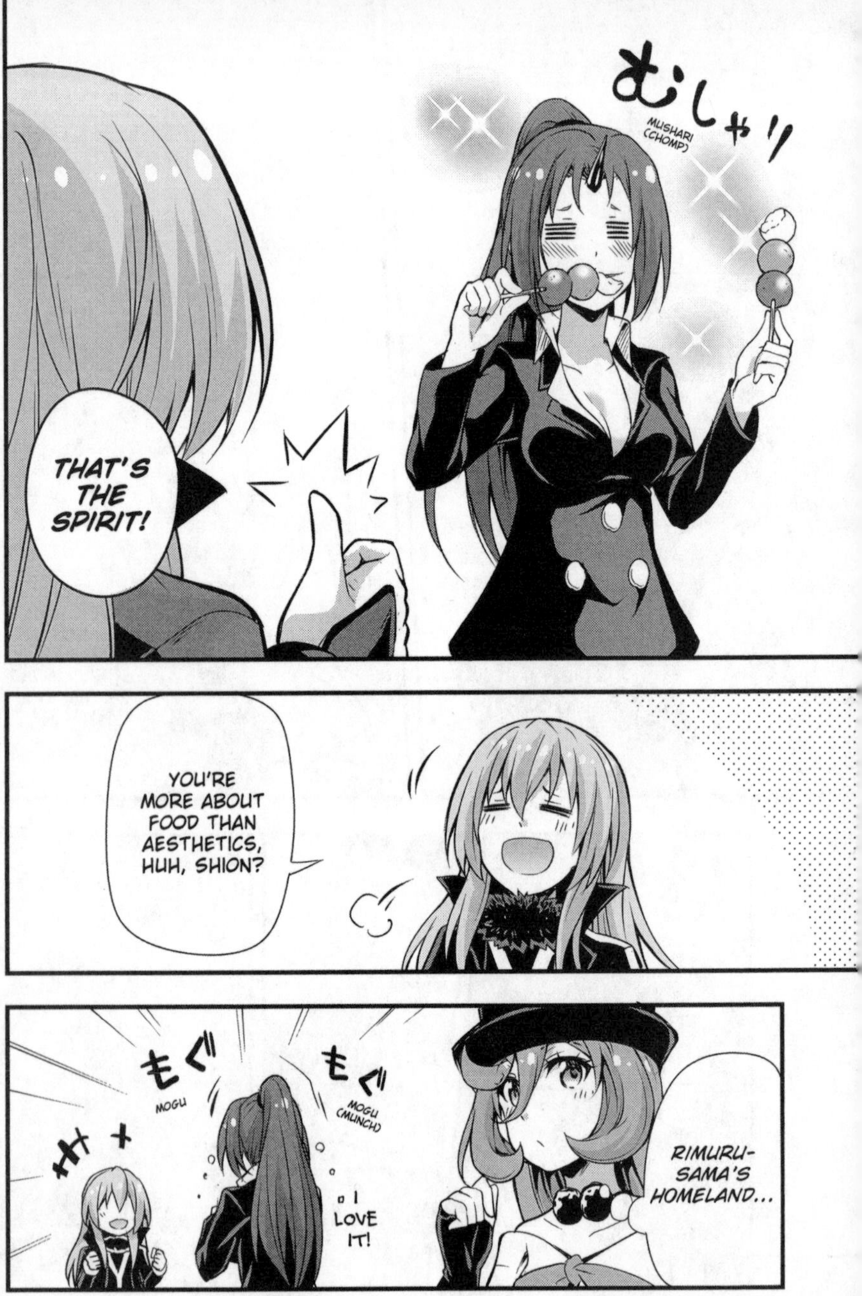
むしゃり
MUSHARI (CHOMP)
THAT'S THE SPIRIT!
YOU'RE MORE ABOUT FOOD THAN AESTHETICS, HUH, SHION?
RIMURU-SAMA'S HOMELAND...
もぐ
MOGU (MUNCH)
もぐ
MOGU
I LOVE IT!

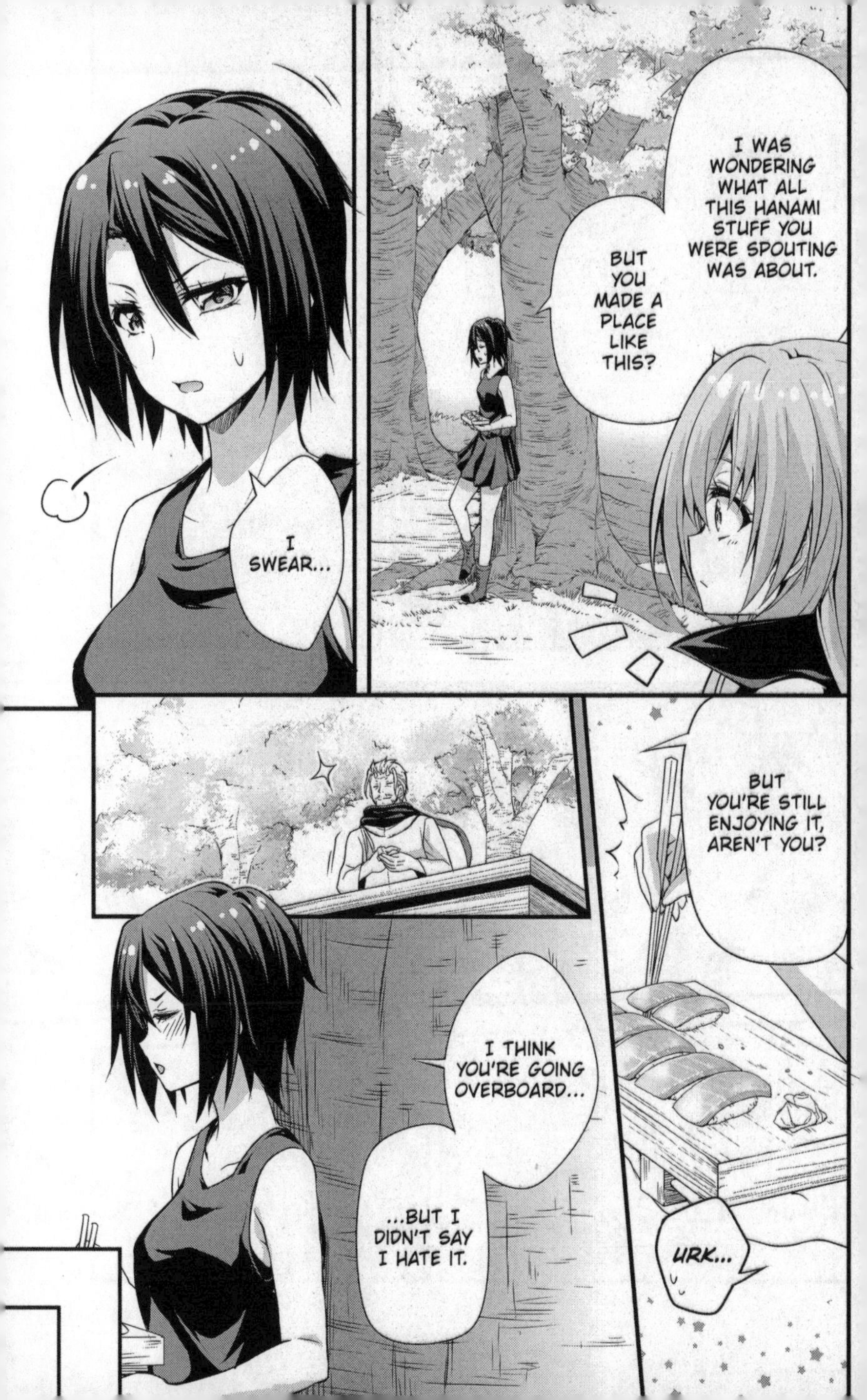
I WAS WONDERING WHAT ALL THIS HANAMI STUFF YOU WERE SPOUTING WAS ABOUT.
BUT YOU MADE A PLACE LIKE THIS?
I SWEAR...
BUT YOU'RE STILL ENJOYING IT, AREN'T YOU?
URK...
I THINK YOU'RE GOING OVERBOARD...
...BUT I DIDN'T SAY I HATE IT.

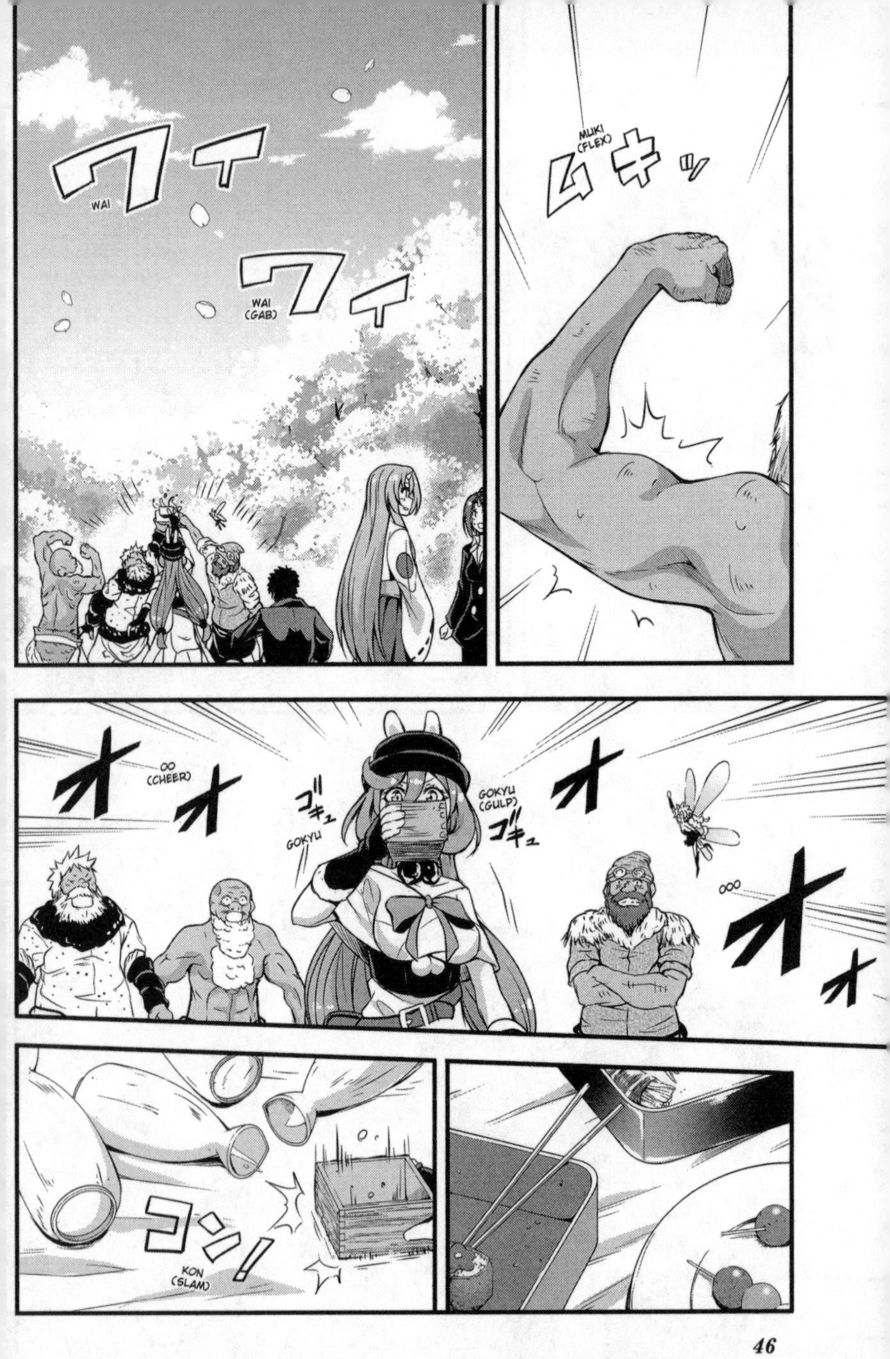
ムキッ
MUKI (FLEX)
ワイ
WAI
ワイ
WAI (GAB)
オオ
OOO
ゴキュ
GOKYU (GULP)
ゴキュ
GOKYU
オオ
OO (CHEER)
コン！
KON (SLAM)

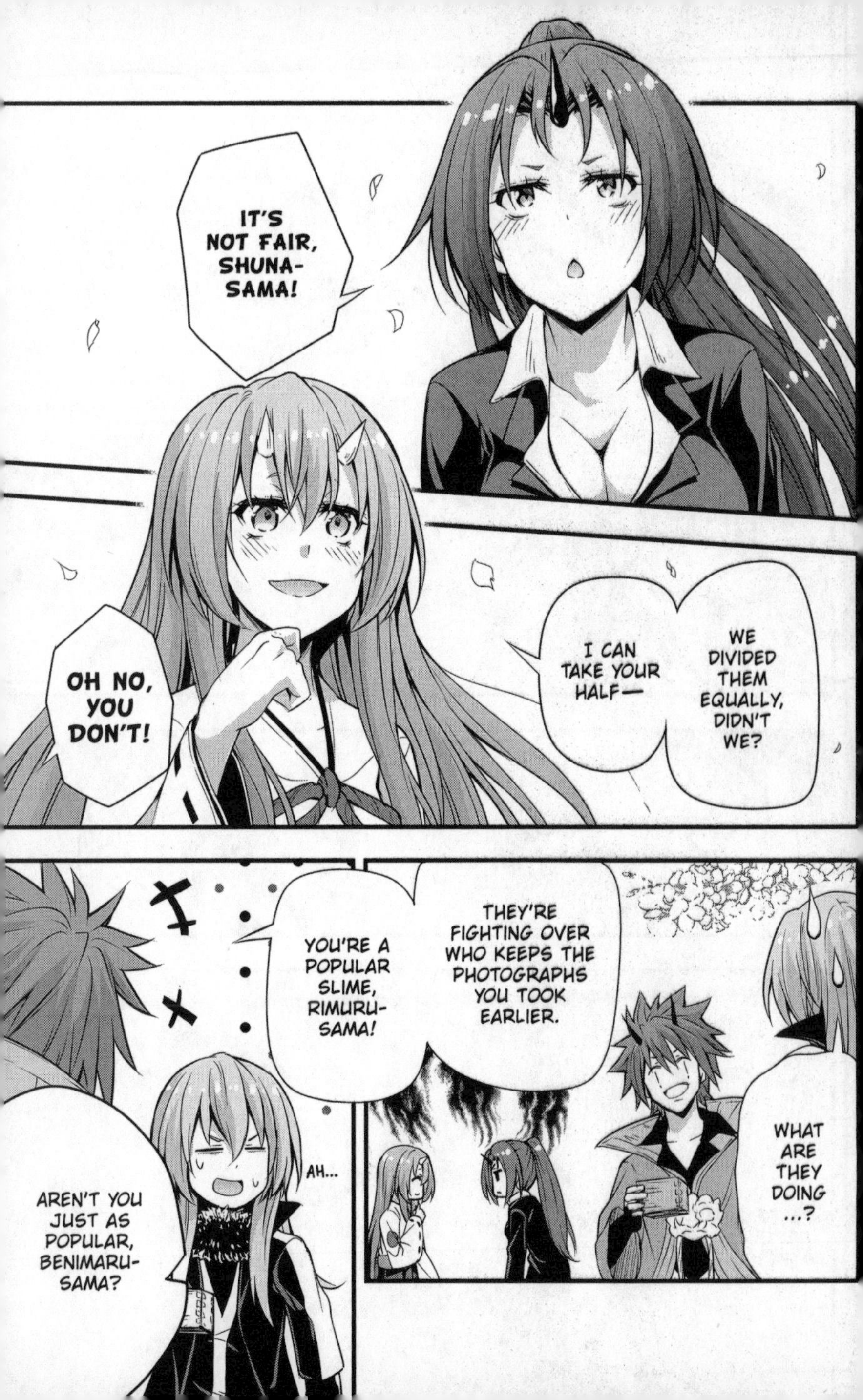
IT'S NOT FAIR, SHUNA-SAMA!
WE DIVIDED THEM EQUALLY, DIDN'T WE?
I CAN TAKE YOUR HALF—
OH NO, YOU DON'T!
WHAT ARE THEY DOING ...?
THEY'RE FIGHTING OVER WHO KEEPS THE PHOTOGRAPHS YOU TOOK EARLIER.
YOU'RE A POPULAR SLIME, RIMURU-SAMA!
AH...
AREN'T YOU JUST AS POPULAR, BENIMARU-SAMA?

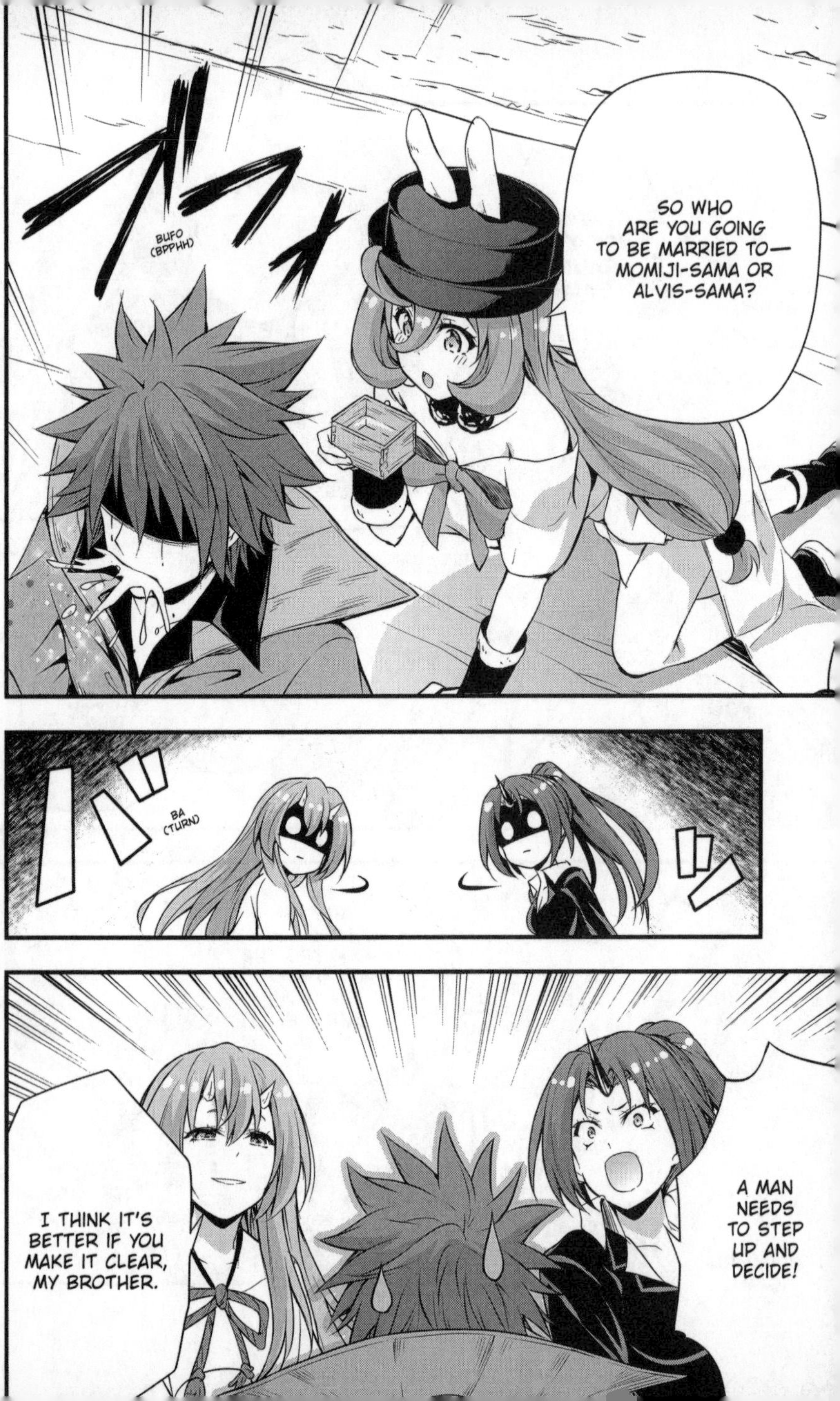
SO WHO ARE YOU GOING TO BE MARRIED TO—MOMIJI-SAMA OR ALVIS-SAMA?
BUFO (BPPHH)
BA (TURN)
A MAN NEEDS TO STEP UP AND DECIDE!
I THINK IT'S BETTER IF YOU MAKE IT CLEAR, MY BROTHER.

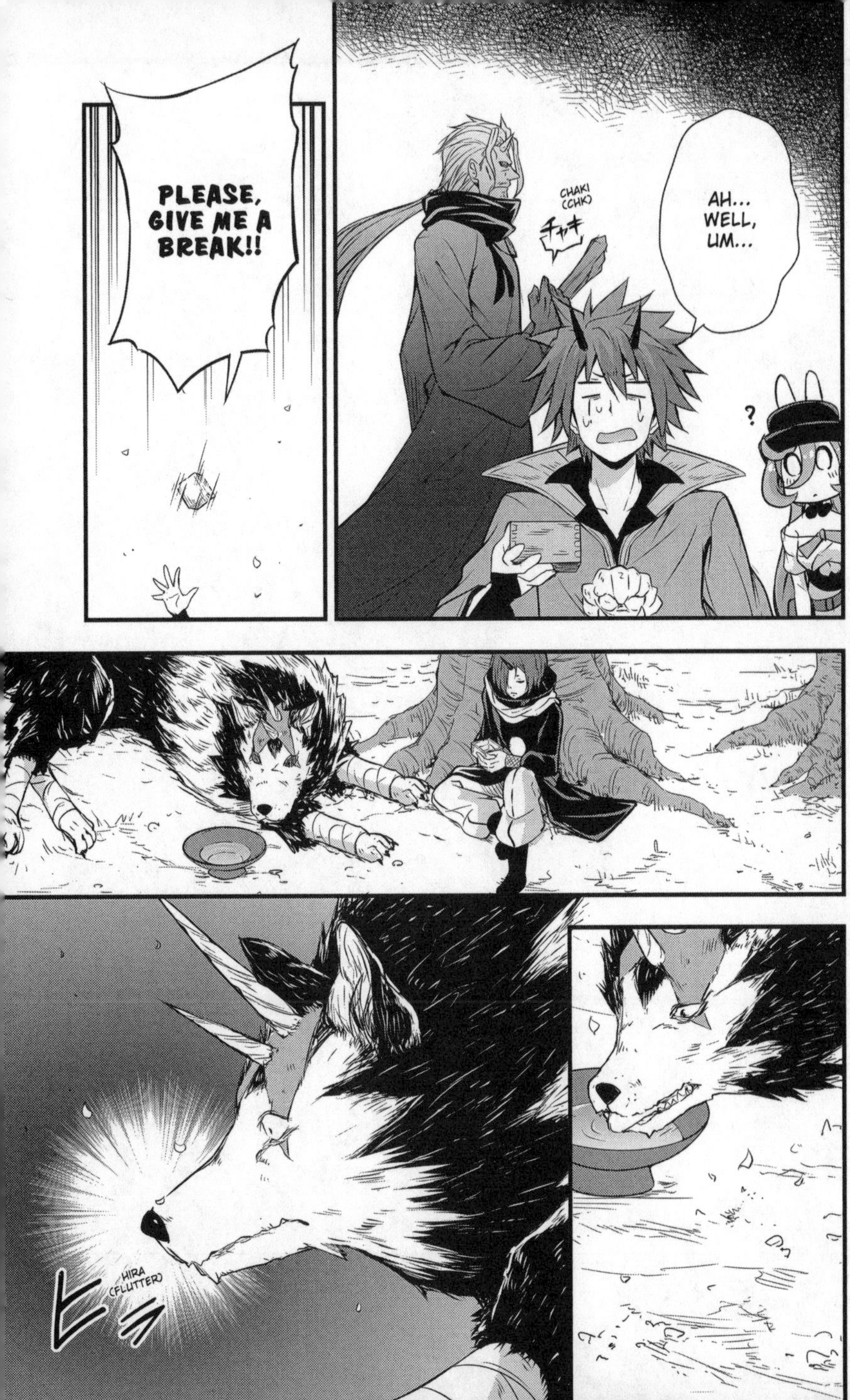
AH... WELL, UM...
CHAKI (CHK)
チャキ
?
PLEASE, GIVE ME A BREAK!!
HIRA (FLUTTER)
ヒラ

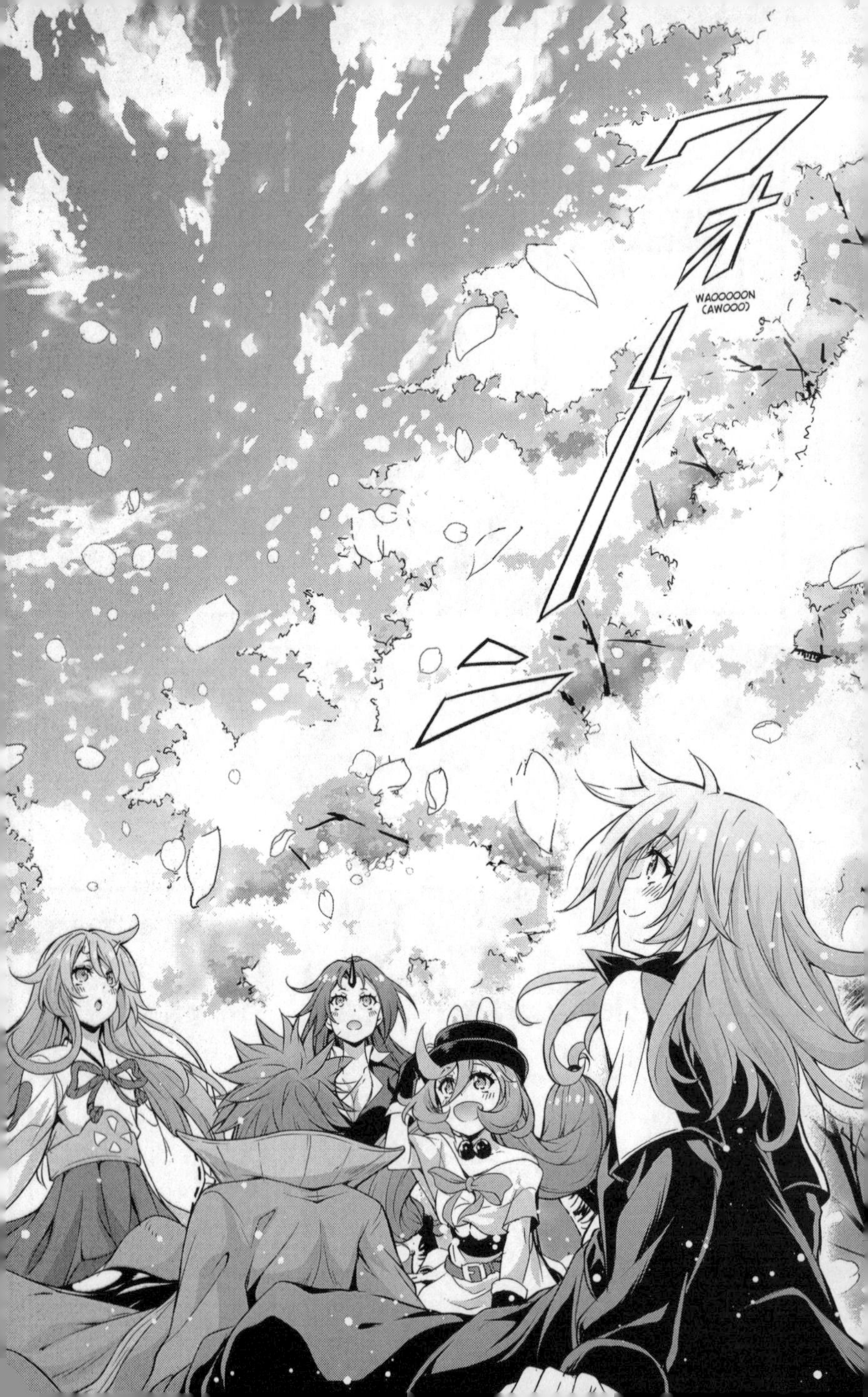
ワオーーン
WAOOOOON (AWOOO)

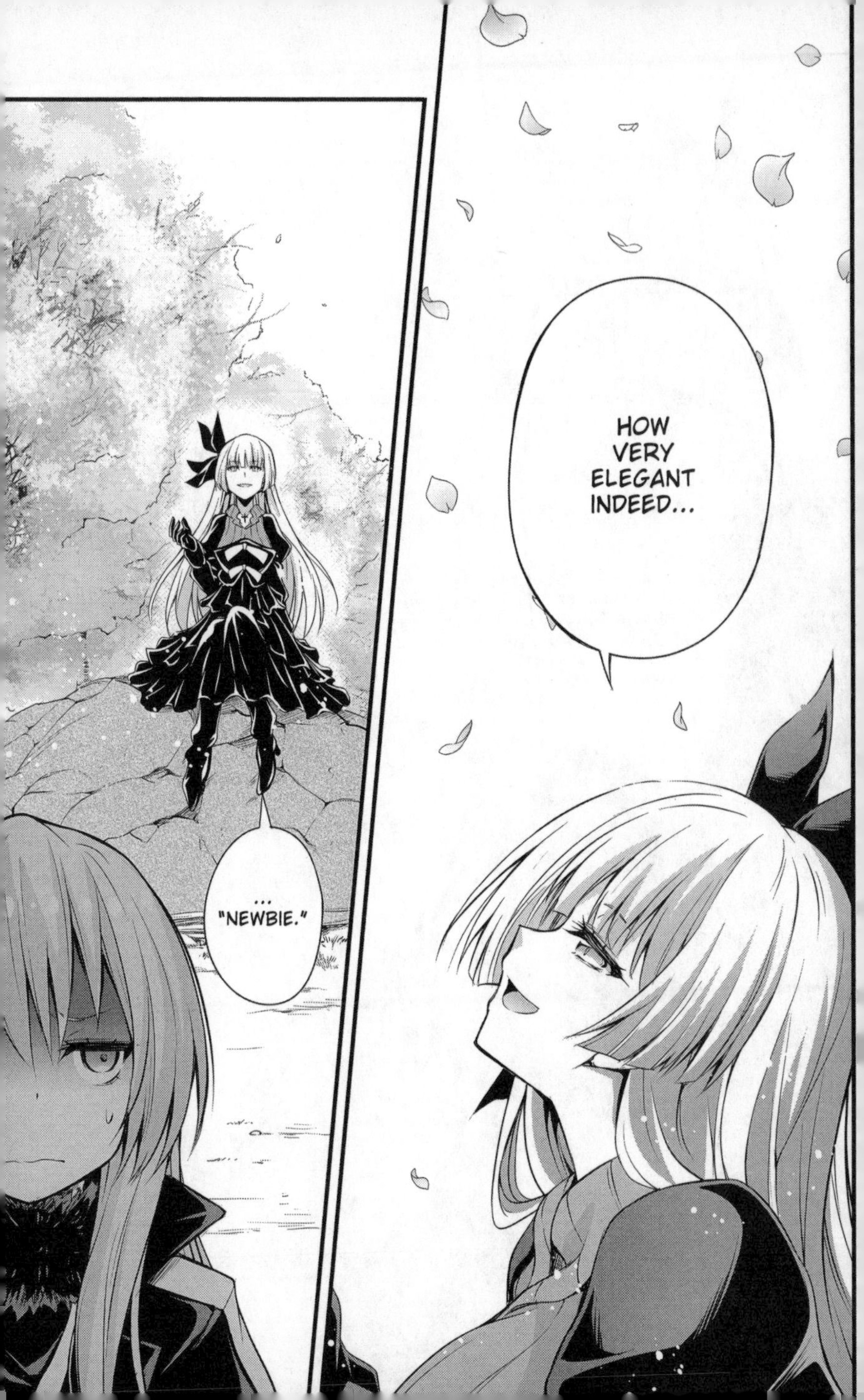
HOW VERY ELEGANT INDEED...
... "NEWBIE."

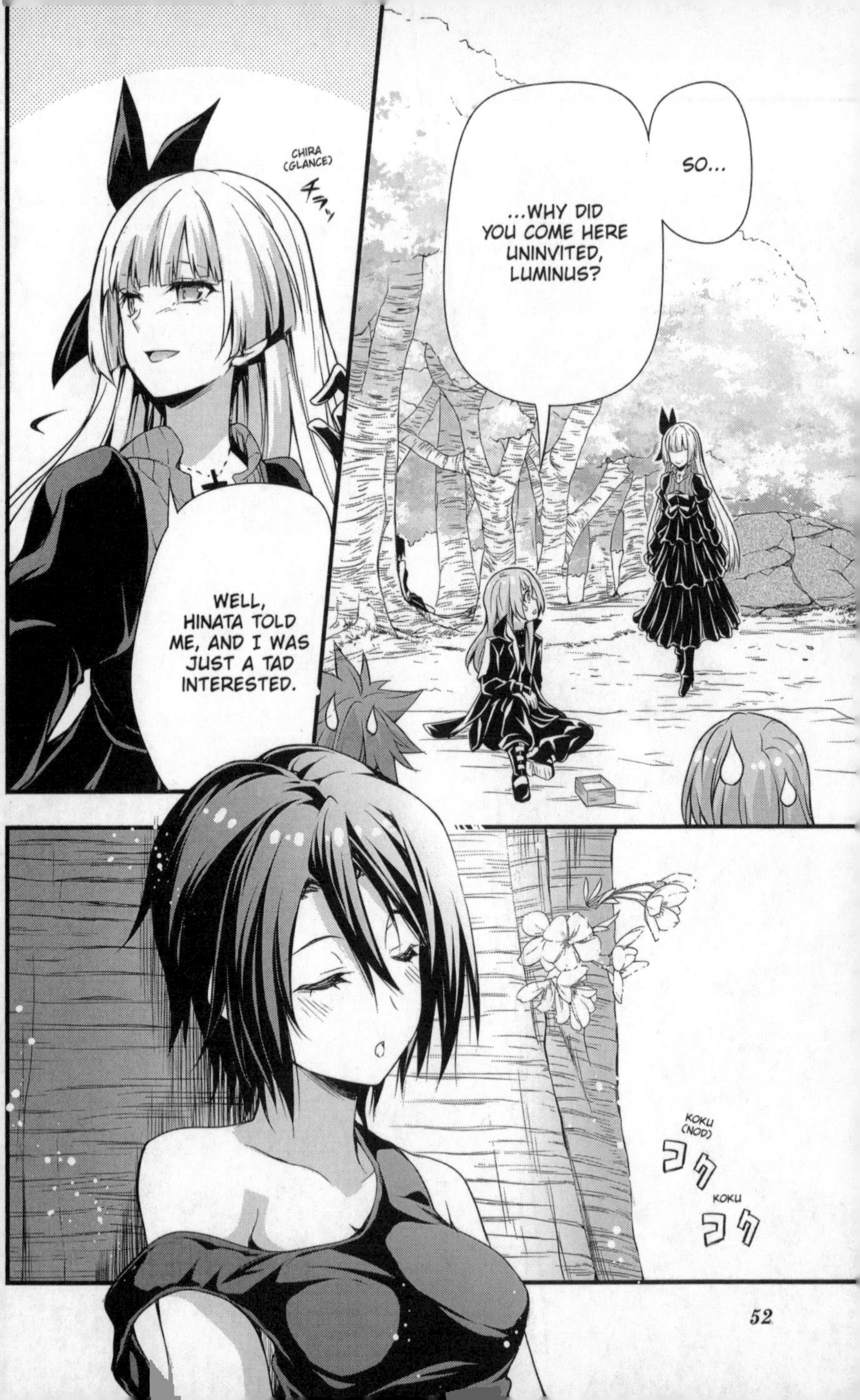
SO...
...WHY DID YOU COME HERE UNINVITED, LUMINUS?
CHIRA (GLANCE)
チラッ
WELL, HINATA TOLD ME, AND I WAS JUST A TAD INTERESTED.
KOKU (NOD)
コク
KOKU
コク

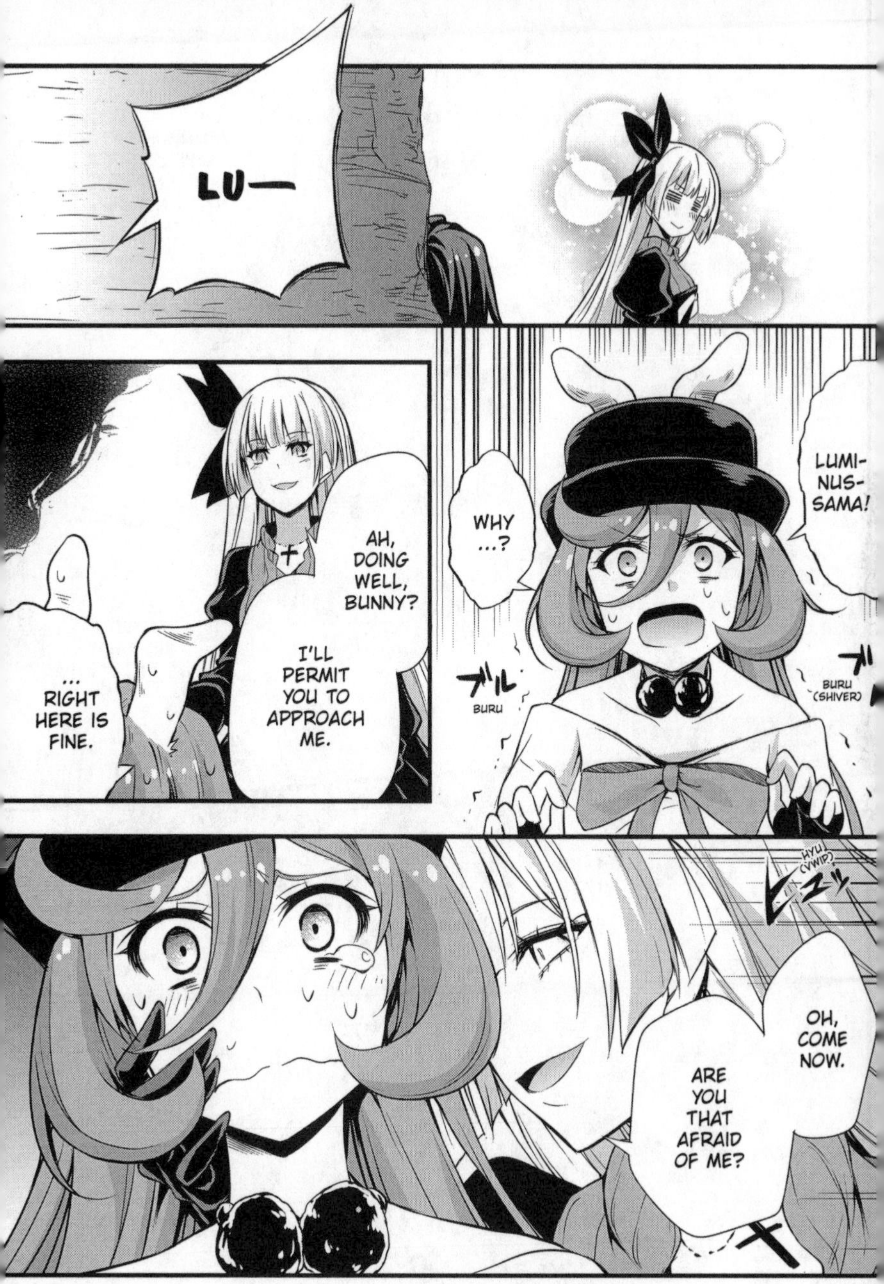
LU—
LUMI-NUS-SAMA!
WHY ...?
BURU (SHIVER)
BURU
AH, DOING WELL, BUNNY?
I'LL PERMIT YOU TO APPROACH ME.
... RIGHT HERE IS FINE.
HYU (VWIP)
OH, COME NOW.
ARE YOU THAT AFRAID OF ME?

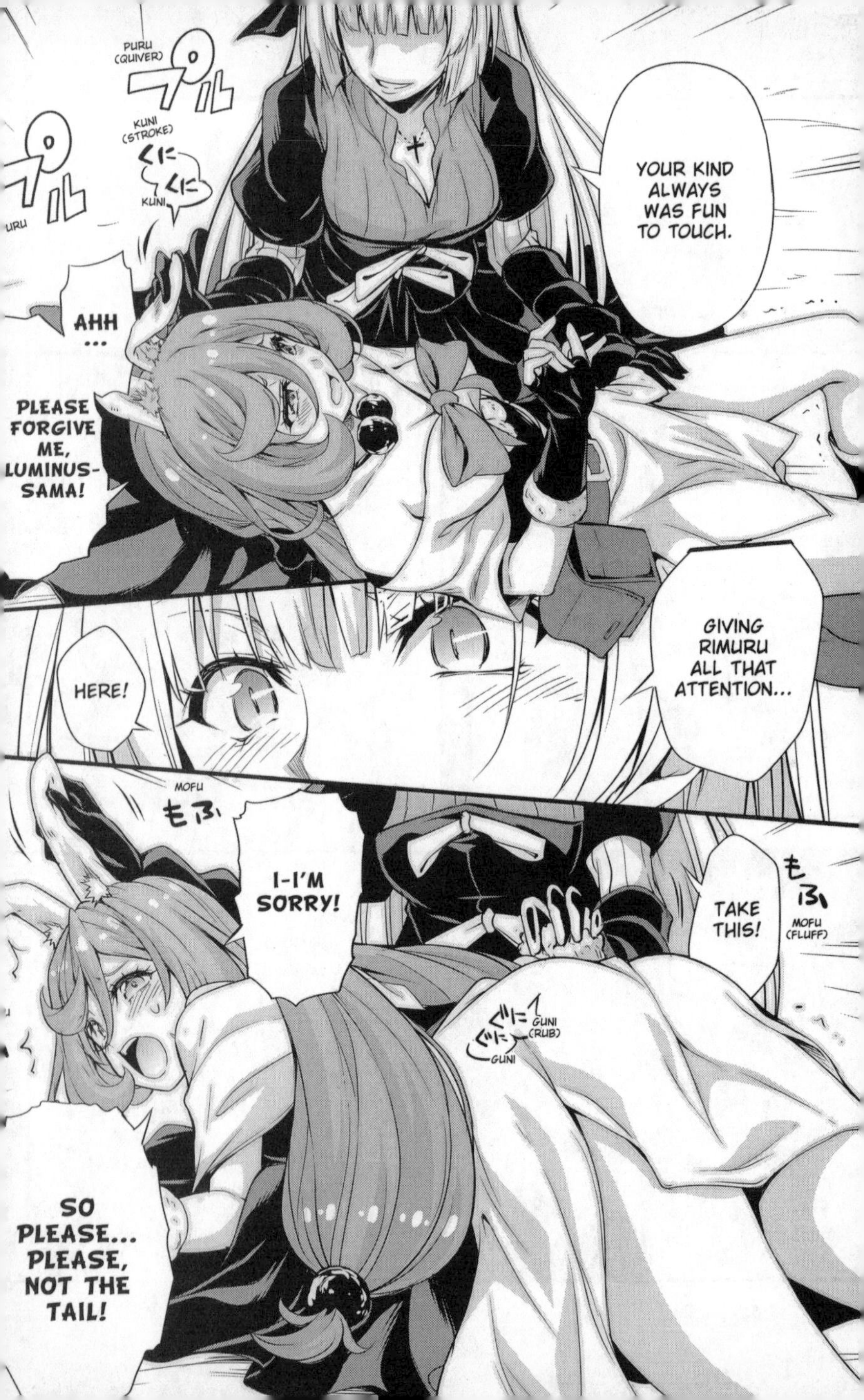
YOUR KIND ALWAYS WAS FUN TO TOUCH.
PURU (QUIVER)
プル
KUNI (STROKE)
くに くに
KUNI
プル
URU
AHH...
PLEASE FORGIVE ME, LUMINUS-SAMA!
GIVING RIMURU ALL THAT ATTENTION...
HERE!
もふ
MOFU (FLUFF)
TAKE THIS!
ぐに ぐに
GUNI (RUB)
GUNI
I-I'M SORRY!
MOFU
もふ
SO PLEASE... PLEASE, NOT THE TAIL!

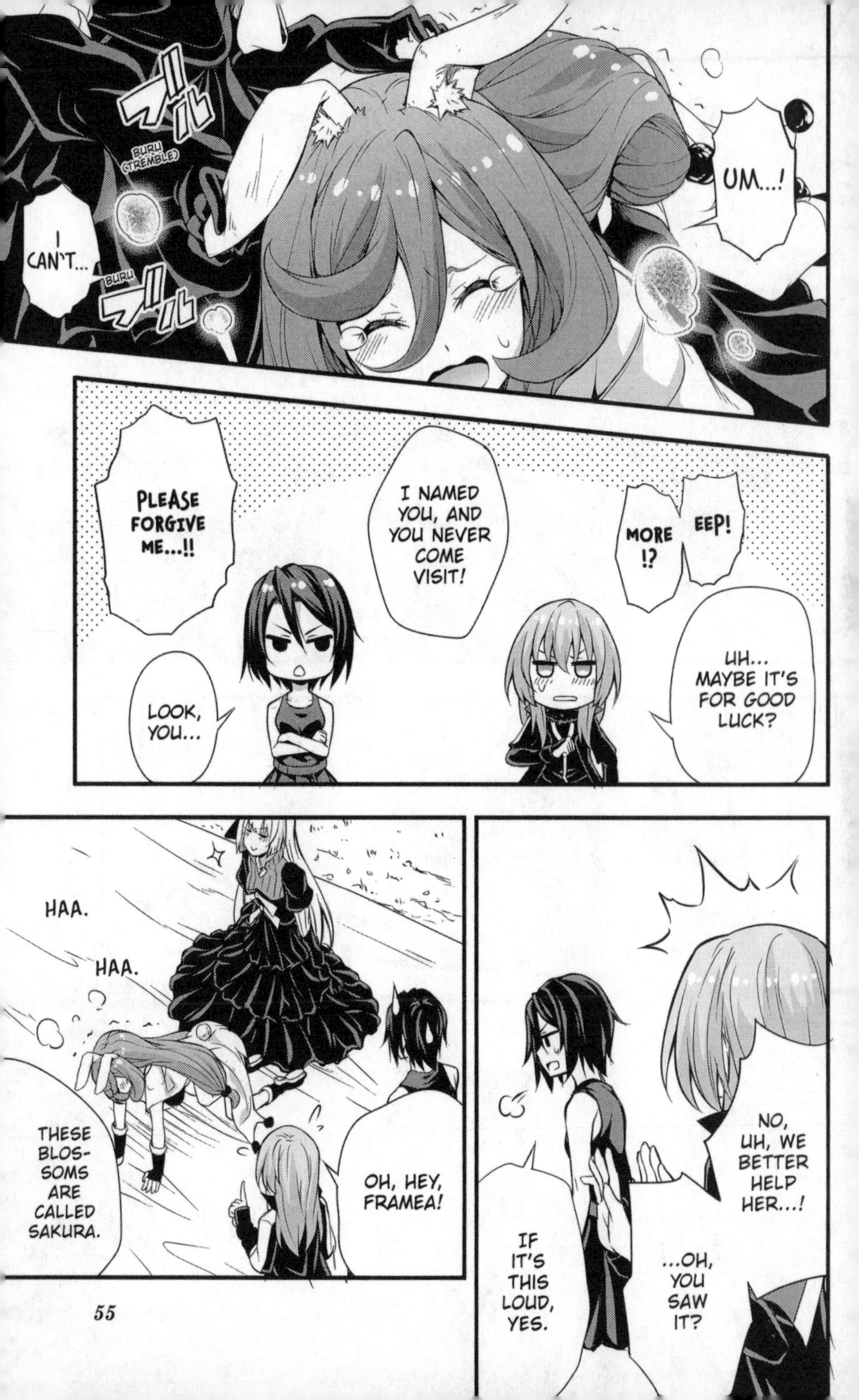
UM...!
BURU (TREMBLE)
I CAN'T...
BURU
EEP!
MORE !?
UH... MAYBE IT'S FOR GOOD LUCK?
I NAMED YOU, AND YOU NEVER COME VISIT!
PLEASE FORGIVE ME...!!
LOOK, YOU...
NO, UH, WE BETTER HELP HER...!
...OH, YOU SAW IT?
IF IT'S THIS LOUD, YES.
OH, HEY, FRAMEA!
HAA.
HAA.
THESE BLOSSOMS ARE CALLED SAKURA.

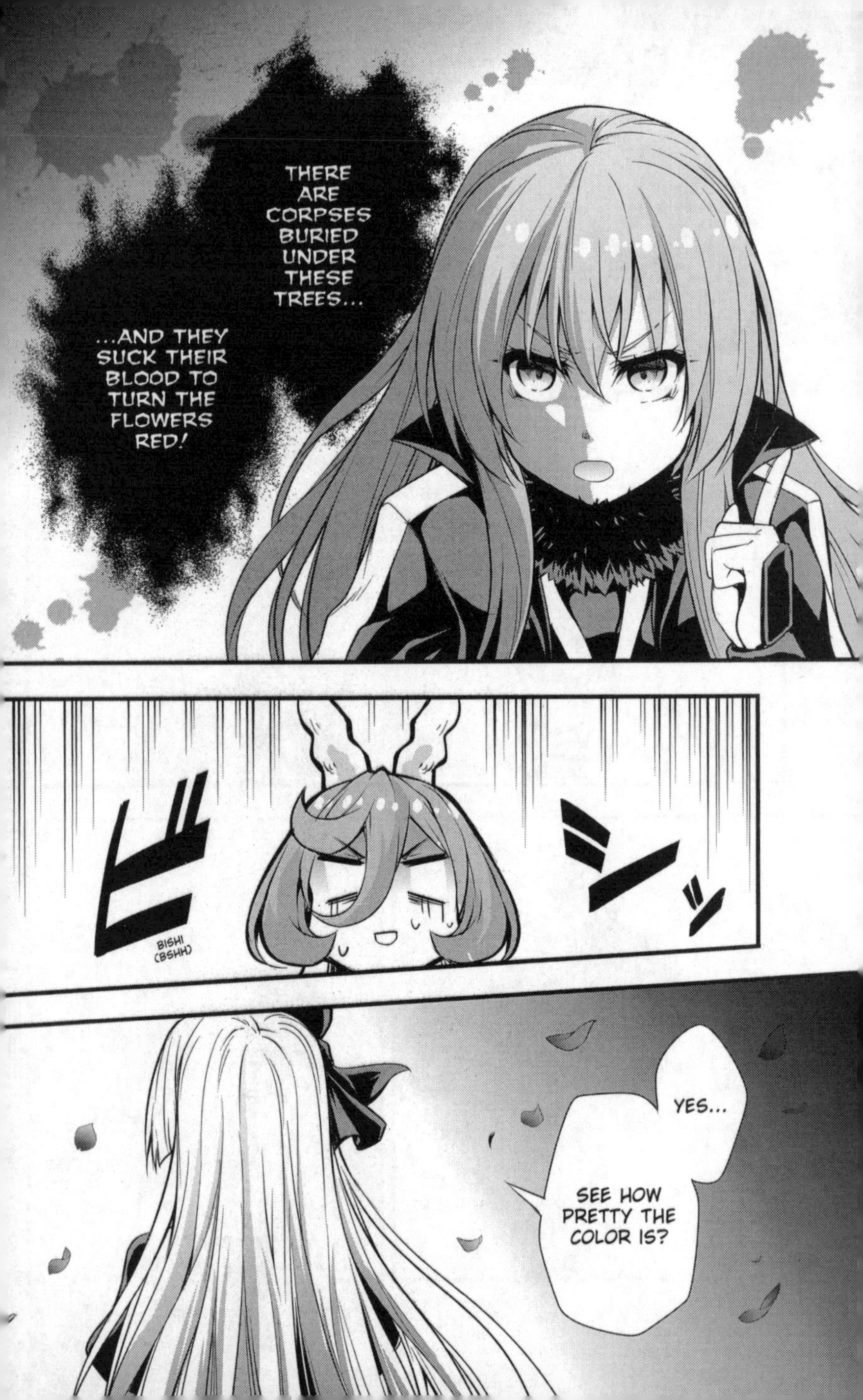
THERE ARE CORPSES BURIED UNDER THESE TREES...
...AND THEY SUCK THEIR BLOOD TO TURN THE FLOWERS RED!
BISHI (BSHH)
YES...
SEE HOW PRETTY THE COLOR IS?

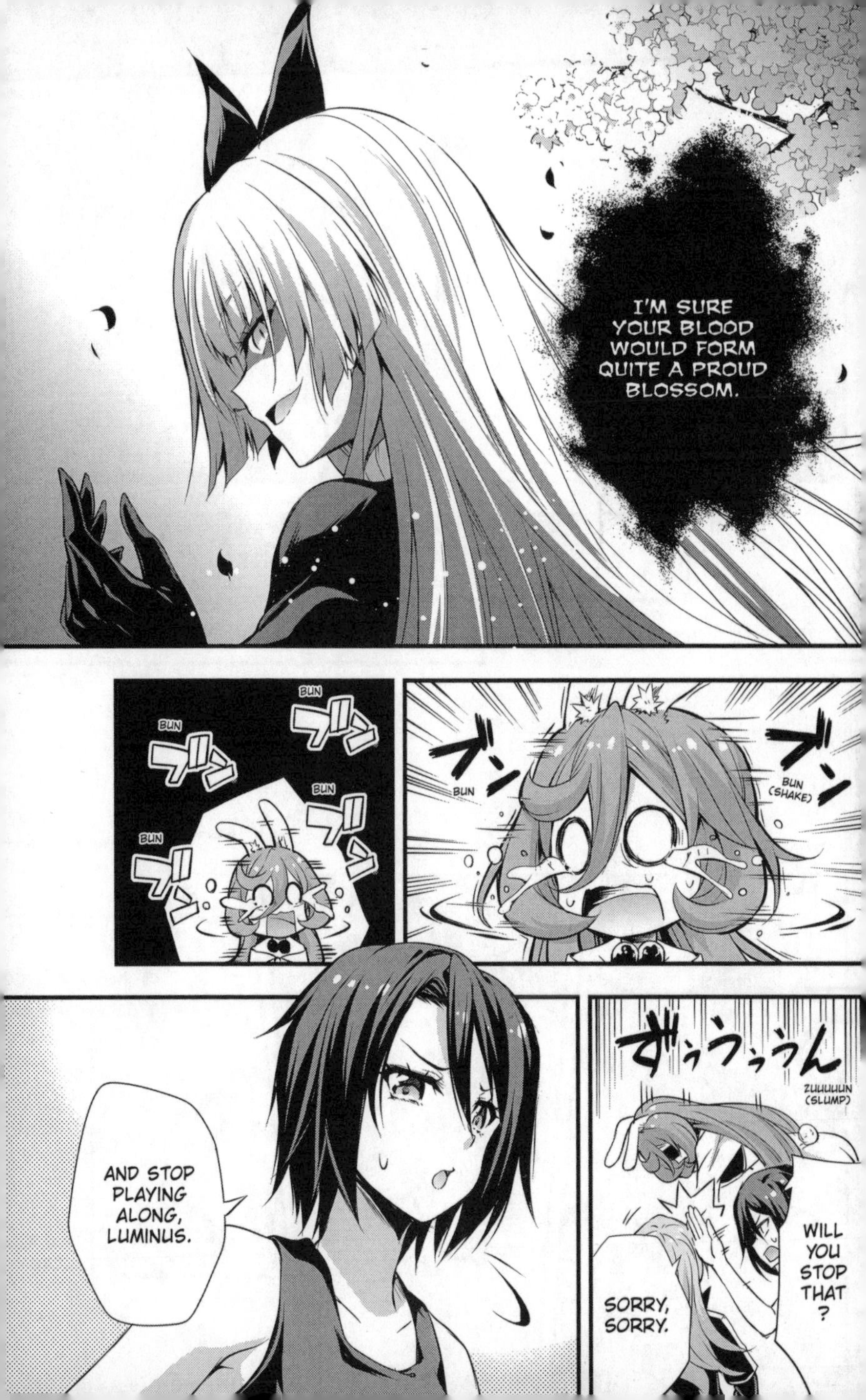
I'M SURE YOUR BLOOD WOULD FORM QUITE A PROUD BLOSSOM.
BUN (SHAKE)
BUN
BUN
BUN
BUN
BUN
ZUUUUUN (SLUMP)
WILL YOU STOP THAT?
SORRY, SORRY.
AND STOP PLAYING ALONG, LUMINUS.

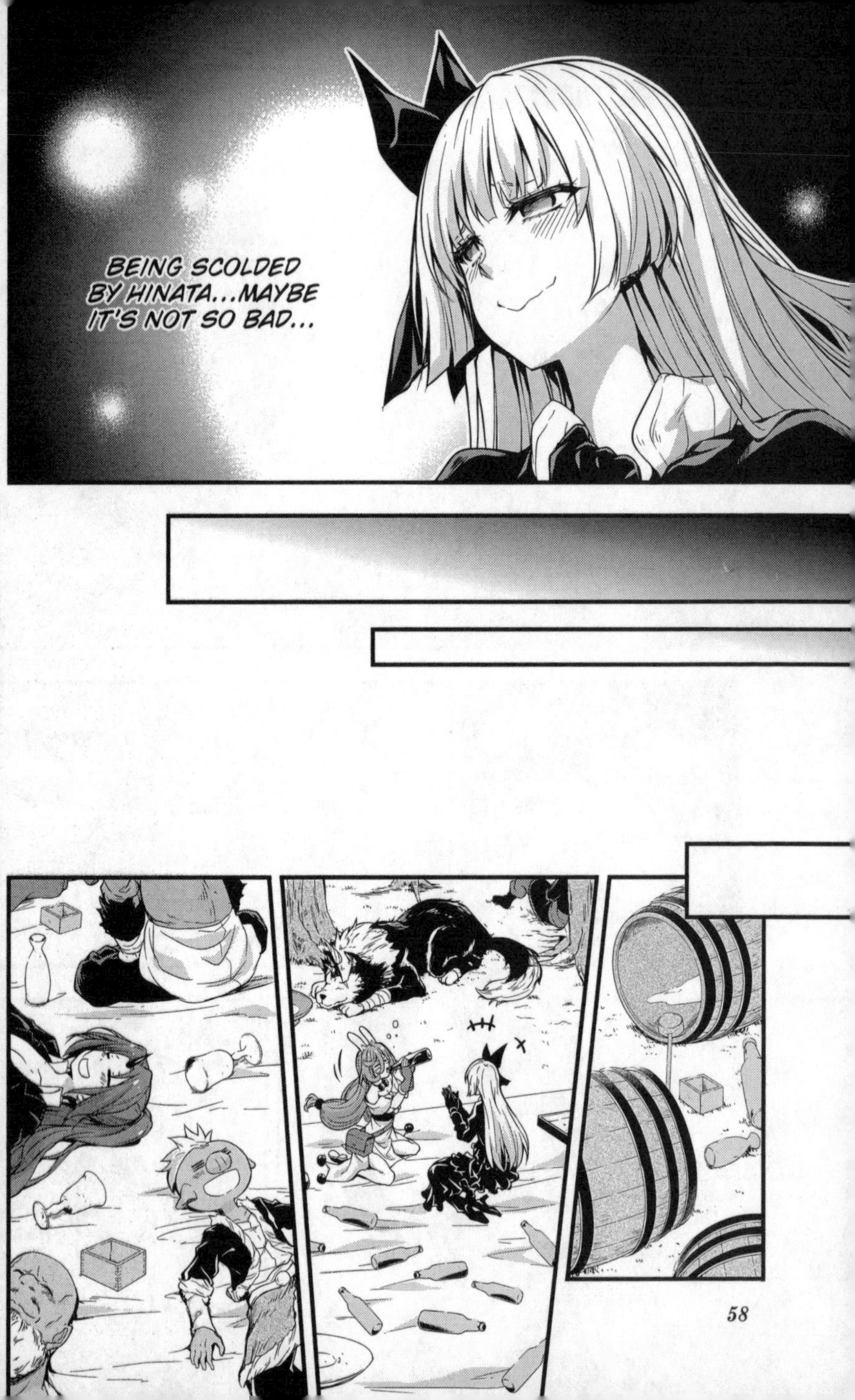
BEING SCOLDED BY HINATA...MAYBE IT'S NOT SO BAD...

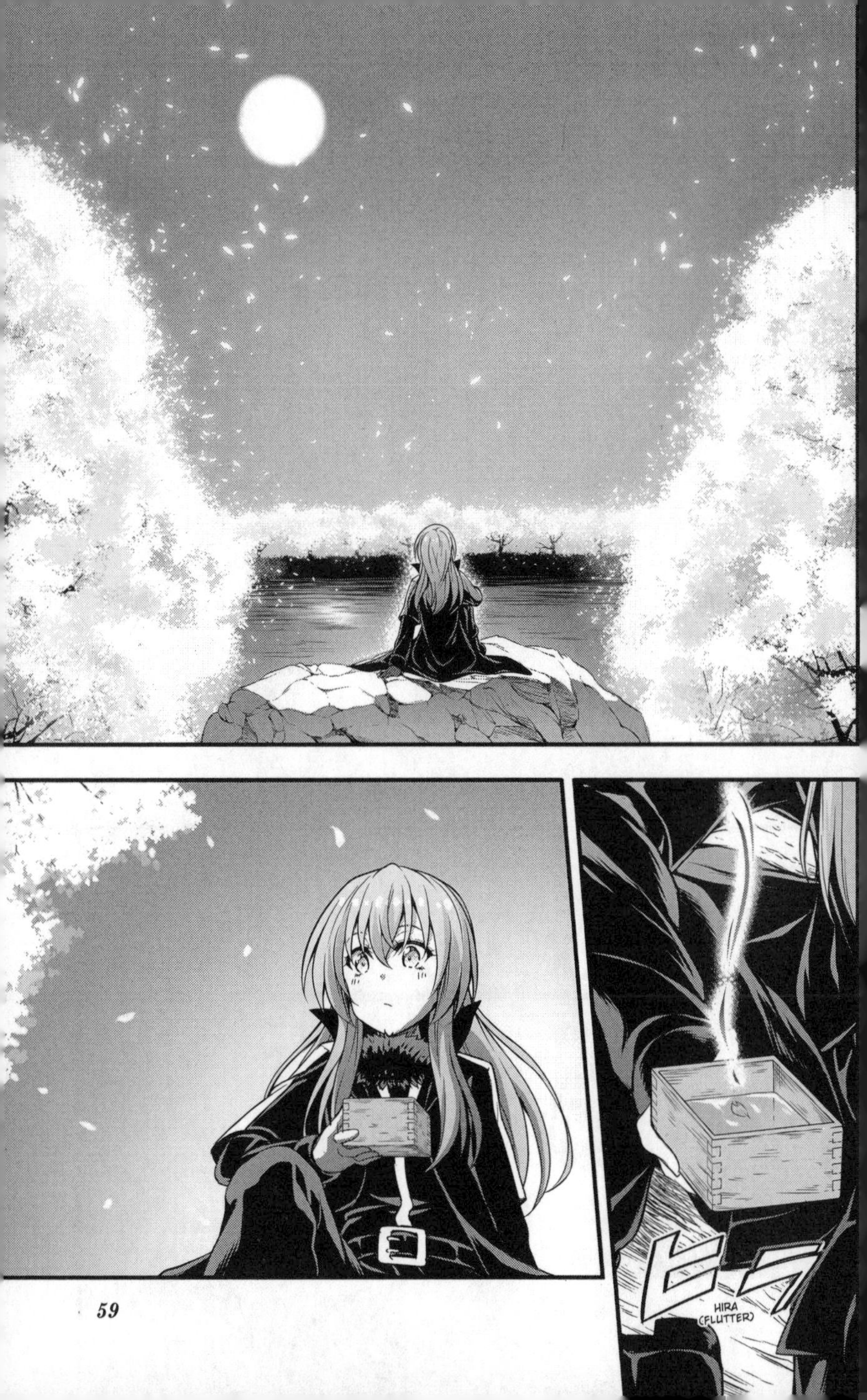
HIRA (FLUTTER)

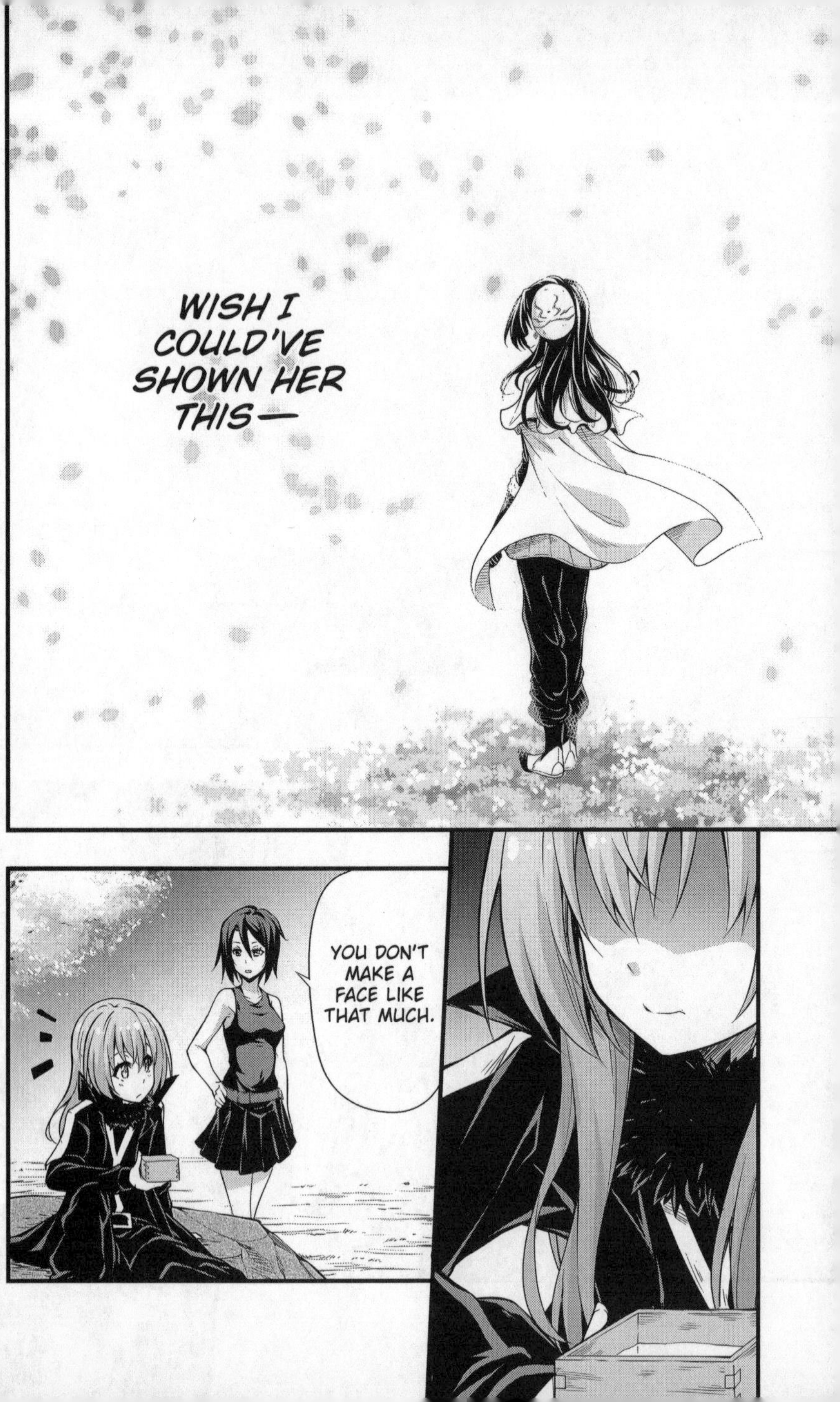
WISH I COULD'VE SHOWN HER THIS—
YOU DON'T MAKE A FACE LIKE THAT MUCH.

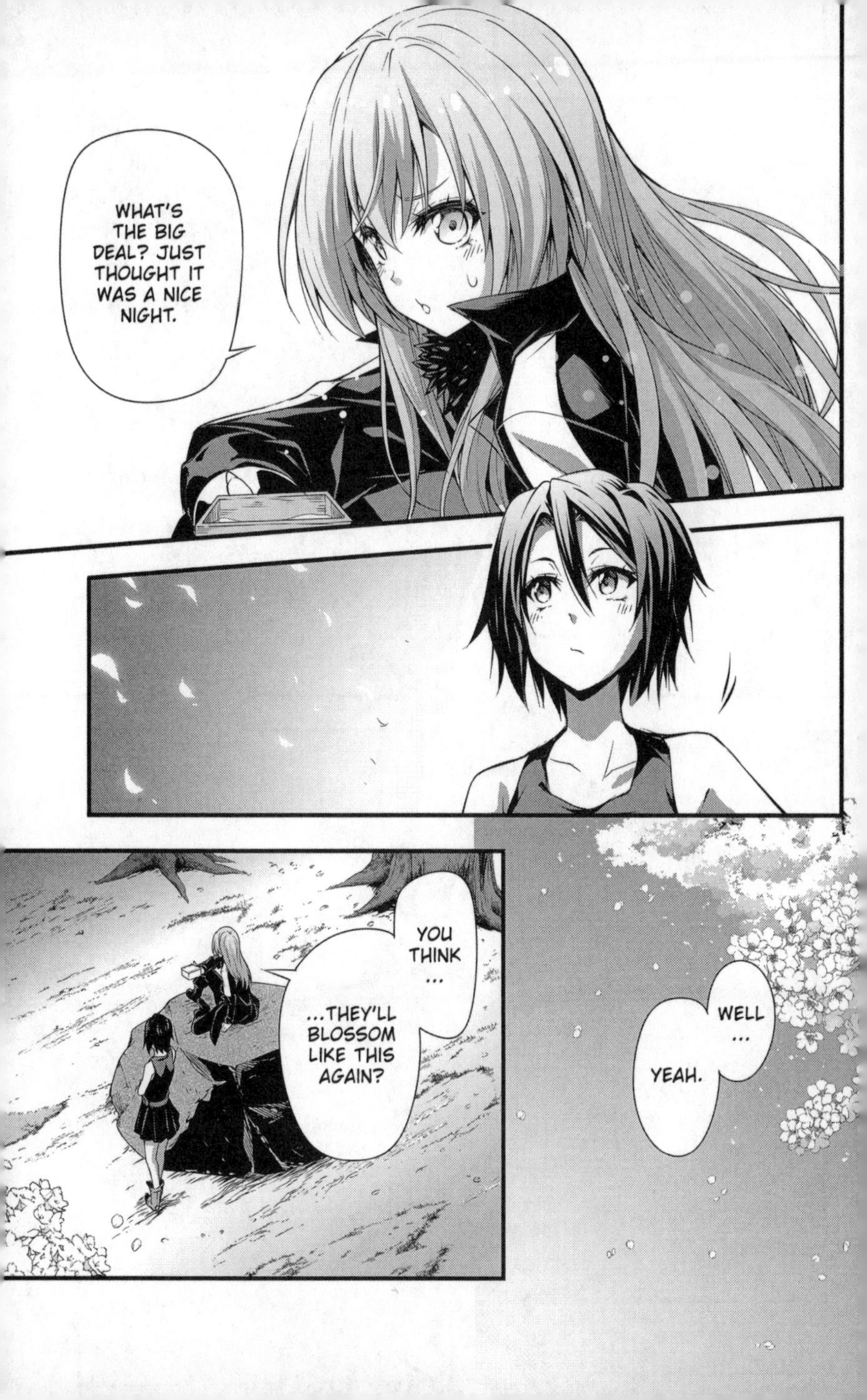
WHAT'S THE BIG DEAL? JUST THOUGHT IT WAS A NICE NIGHT.
WELL ... YEAH.
YOU THINK ...
...THEY'LL BLOSSOM LIKE THIS AGAIN?

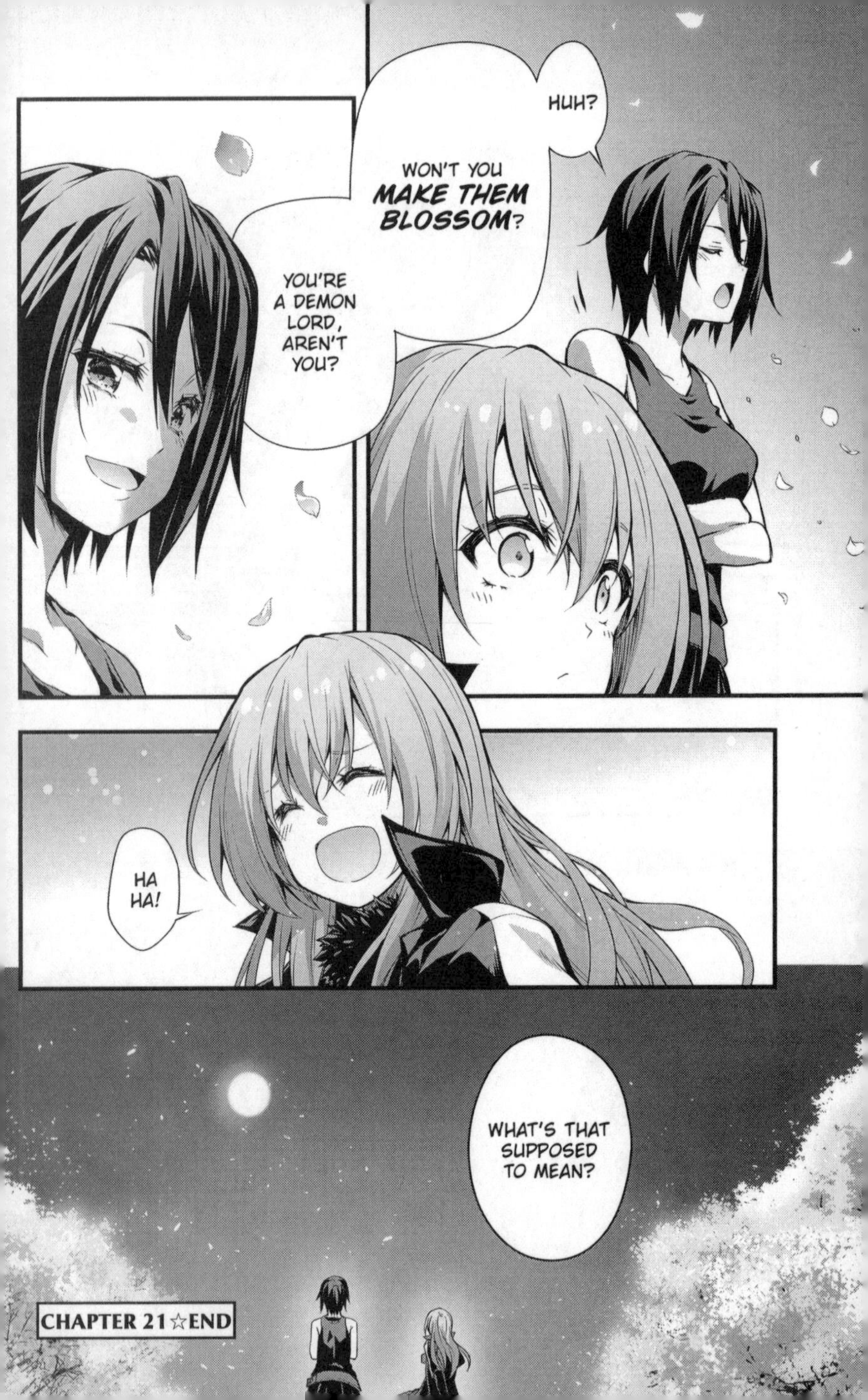
HUH?
WON'T YOU MAKE THEM BLOSSOM?
YOU'RE A DEMON LORD, AREN'T YOU?
HA HA!
WHAT'S THAT SUPPOSED TO MEAN?
CHAPTER 21☆END

That **Time I Got**
Rèincarnated
as a SLIME
The Ways of the Monster Nation

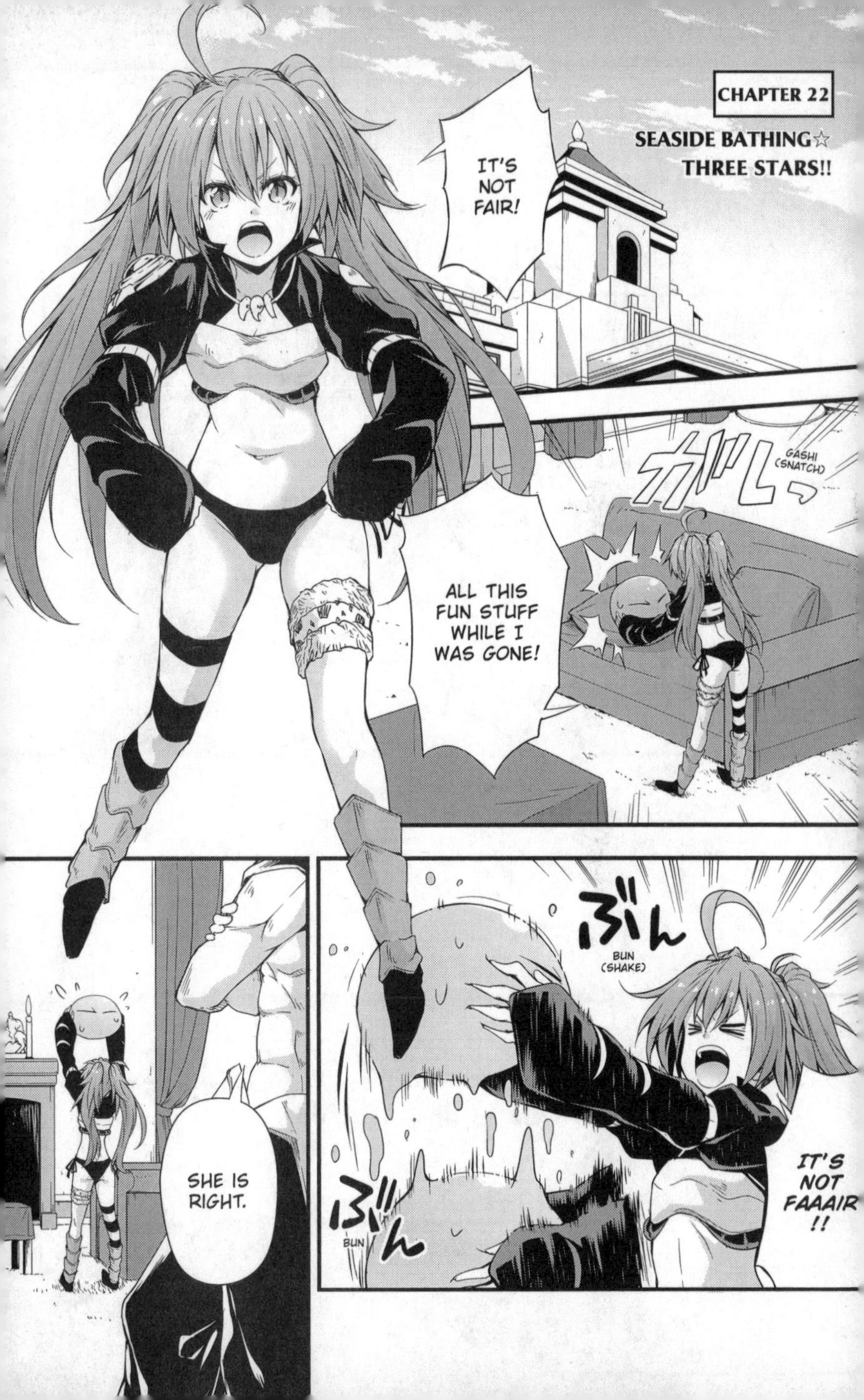
CHAPTER 22
SEASIDE BATHING☆ THREE STARS!!
IT'S NOT FAIR!
GASHI (SNATCH)
ALL THIS FUN STUFF WHILE I WAS GONE!
BUN (SHAKE)
IT'S NOT FAAAIR!!
BUN
SHE IS RIGHT.

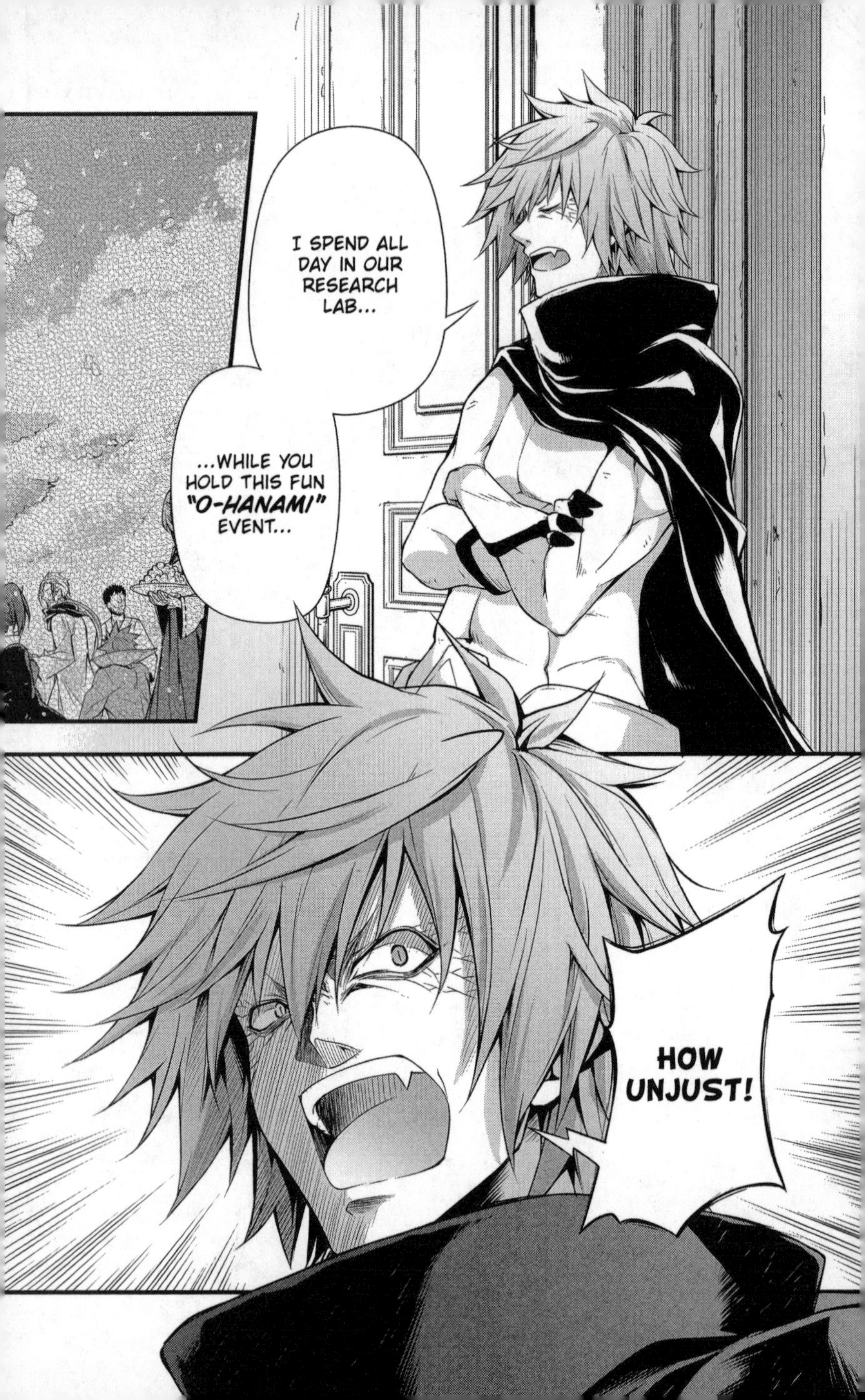
I SPEND ALL DAY IN OUR RESEARCH LAB...
...WHILE YOU HOLD THIS FUN "O-HANAMI" EVENT...
HOW UNJUST!

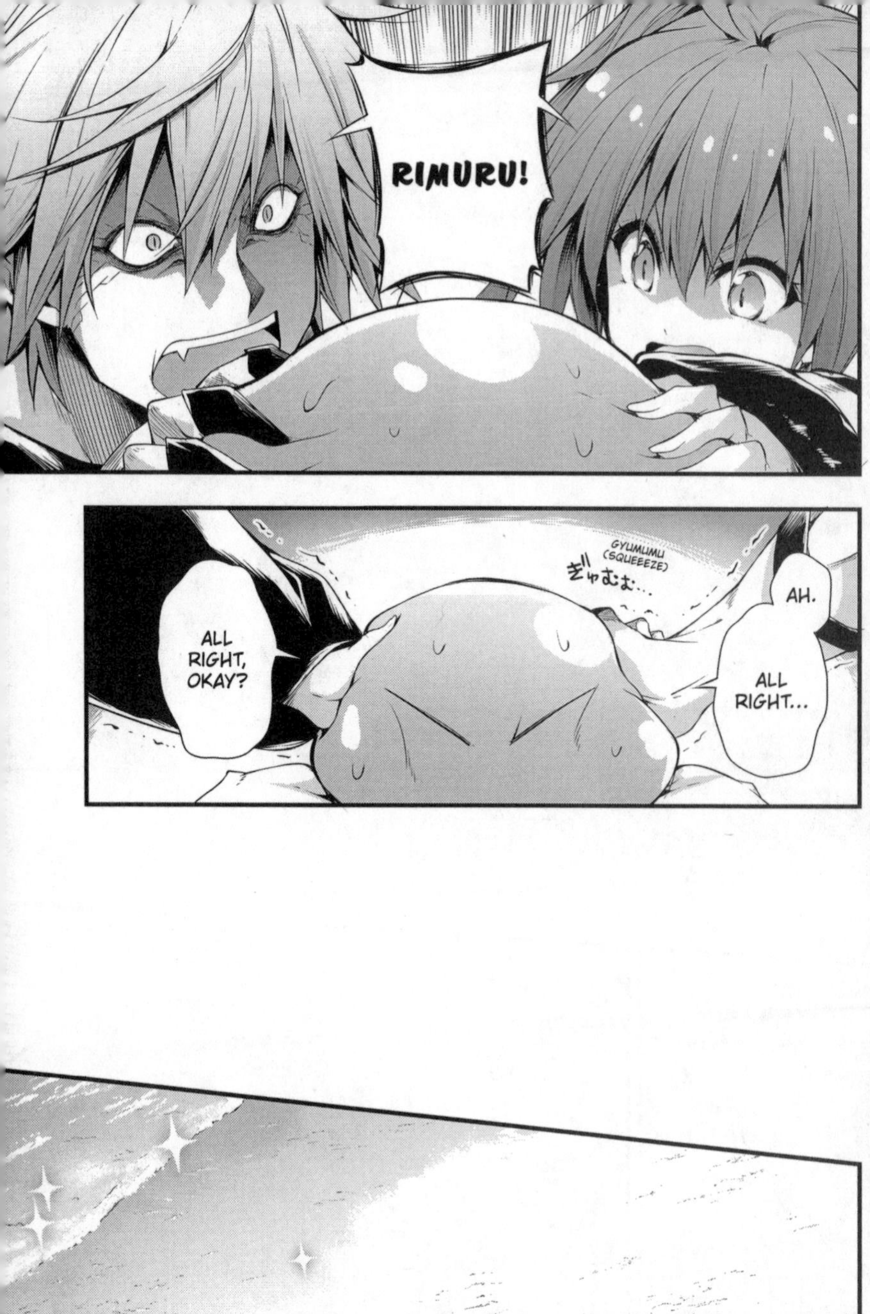
RIMURU!
AH.
ALL RIGHT...
GYUMUMU (SQUEEEZE)
ぎゅむむ…
ALL RIGHT, OKAY?

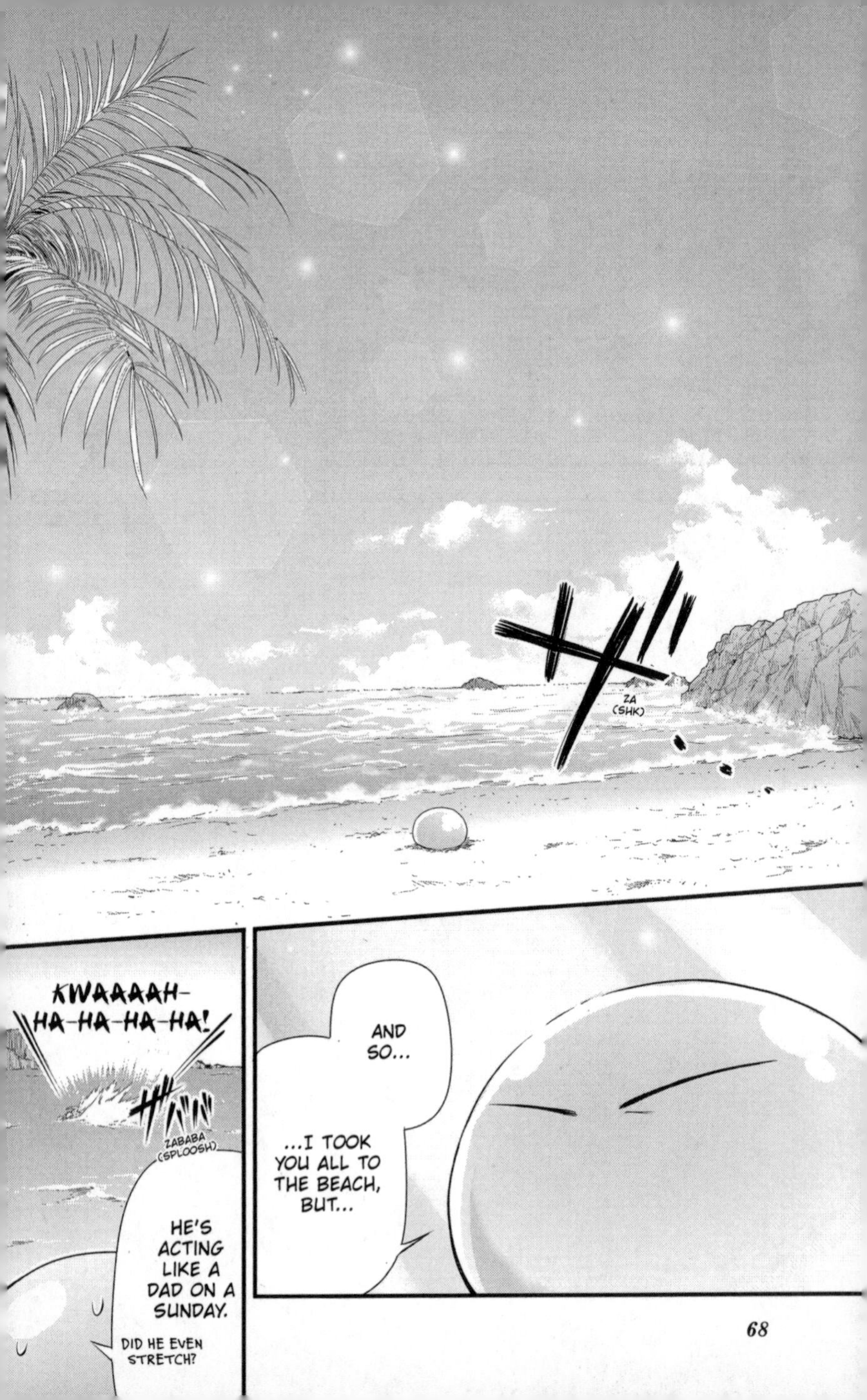
ZA (SHK)
AND SO...
...I TOOK YOU ALL TO THE BEACH, BUT...
KWAAAAH-HA-HA-HA-HA!
ZABABA (SPLOOSH)
HE'S ACTING LIKE A DAD ON A SUNDAY.
DID HE EVEN STRETCH?

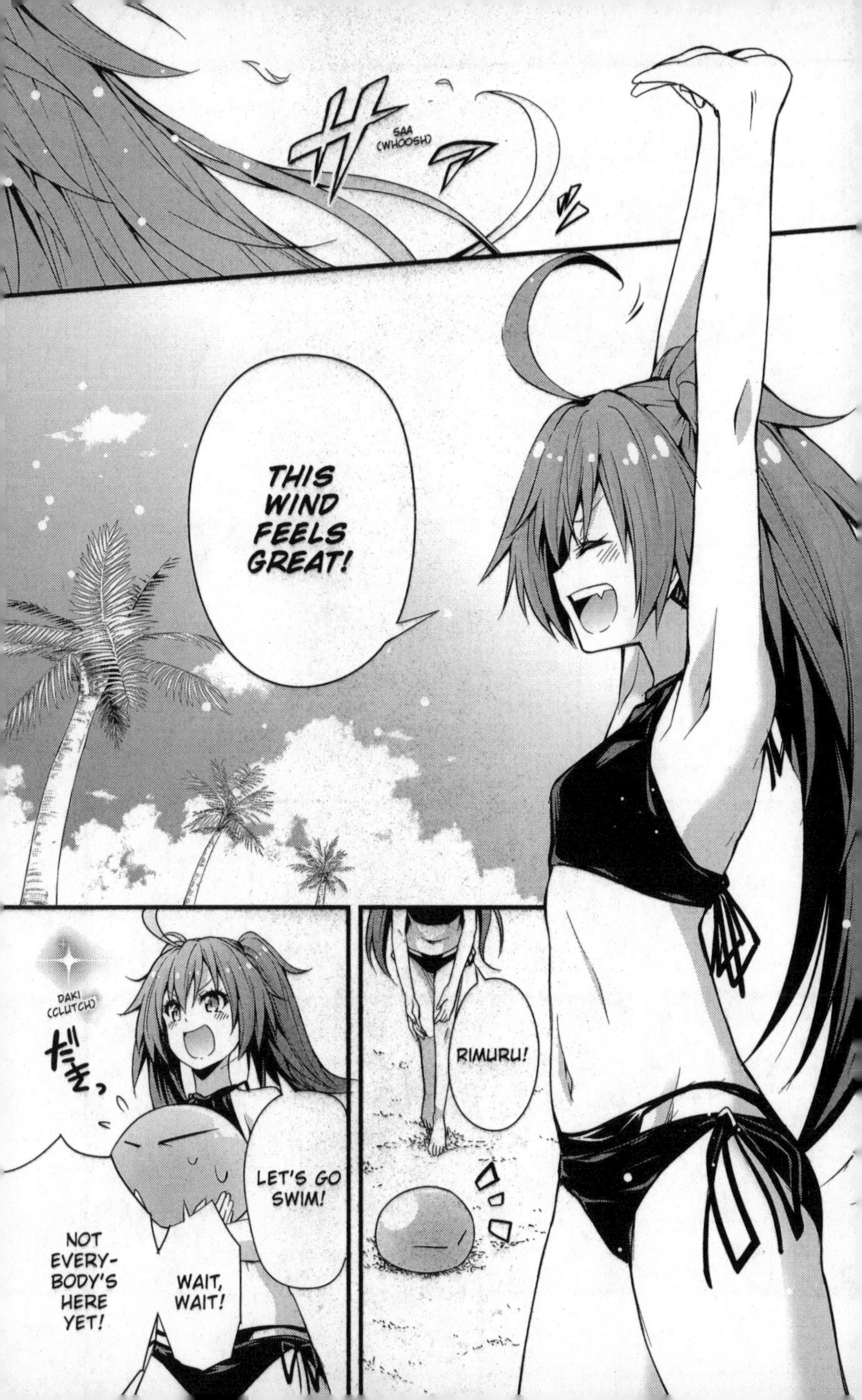
SAA (WHOOSH)
THIS WIND FEELS GREAT!
RIMURU!
DAKI (CLUTCH)
LET'S GO SWIM!
WAIT, WAIT!
NOT EVERYBODY'S HERE YET!

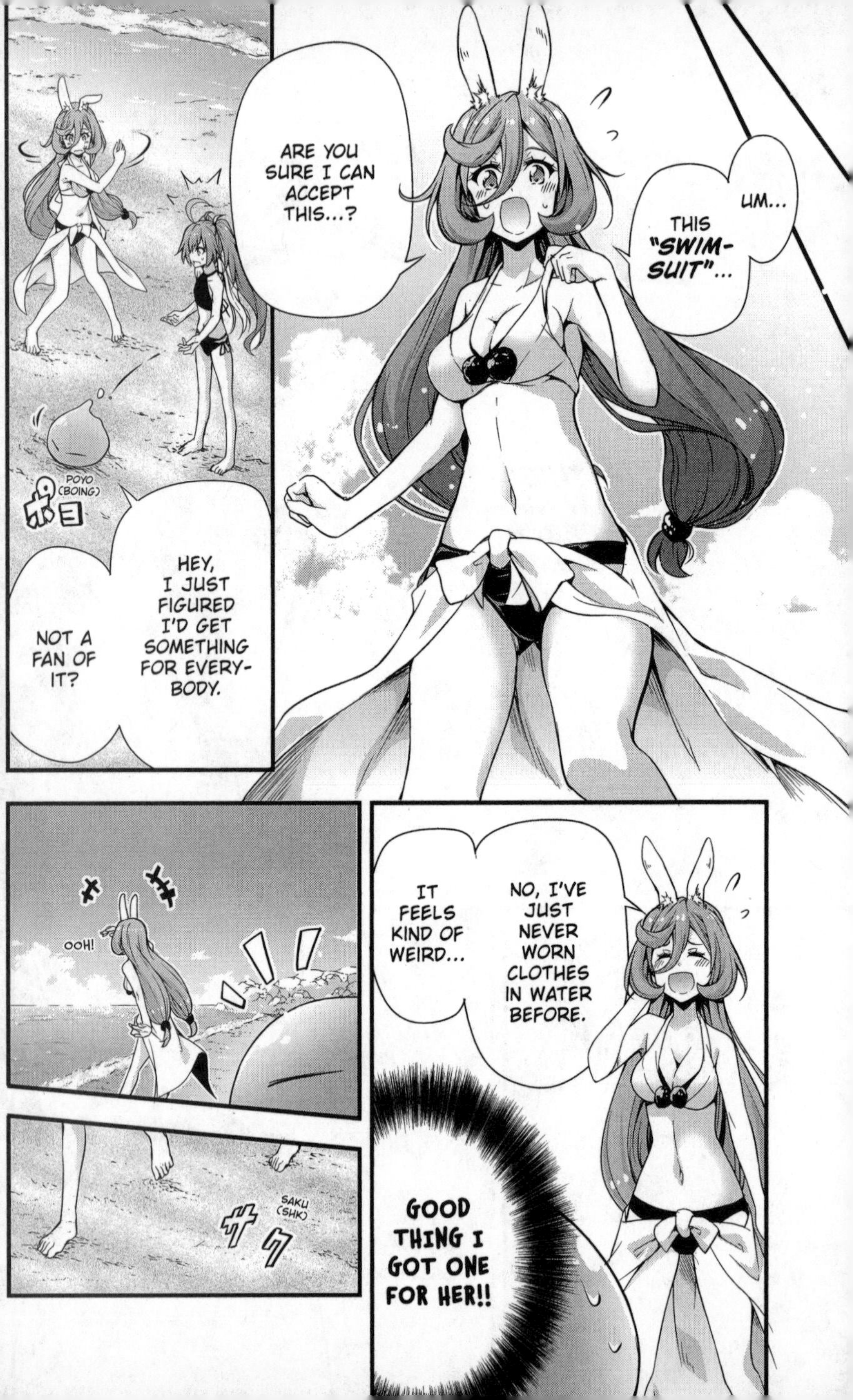
UM... THIS "SWIM-SUIT"...
ARE YOU SURE I CAN ACCEPT THIS...?
POYO (BOING)
HEY, I JUST FIGURED I'D GET SOMETHING FOR EVERY-BODY.
NOT A FAN OF IT?
NO, I'VE JUST NEVER WORN CLOTHES IN WATER BEFORE.
IT FEELS KIND OF WEIRD...
GOOD THING I GOT ONE FOR HER!!
OOH!
SAKU (SHK)

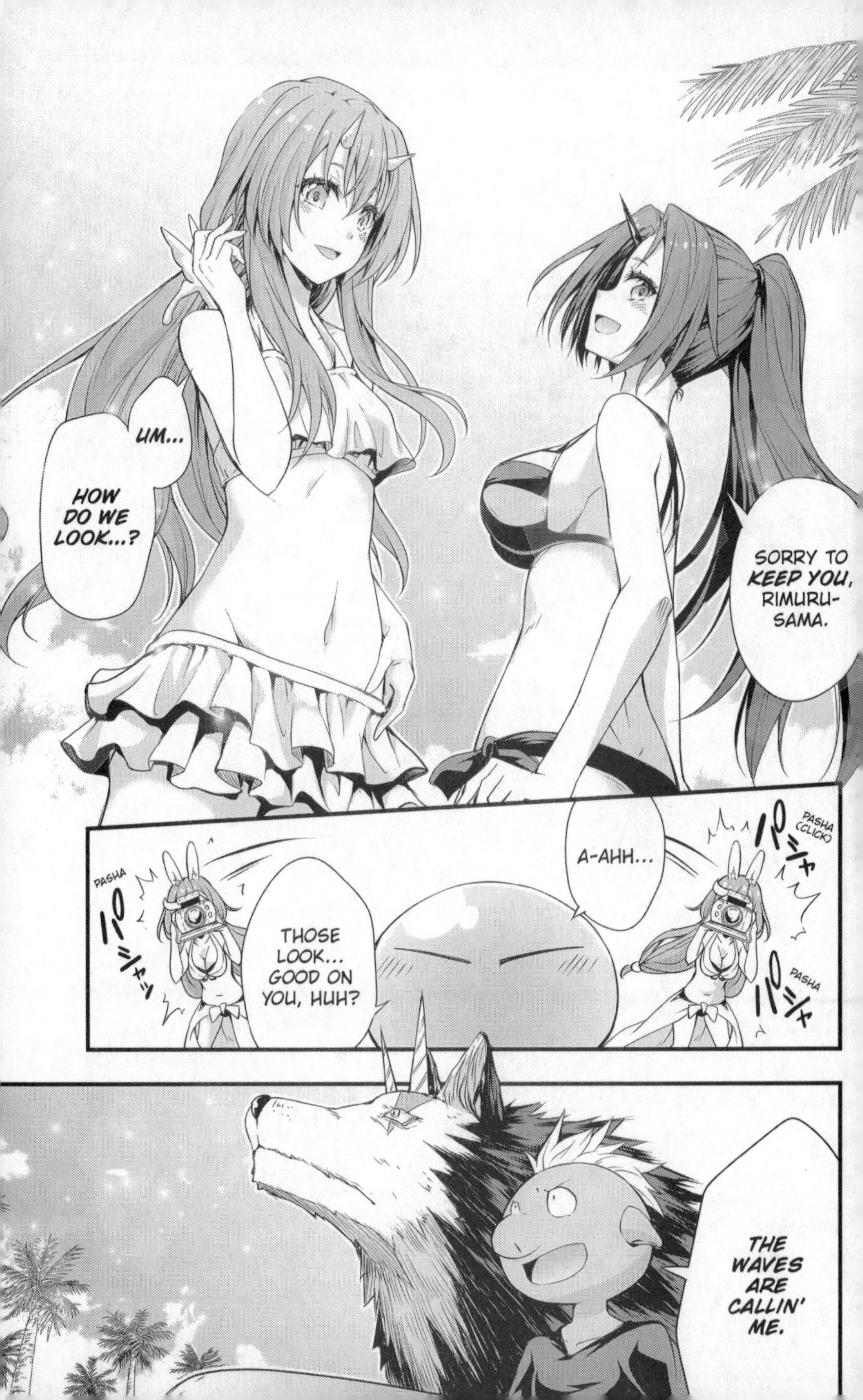
SORRY TO KEEP YOU, RIMURU-SAMA.
UM...
HOW DO WE LOOK...?
PASHA (CLICK)
パシャ
A-AHH...
PASHA
パシャ
THOSE LOOK... GOOD ON YOU, HUH?
PASHA
パシャッ
THE WAVES ARE CALLIN' ME.

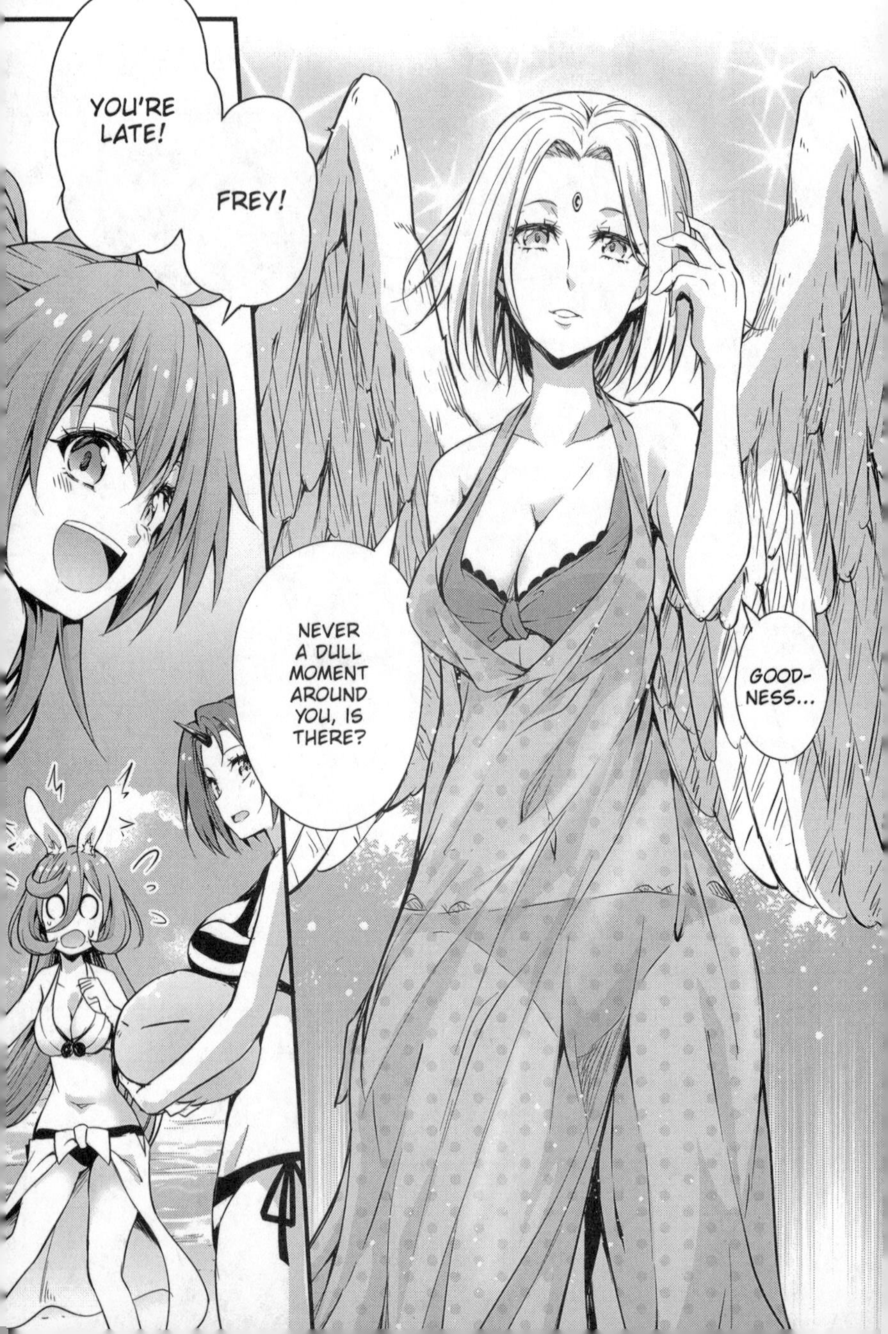
YOU'RE LATE!
FREY!
GOOD-NESS...
NEVER A DULL MOMENT AROUND YOU, IS THERE?

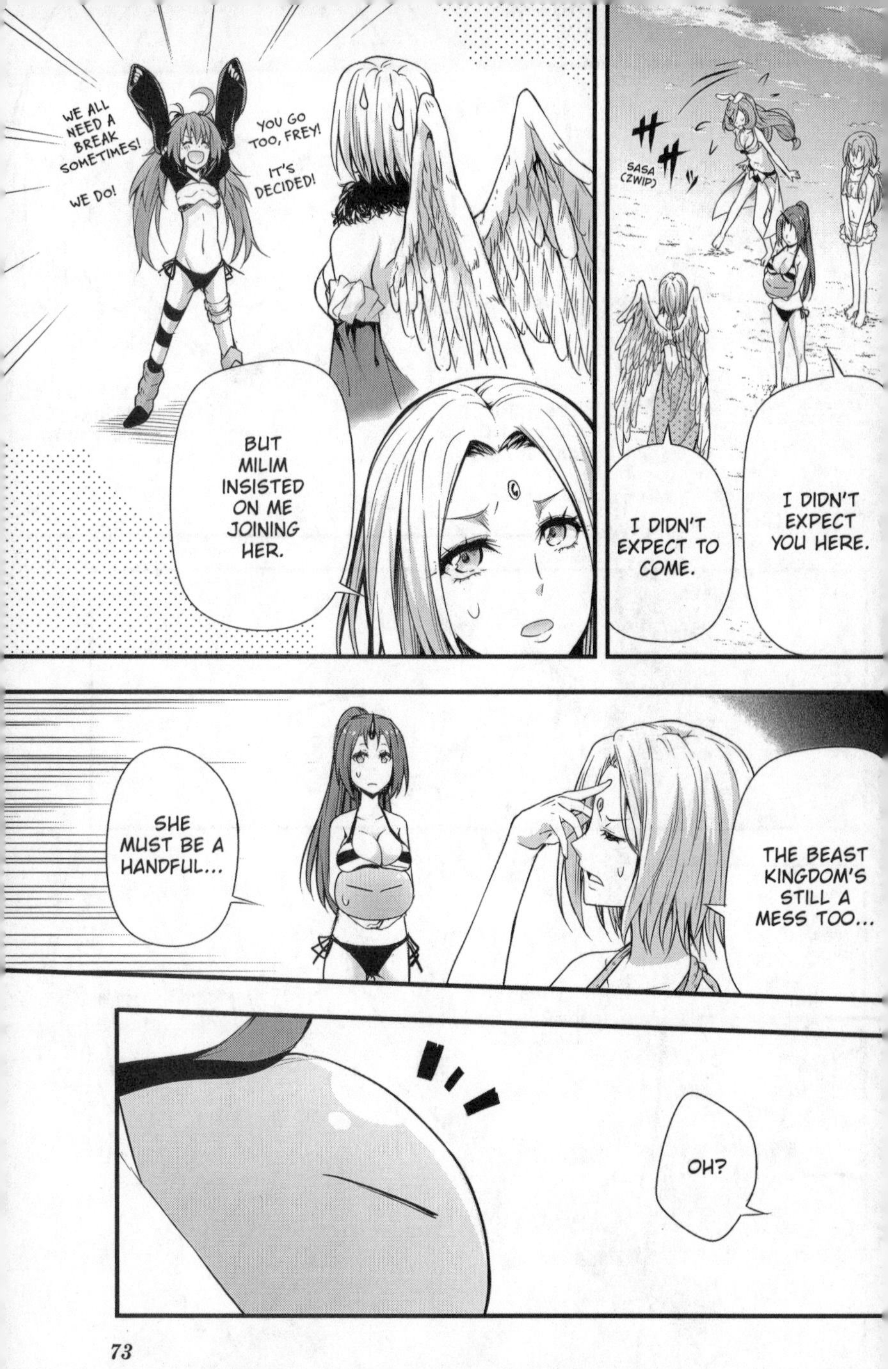
SASA (ZWIP)
I DIDN'T EXPECT YOU HERE.
I DIDN'T EXPECT TO COME.
YOU GO TOO, FREY!
IT'S DECIDED!
WE ALL NEED A BREAK SOMETIMES!
WE DO!
BUT MILIM INSISTED ON ME JOINING HER.
THE BEAST KINGDOM'S STILL A MESS TOO...
SHE MUST BE A HANDFUL...
OH?

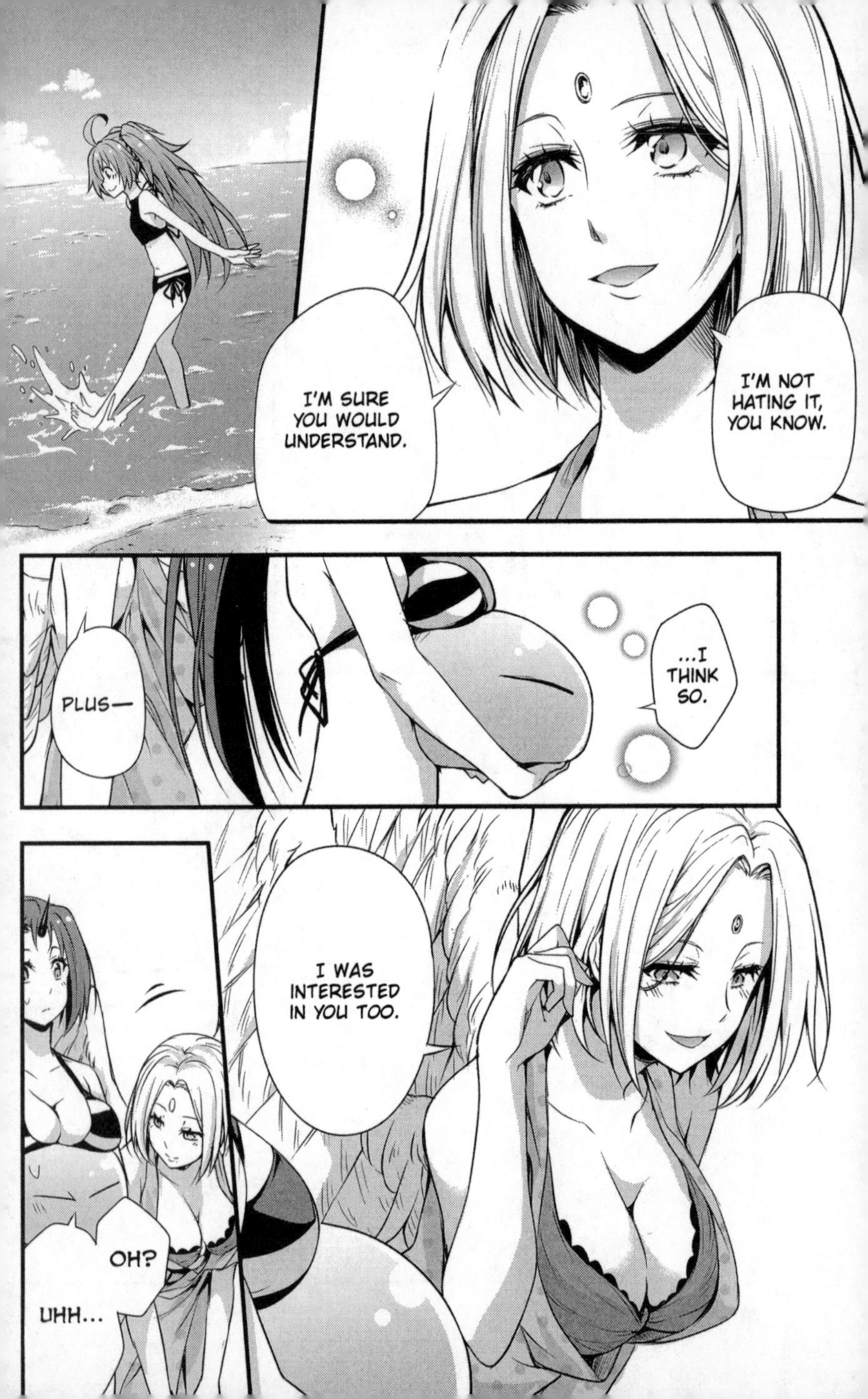
I'M NOT HATING IT, YOU KNOW.
I'M SURE YOU WOULD UNDERSTAND.
...I THINK SO.
PLUS—
I WAS INTERESTED IN YOU TOO.
OH?
UHH...

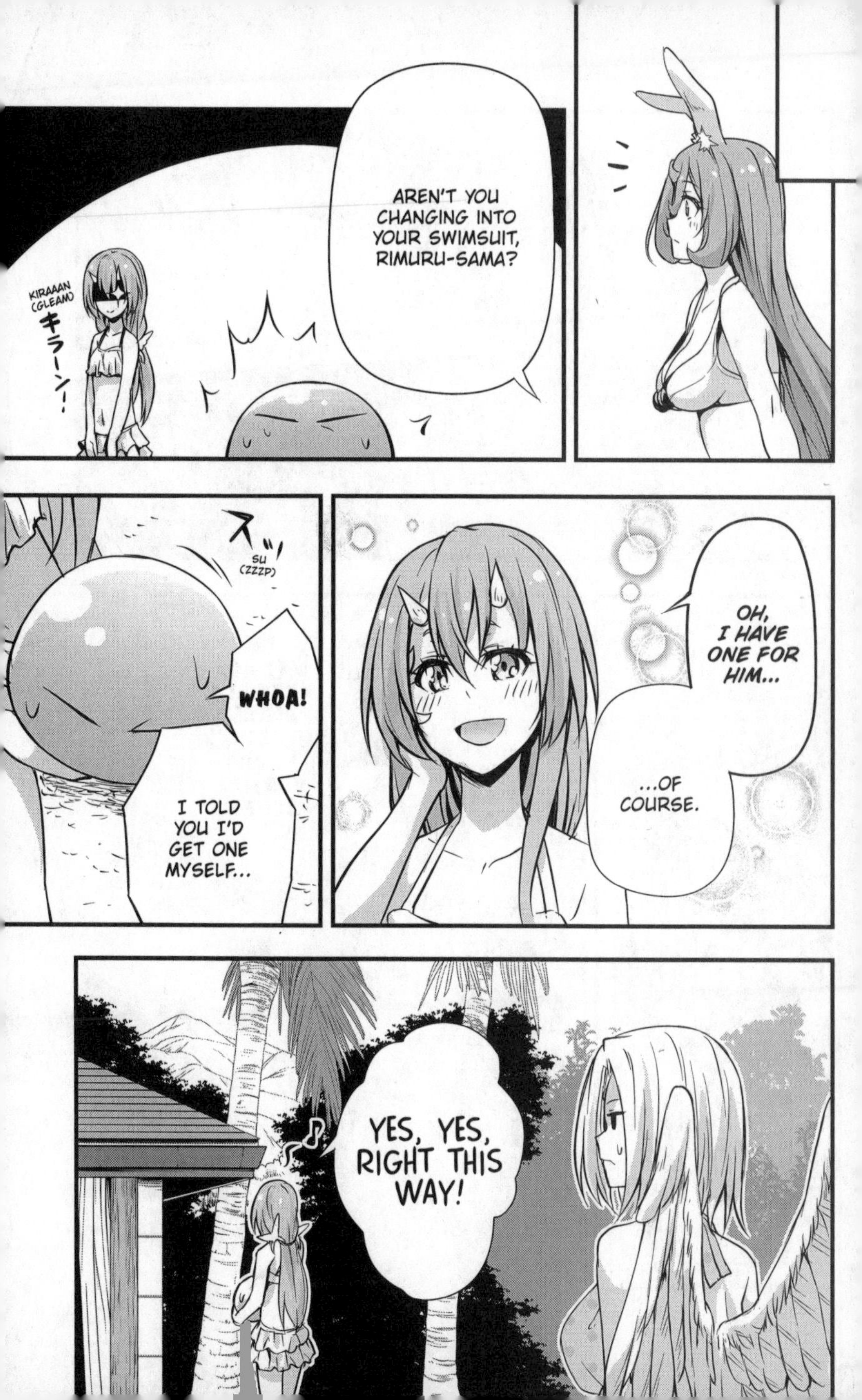
AREN'T YOU CHANGING INTO YOUR SWIMSUIT, RIMURU-SAMA?
KIRAAAN (GLEAM)
キラーン!
OH, I HAVE ONE FOR HIM...
...OF COURSE.
ス
SU (ZZZP)
WHOA!
I TOLD YOU I'D GET ONE MYSELF...
YES, YES, RIGHT THIS WAY!

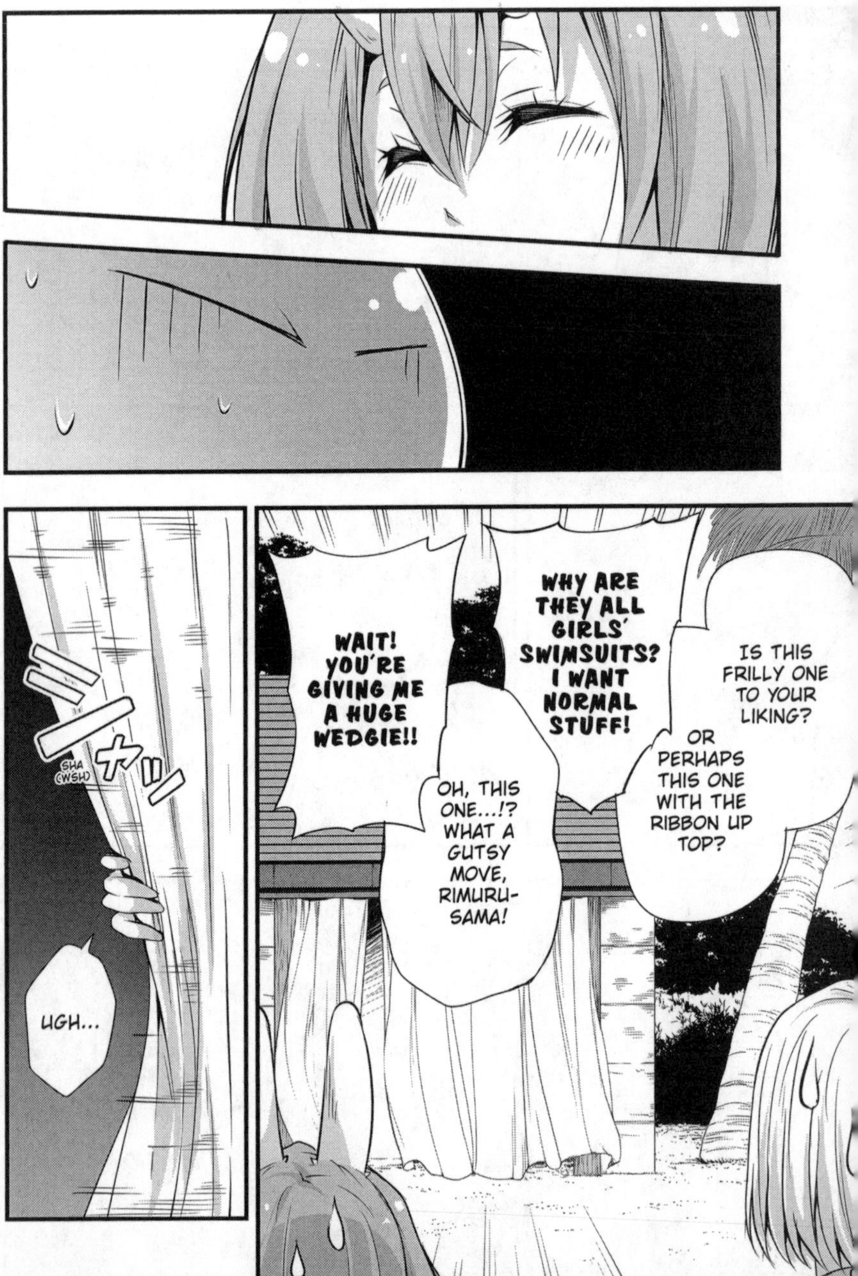
IS THIS FRILLY ONE TO YOUR LIKING?
OR PERHAPS THIS ONE WITH THE RIBBON UP TOP?
WHY ARE THEY ALL GIRLS' SWIMSUITS? I WANT NORMAL STUFF!
OH, THIS ONE...!? WHAT A GUTSY MOVE, RIMURU-SAMA!
WAIT! YOU'RE GIVING ME A HUGE WEDGIE!!
SHA (WSH)
UGH...

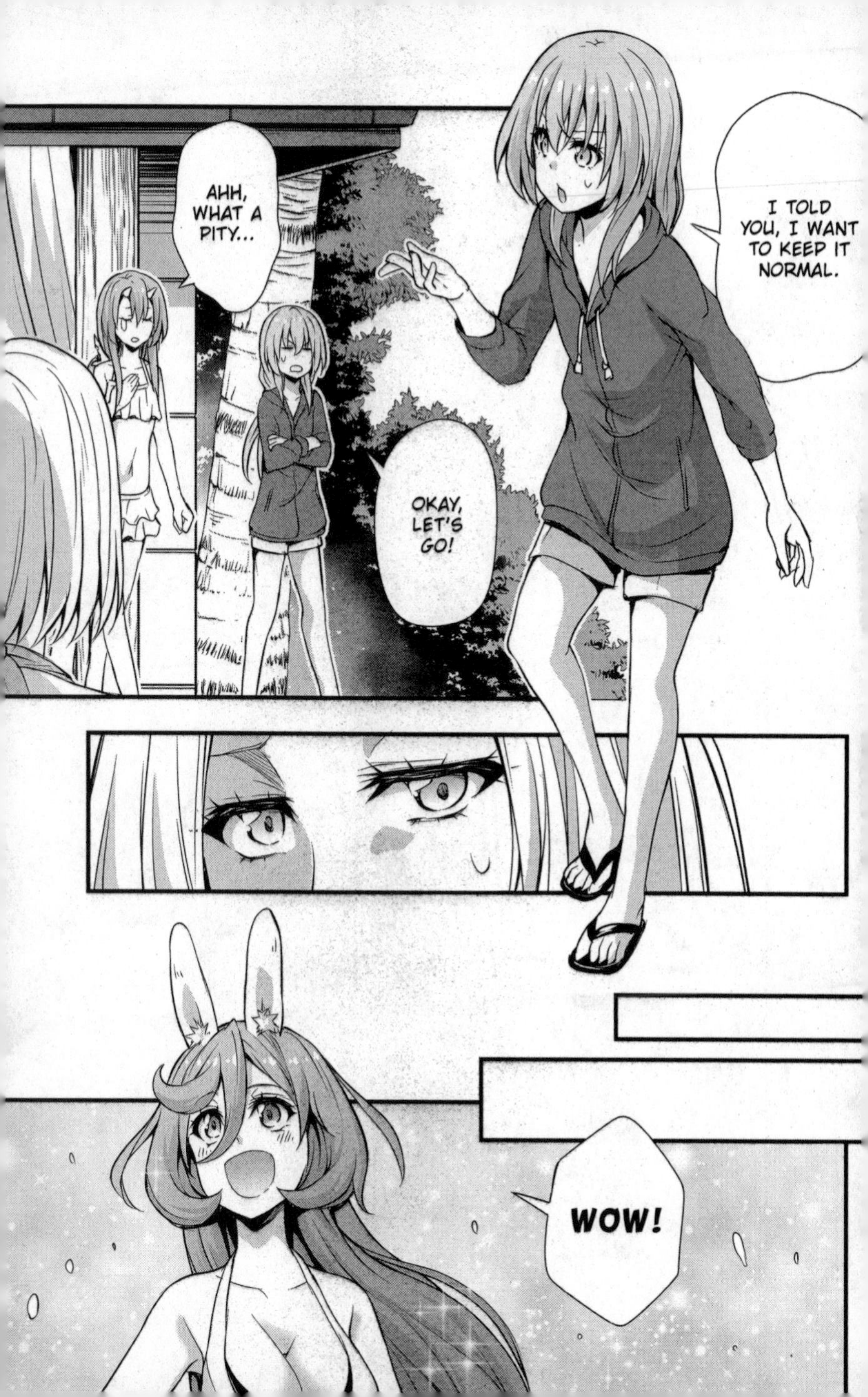
I TOLD YOU, I WANT TO KEEP IT NORMAL.
AHH, WHAT A PITY...
OKAY, LET'S GO!
WOW!

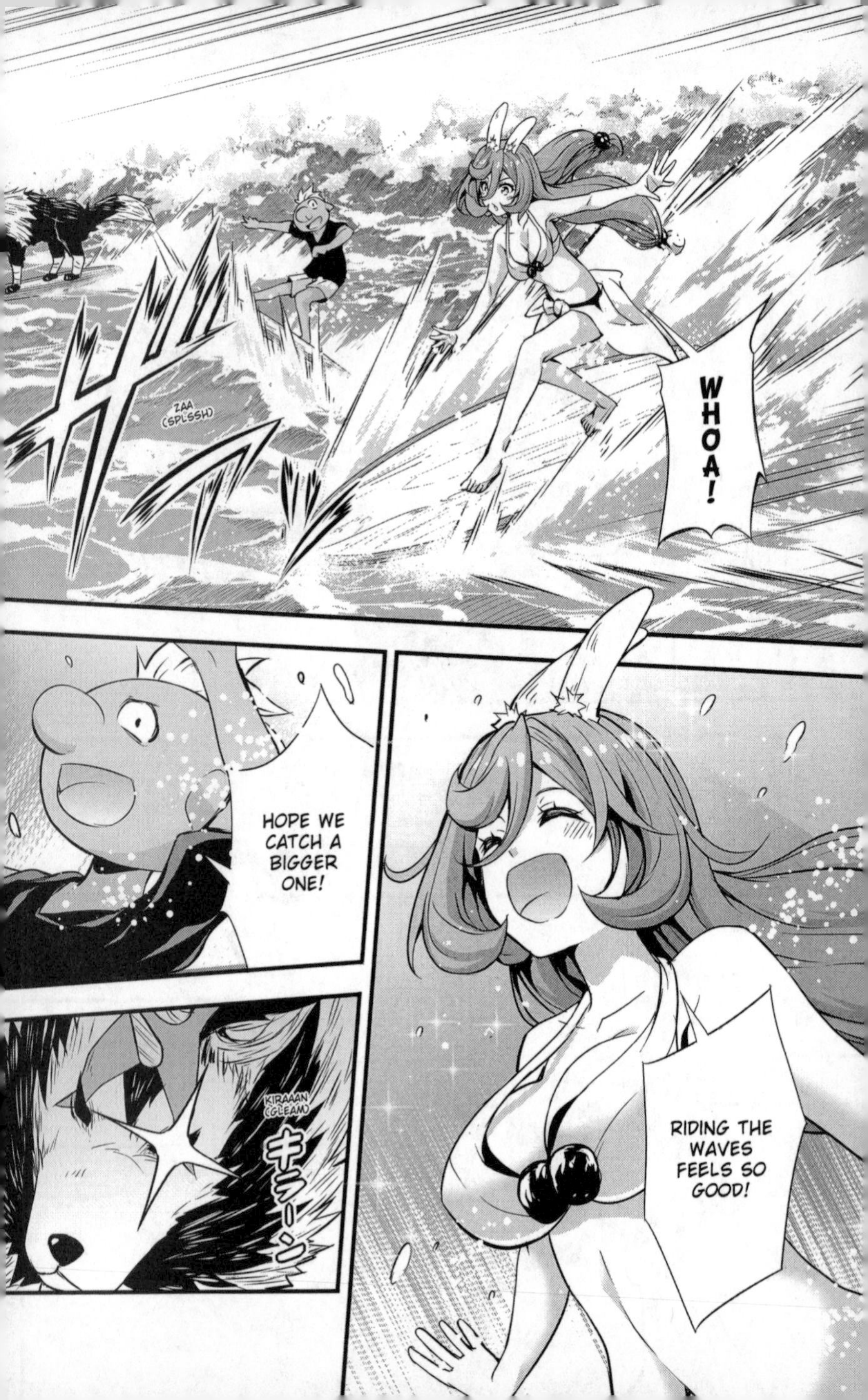
WHOA!
ZAA (SPLSSH)
RIDING THE WAVES FEELS SO GOOD!
HOPE WE CATCH A BIGGER ONE!
KIRAAAN (GLEAM)
キラーン

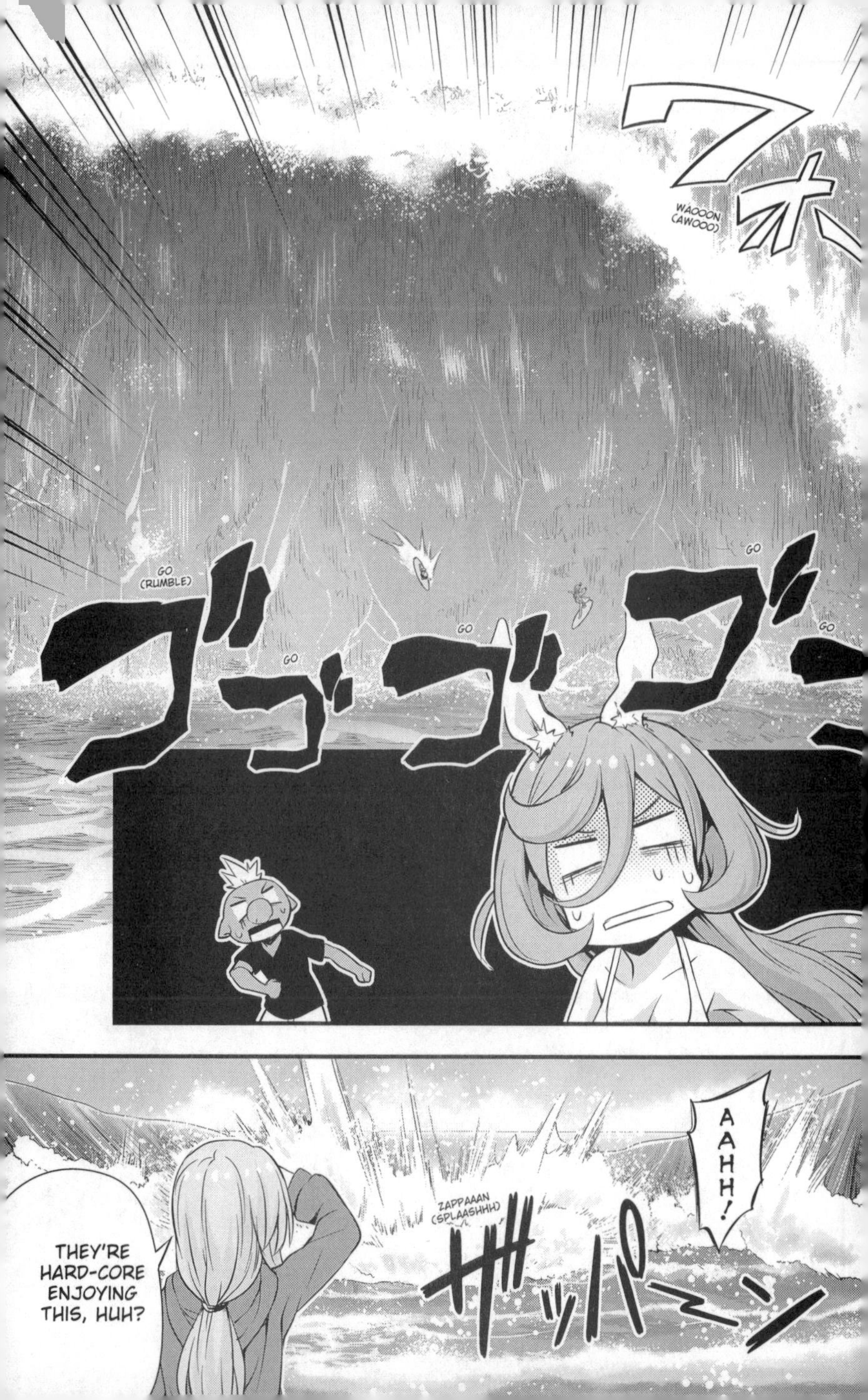
WAOOON (AWOOO)
GO (RUMBLE)
GO
GO
GO
GO
AAHH!
ZAPPAAN (SPLAASHHH)
THEY'RE HARD-CORE ENJOYING THIS, HUH?

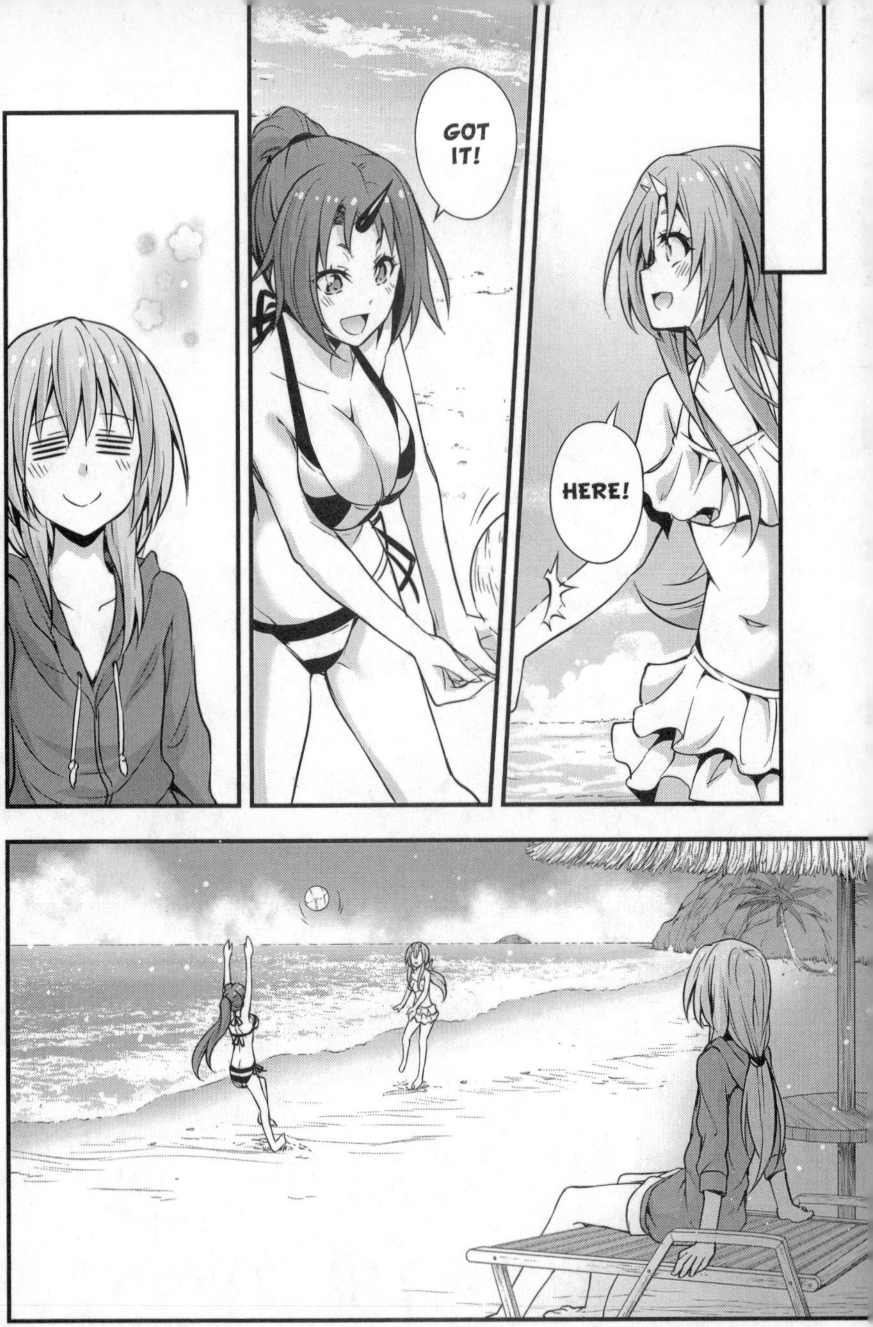
HERE!
GOT IT!

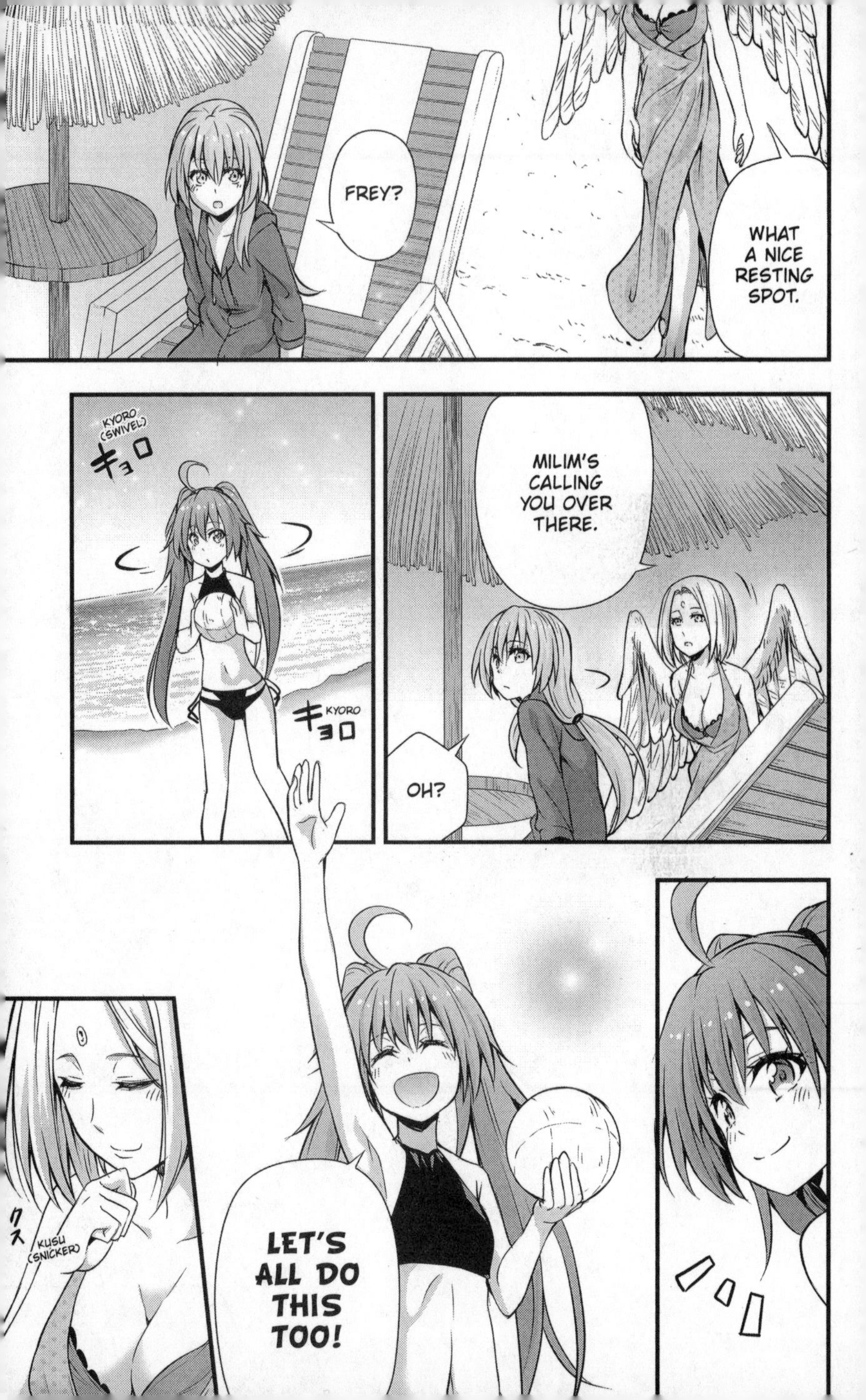

WHAT A NICE RESTING SPOT.
FREY?
MILIM'S CALLING YOU OVER THERE.
OH?
キョロ
KYORO (SWIVEL)
キョロ
KYORO
LET'S ALL DO THIS TOO!
クス
KUSU (SNICKER)

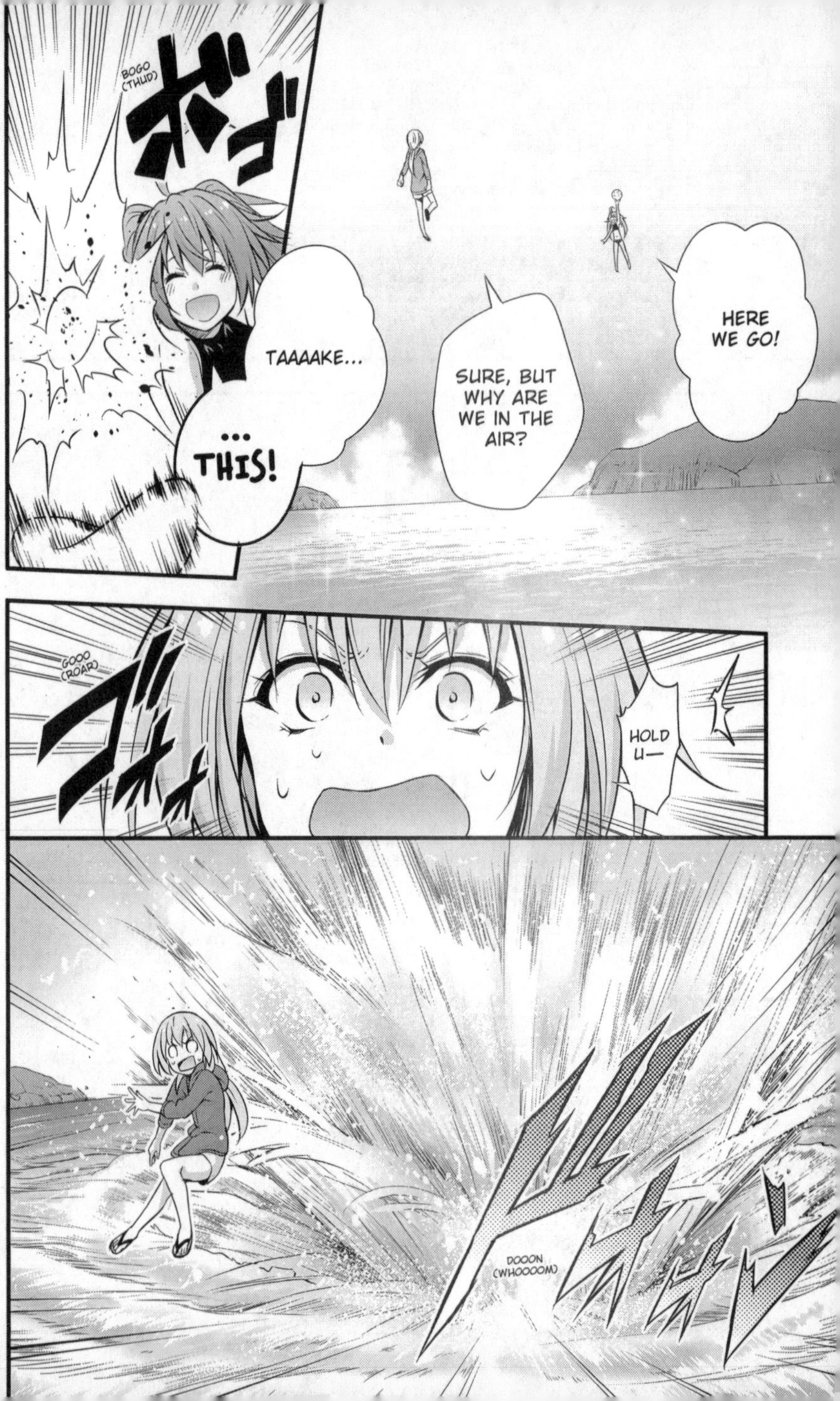
HERE WE GO!
SURE, BUT WHY ARE WE IN THE AIR?
TAAAAKE...
...THIS!
BOGO (THUD)
HOLD U—
GOOO (ROAR)
DOOON (WHOOOOM)

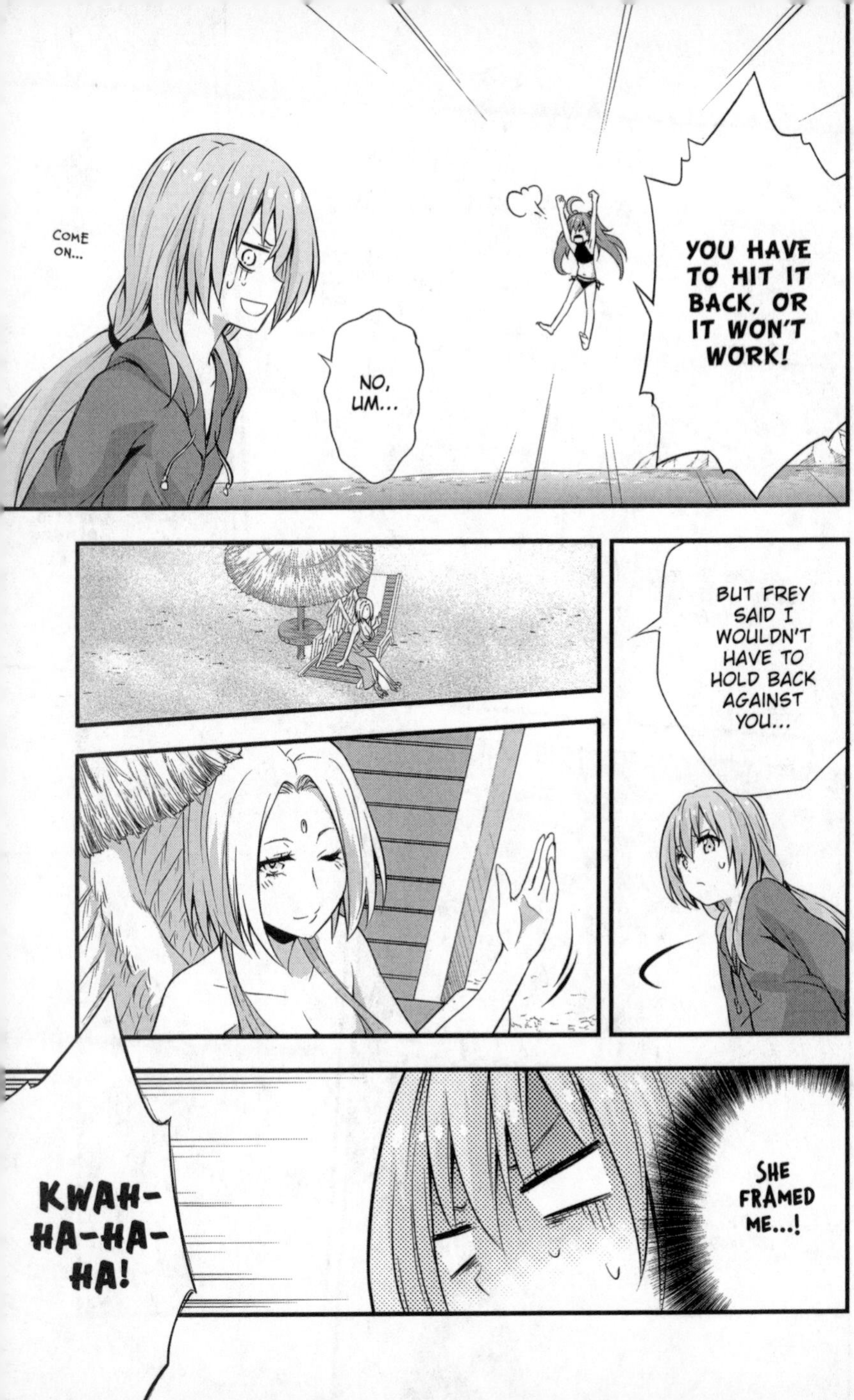
YOU HAVE TO HIT IT BACK, OR IT WON'T WORK!
NO, UM...
COME ON...
BUT FREY SAID I WOULDN'T HAVE TO HOLD BACK AGAINST YOU...
SHE FRAMED ME...!
KWAH-HA-HA-HA!

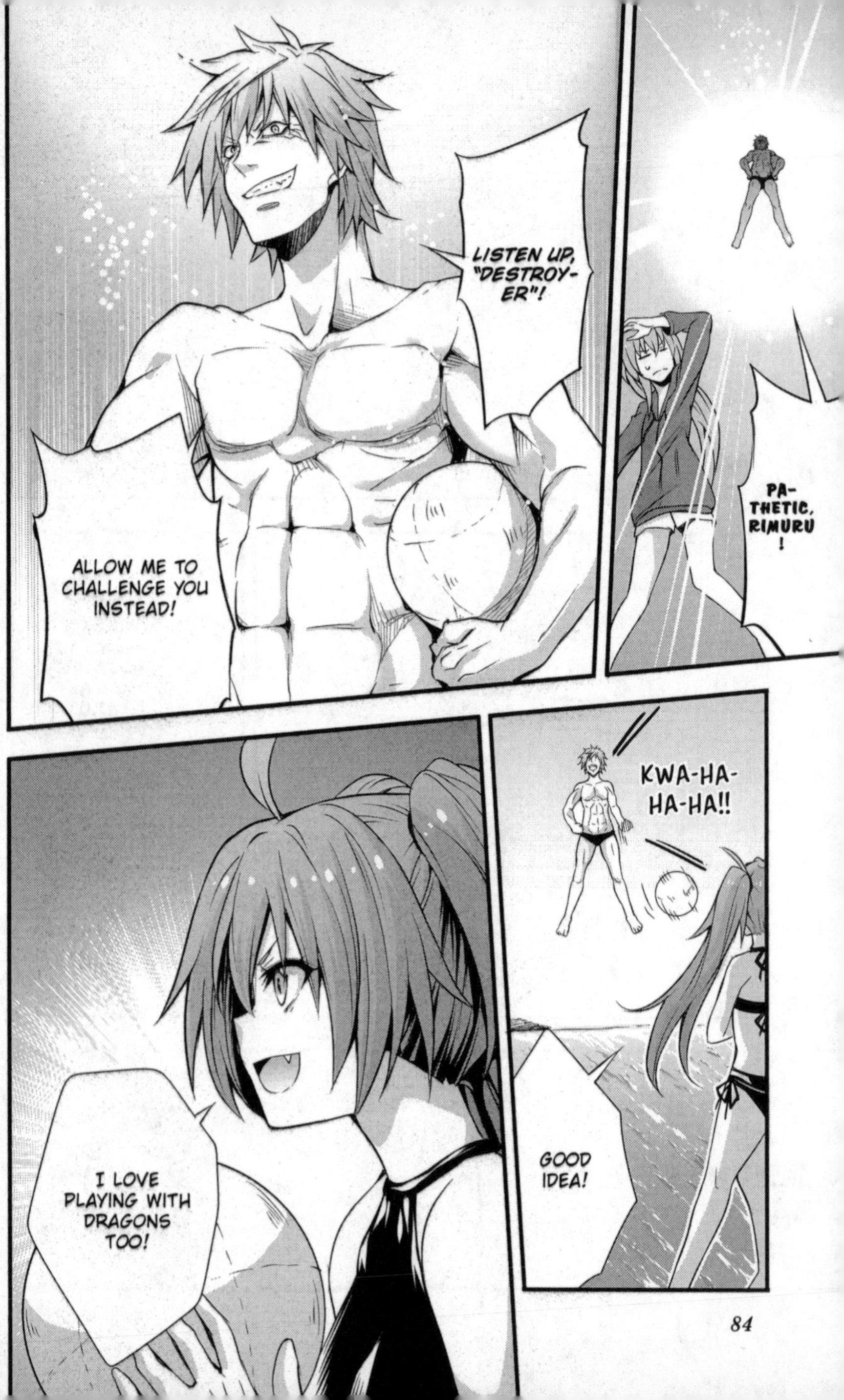
PA-THETIC, RIMURU!
LISTEN UP, "DESTROYER"!
ALLOW ME TO CHALLENGE YOU INSTEAD!
KWA-HA-HA-HA!!
GOOD IDEA!
I LOVE PLAYING WITH DRAGONS TOO!

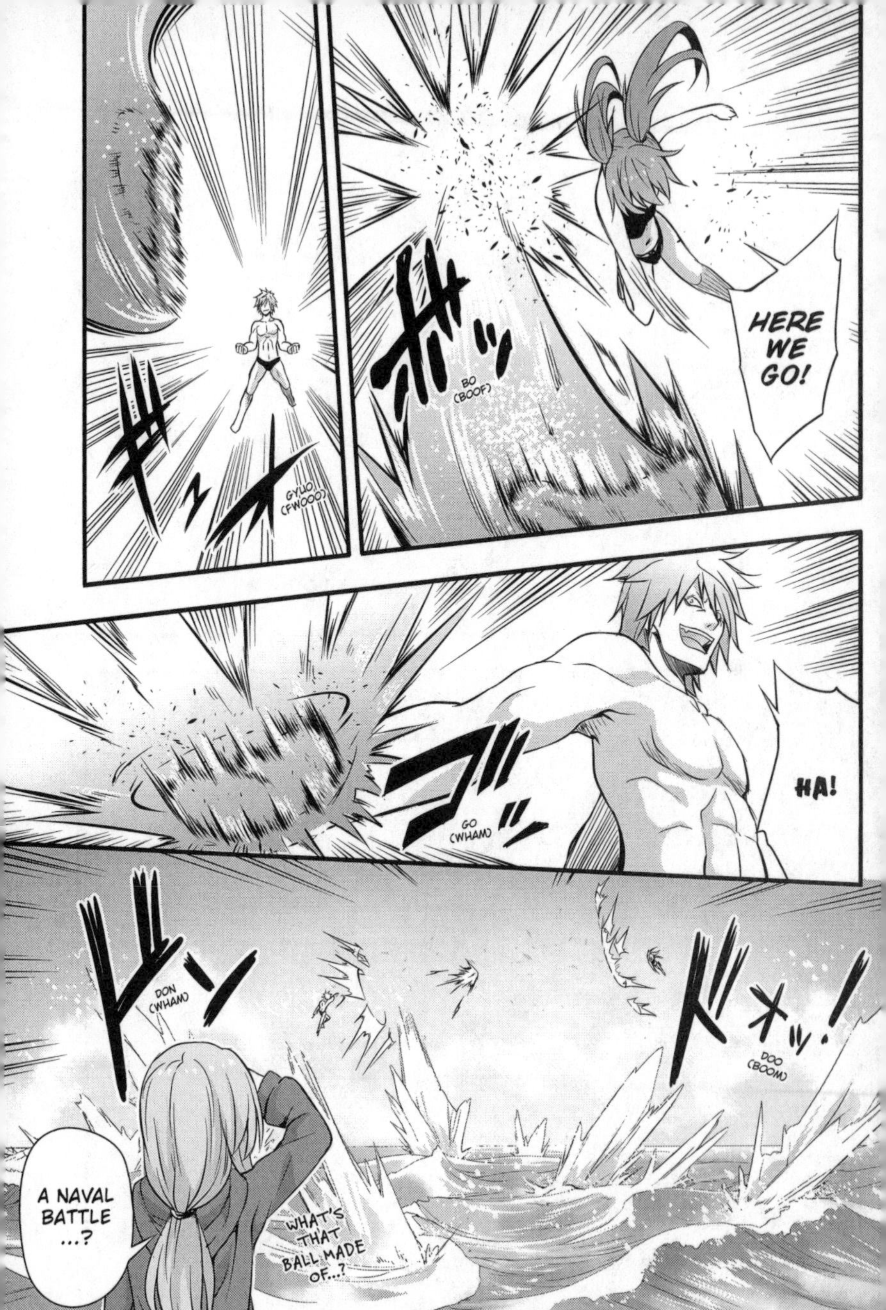
HERE WE GO!
BO (BOOF)
GYUO (FWOOO)
HA!
GO (WHAM)
DOO (BOOM)
DON (WHAM)
WHAT'S THAT BALL MADE OF...?
A NAVAL BATTLE ...?

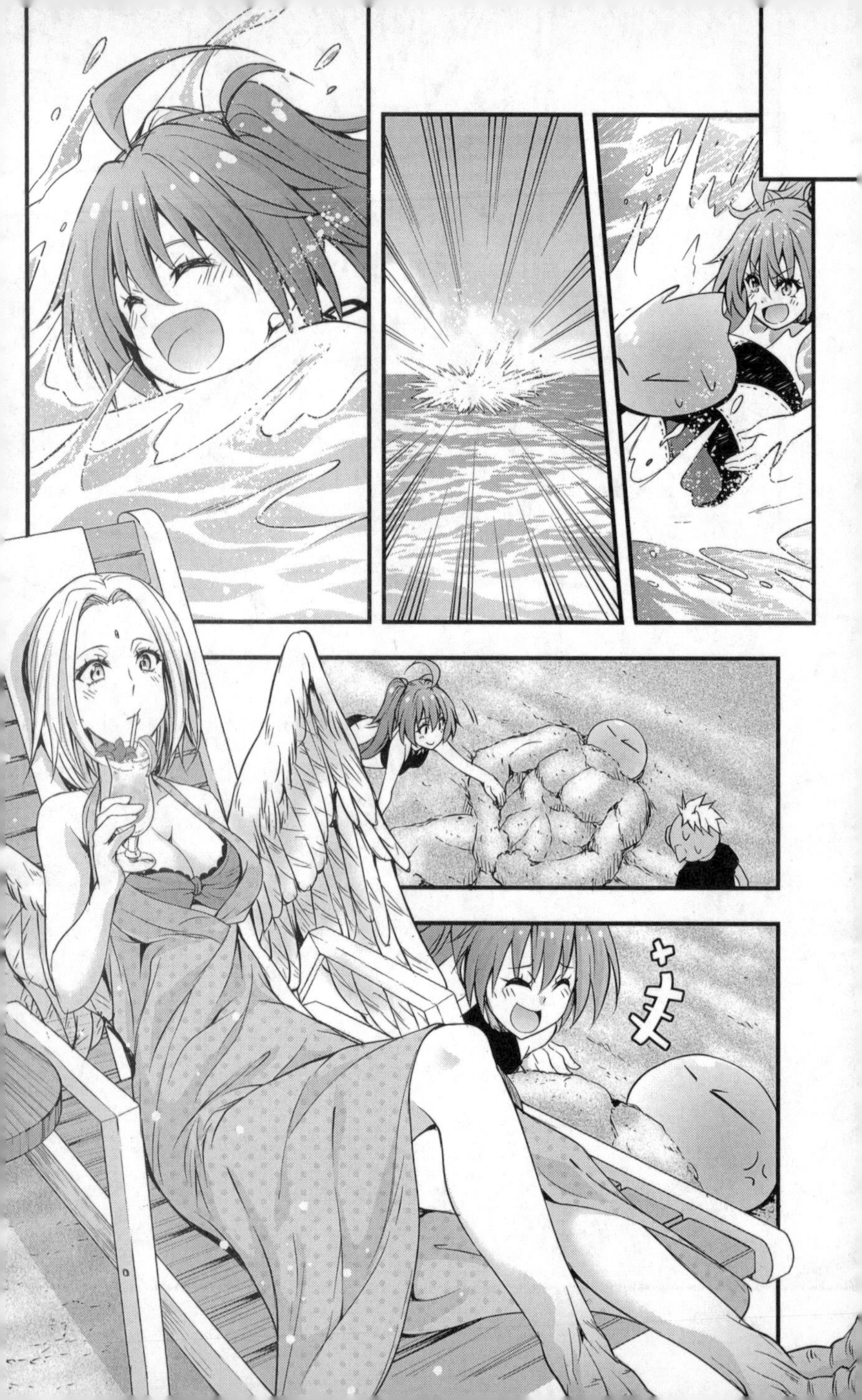

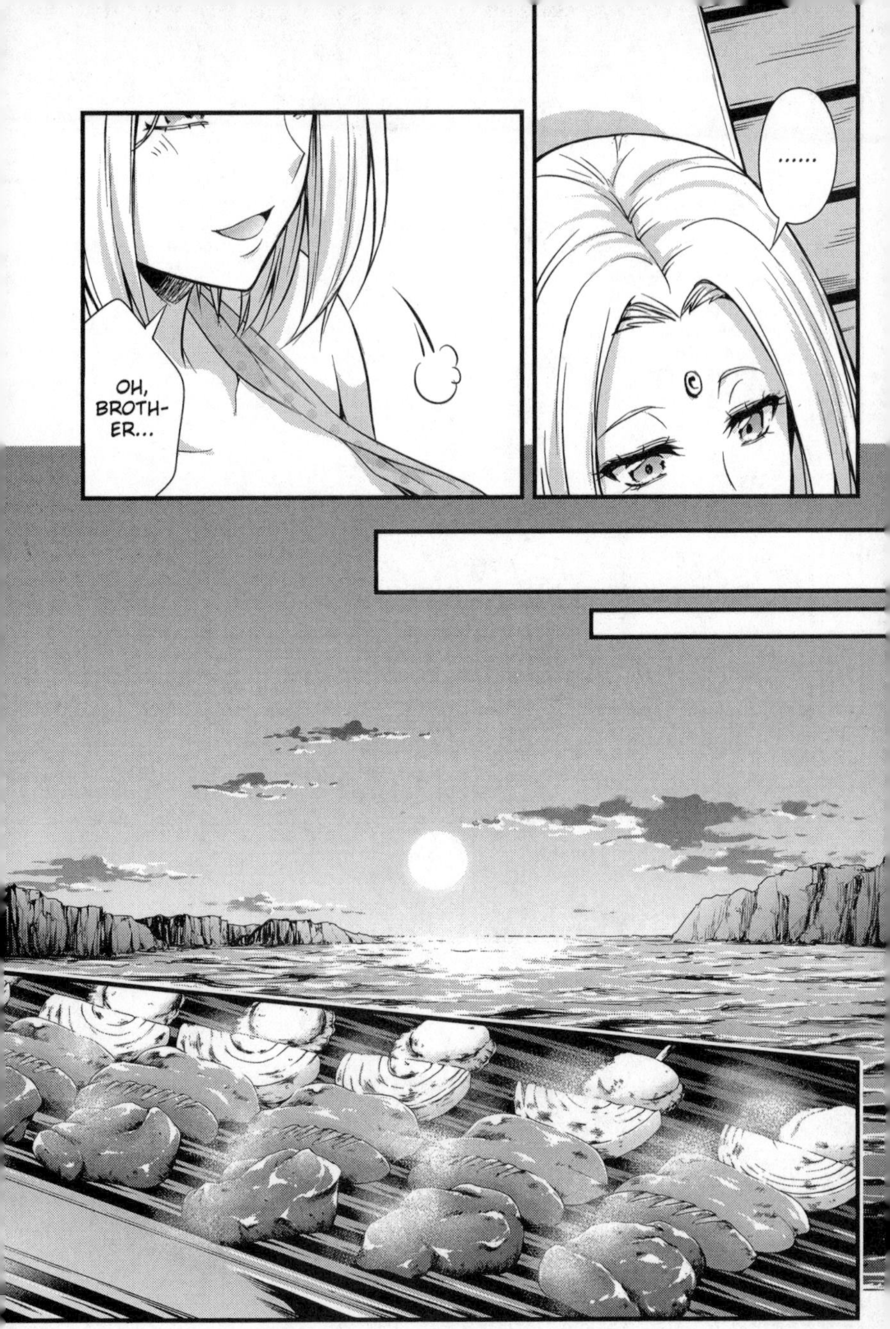
......
OH, BROTHER...

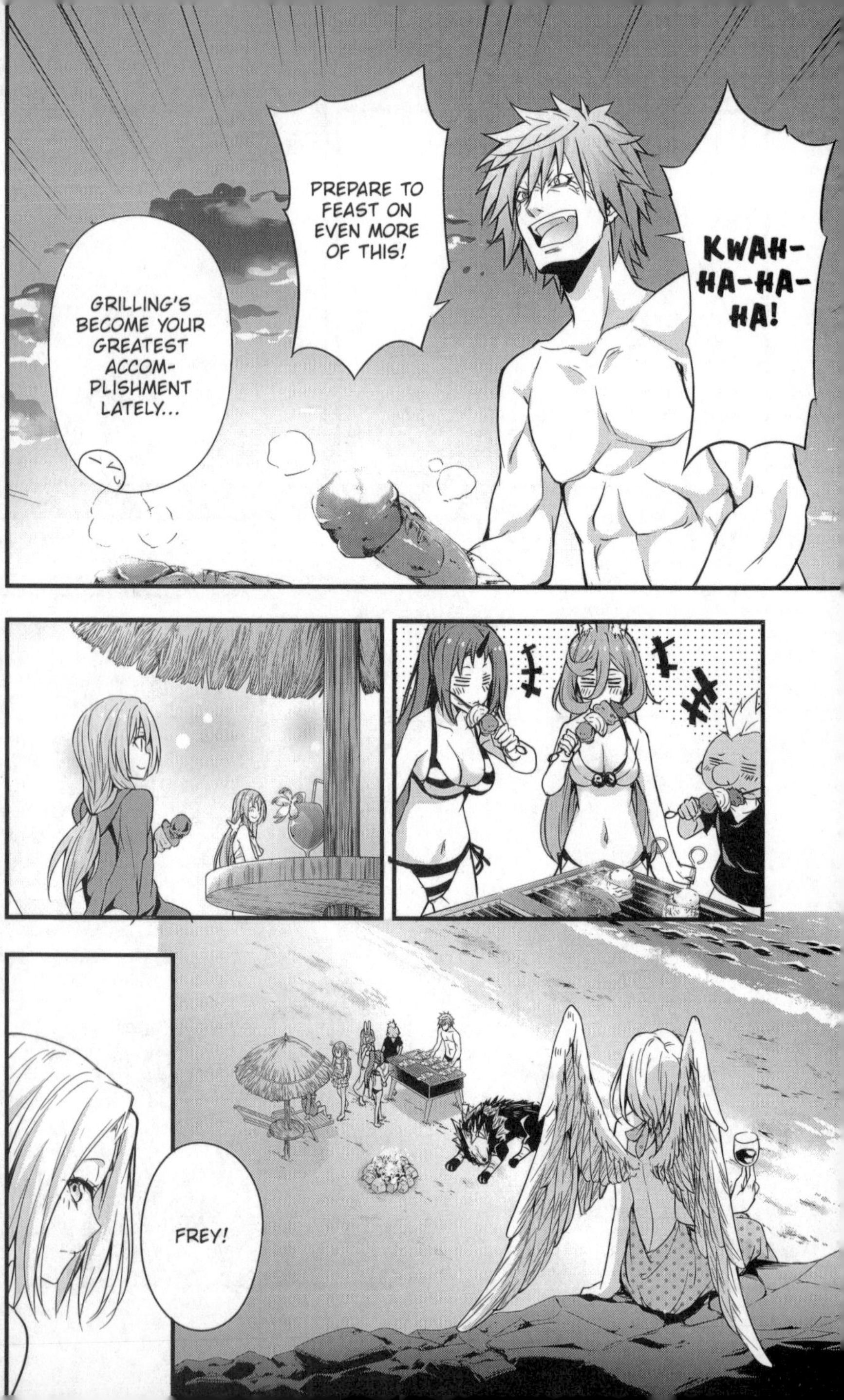
KWAH-HA-HA-HA!
PREPARE TO FEAST ON EVEN MORE OF THIS!
GRILLING'S BECOME YOUR GREATEST ACCOM-PLISHMENT LATELY...
FREY!

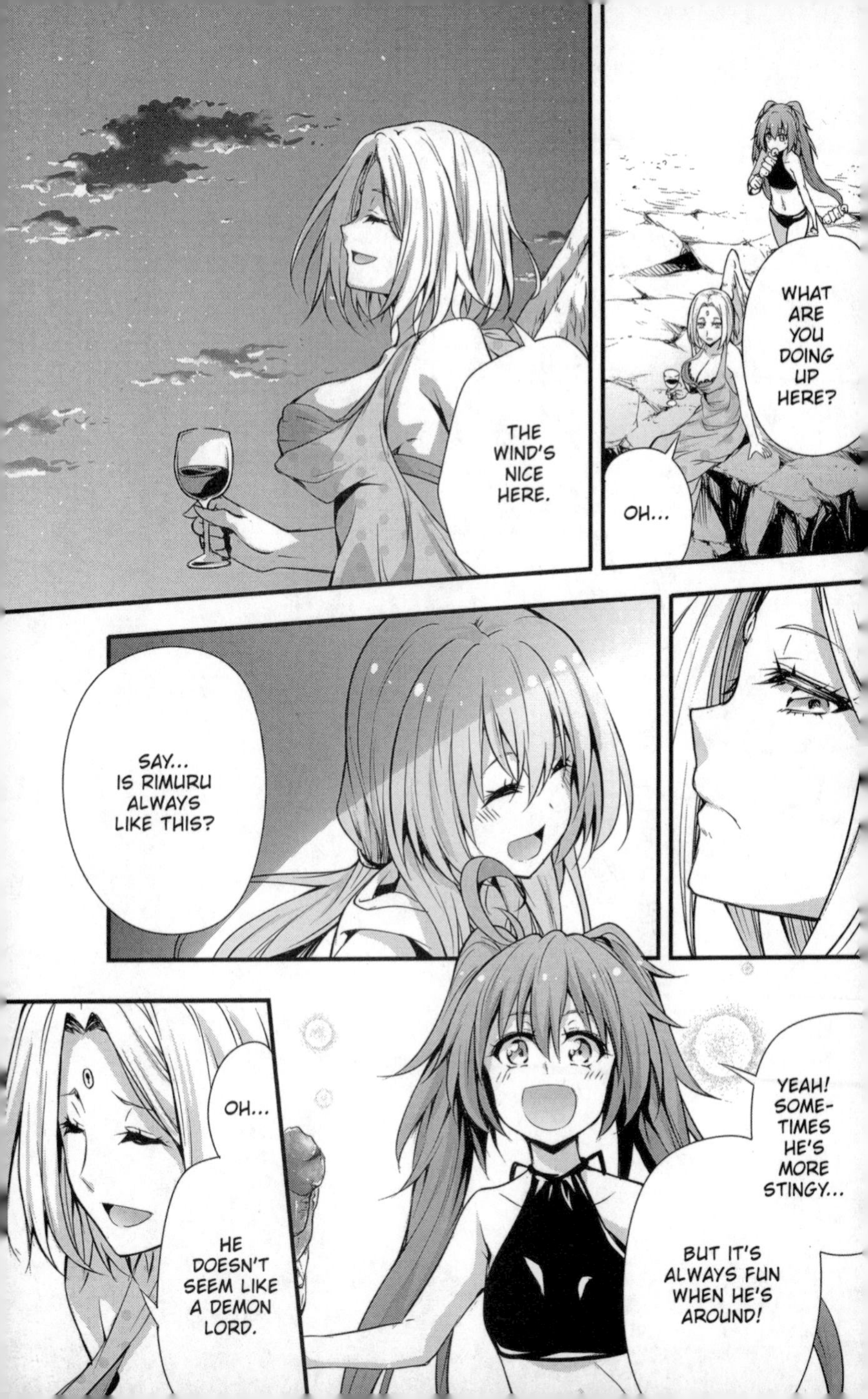
WHAT ARE YOU DOING UP HERE?
OH...
THE WIND'S NICE HERE.
SAY... IS RIMURU ALWAYS LIKE THIS?
YEAH! SOME-TIMES HE'S MORE STINGY...
BUT IT'S ALWAYS FUN WHEN HE'S AROUND!
OH...
HE DOESN'T SEEM LIKE A DEMON LORD.

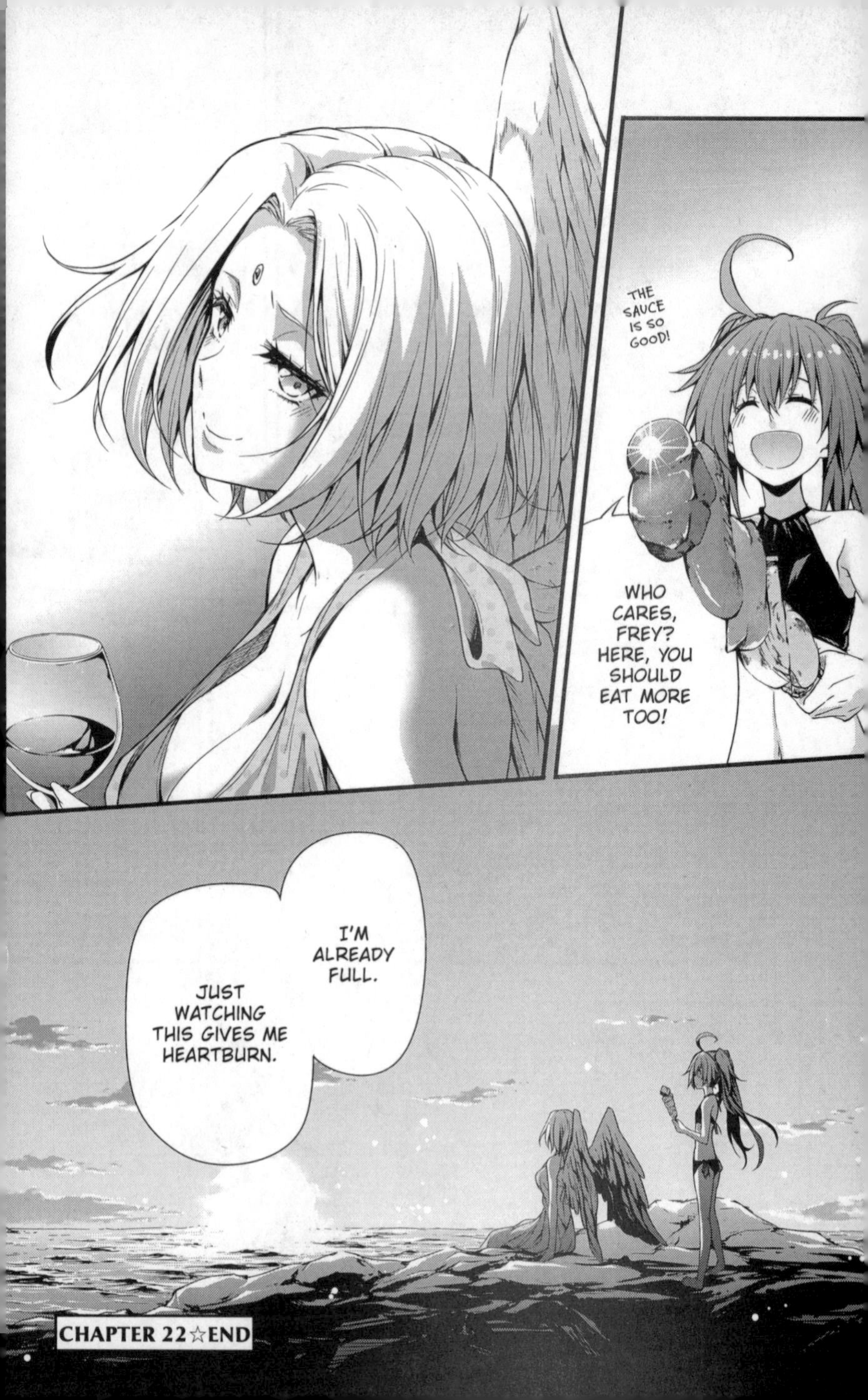
THE SAUCE IS SO GOOD!
WHO CARES, FREY? HERE, YOU SHOULD EAT MORE TOO!
I'M ALREADY FULL.
JUST WATCHING THIS GIVES ME HEARTBURN.
CHAPTER 22☆END

That Time I Got Reincarnated as a SLIME
The Ways of the Monster Nation

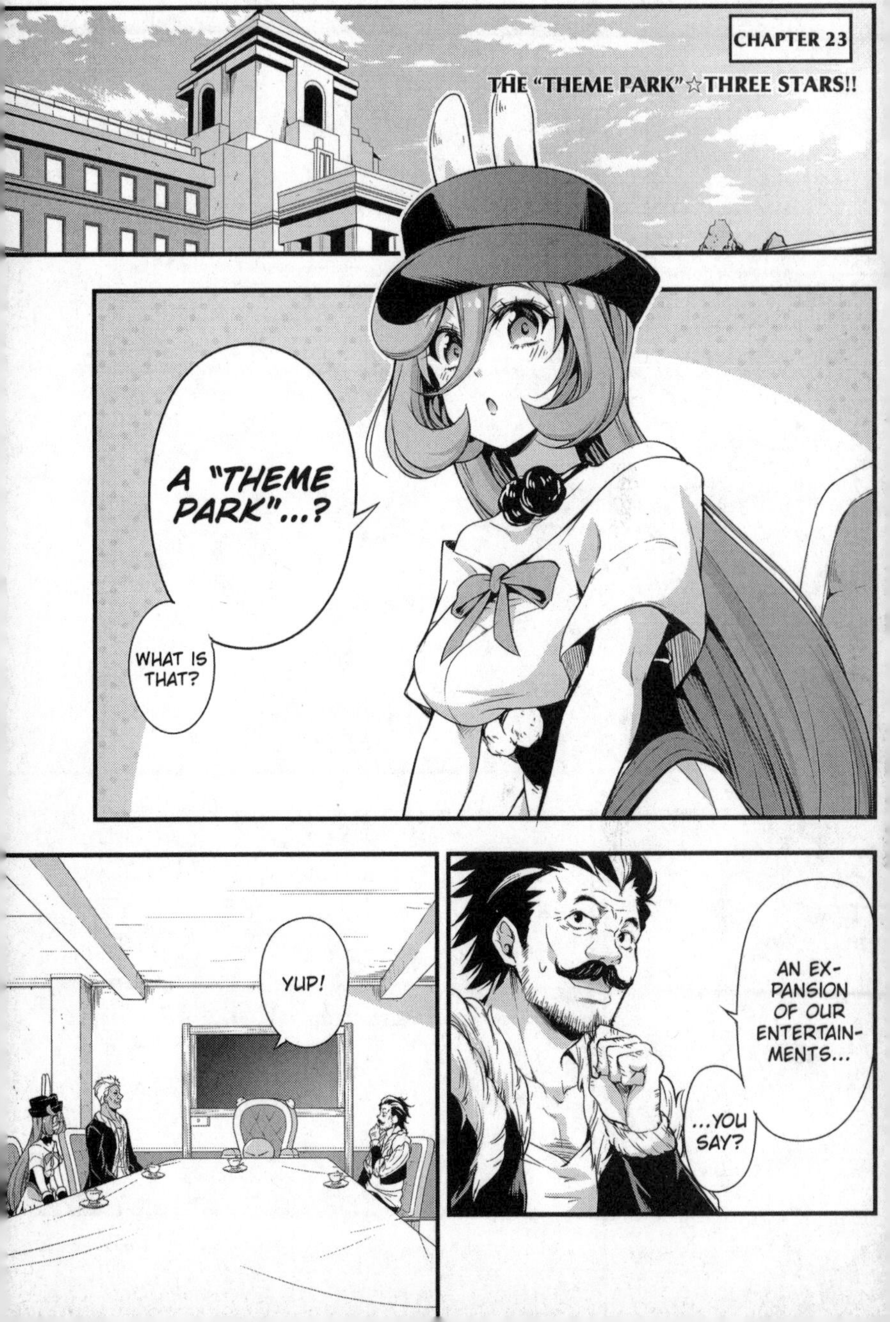
CHAPTER 23
THE "THEME PARK"☆THREE STARS!!
A "THEME PARK"...?
WHAT IS THAT?
AN EXPANSION OF OUR ENTERTAINMENTS...
...YOU SAY?
YUP!

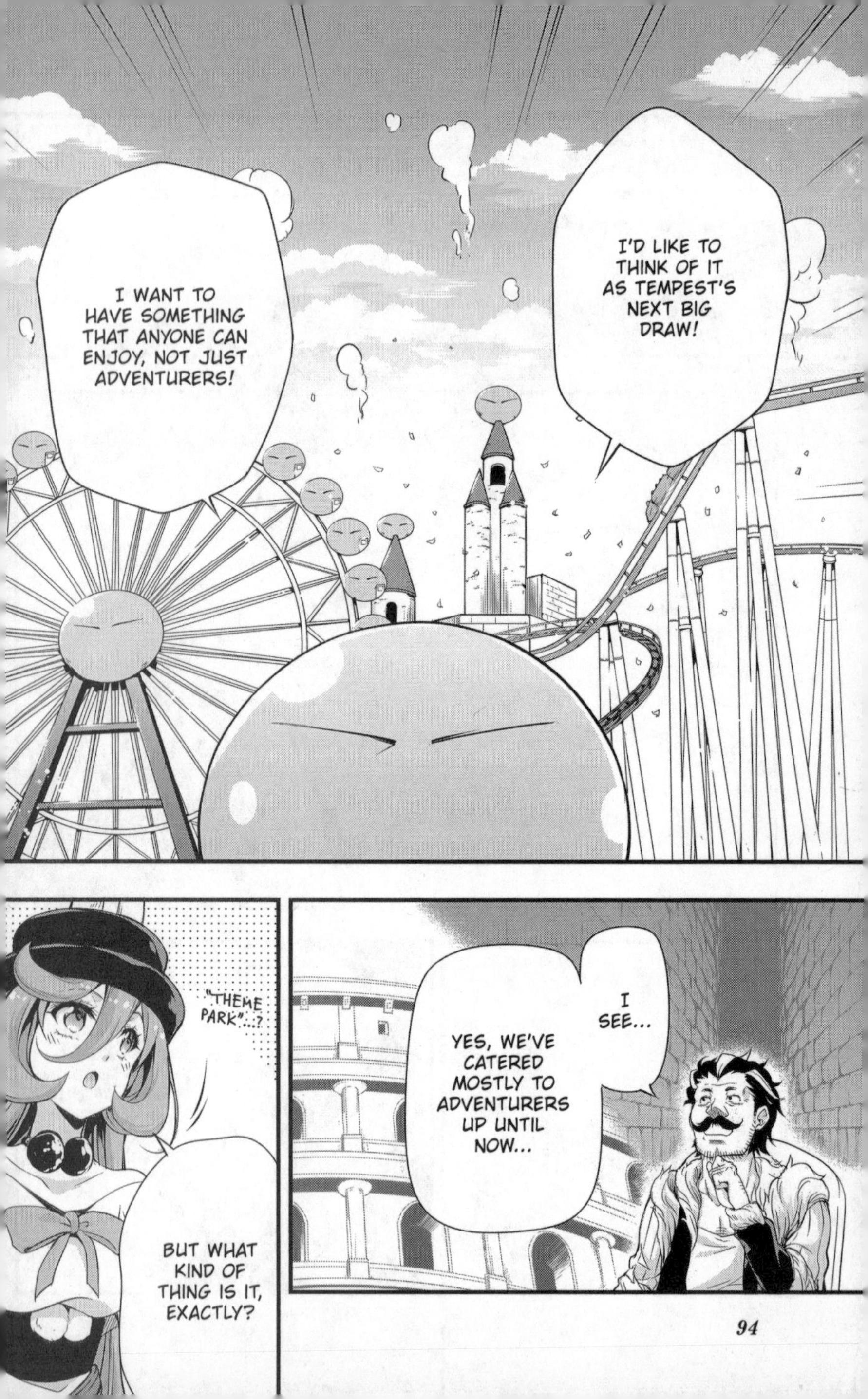
I'D LIKE TO THINK OF IT AS TEMPEST'S NEXT BIG DRAW!
I WANT TO HAVE SOMETHING THAT ANYONE CAN ENJOY, NOT JUST ADVENTURERS!
I SEE...
YES, WE'VE CATERED MOSTLY TO ADVENTURERS UP UNTIL NOW...
"THEME PARK"...?
BUT WHAT KIND OF THING IS IT, EXACTLY?

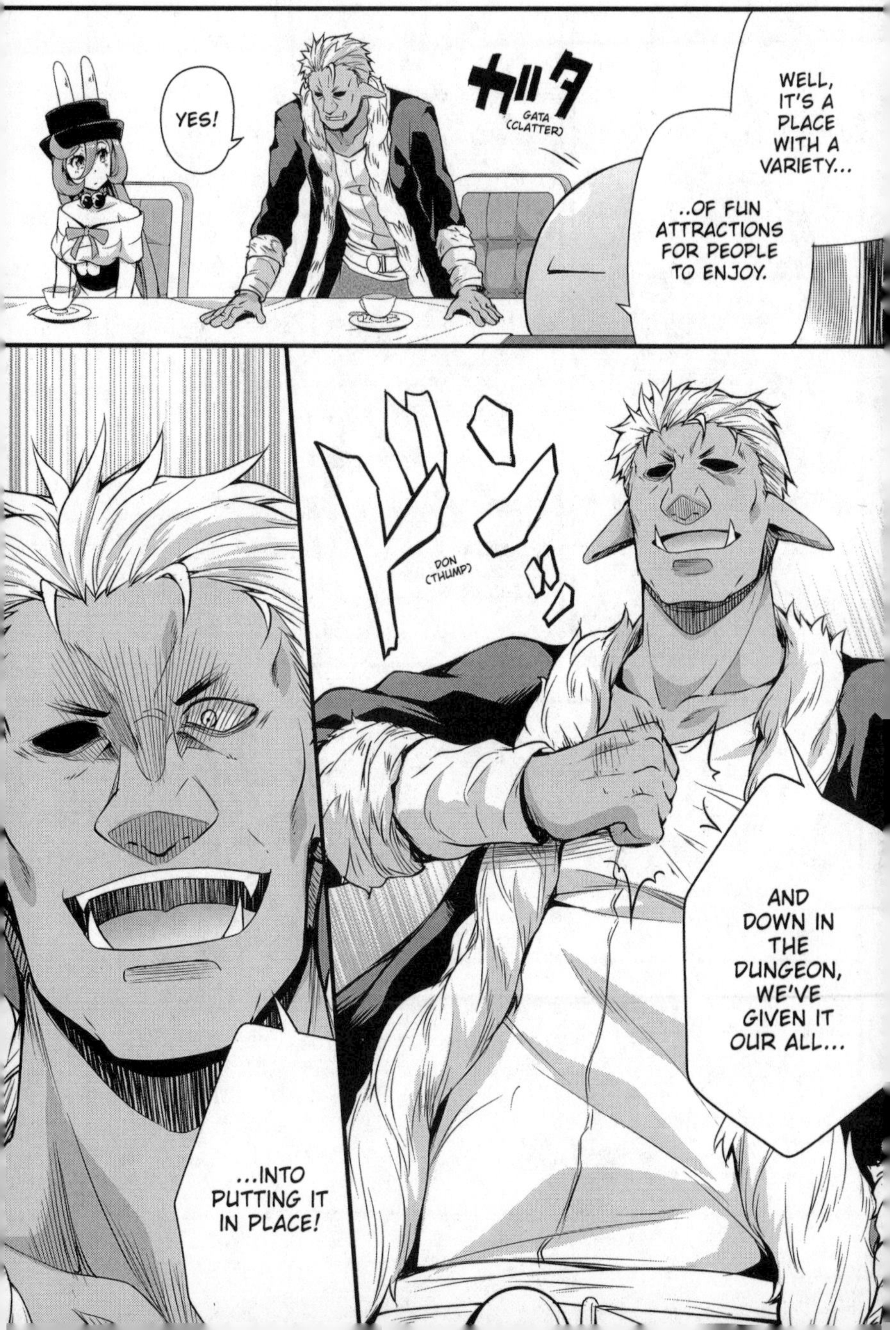
WELL, IT'S A PLACE WITH A VARIETY...
..OF FUN ATTRACTIONS FOR PEOPLE TO ENJOY.
ガタ
GATA (CLATTER)
YES!
ドン
DON (THUMP)
AND DOWN IN THE DUNGEON, WE'VE GIVEN IT OUR ALL...
...INTO PUTTING IT IN PLACE!

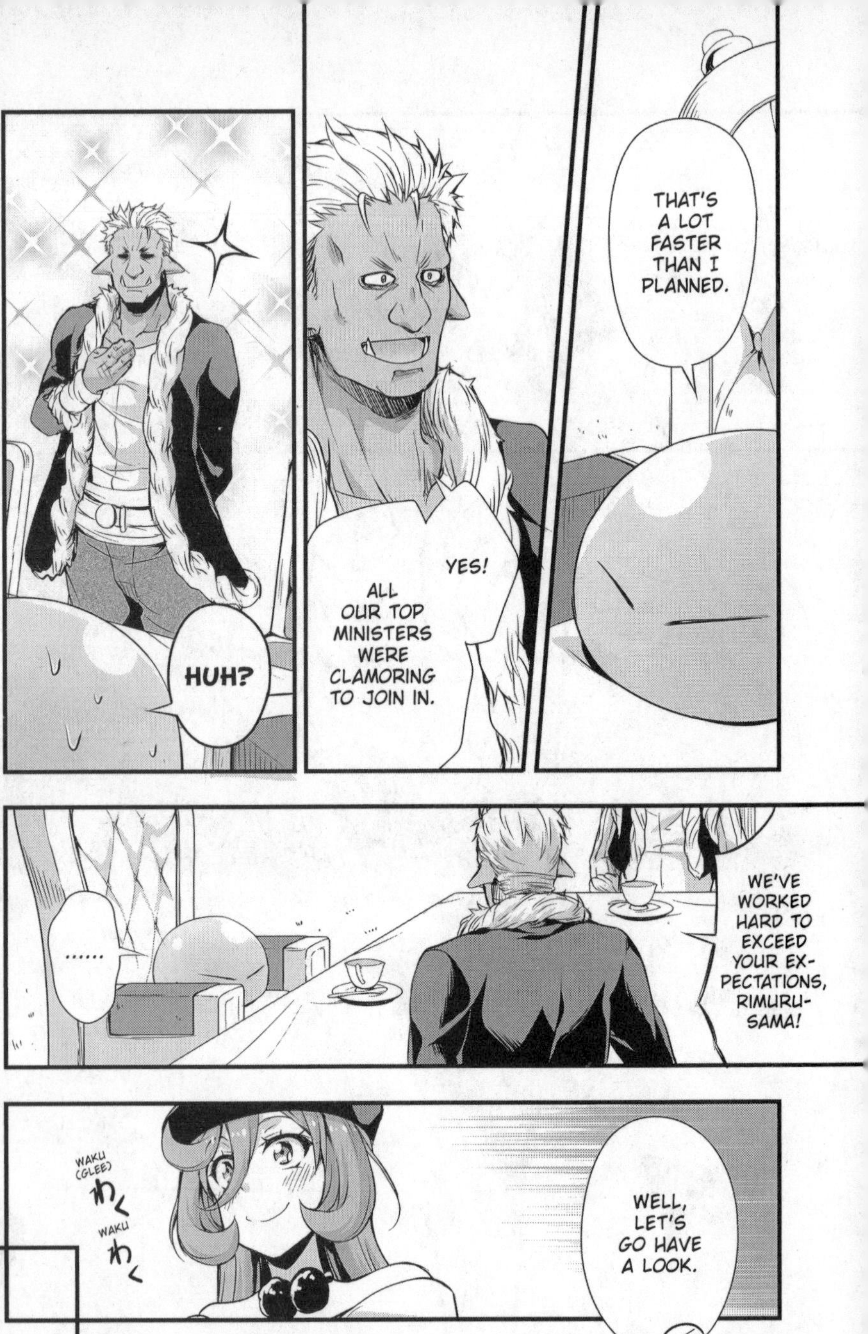
THAT'S A LOT FASTER THAN I PLANNED.
YES!
ALL OUR TOP MINISTERS WERE CLAMORING TO JOIN IN.
HUH?
WE'VE WORKED HARD TO EXCEED YOUR EX-PECTATIONS, RIMURU-SAMA!
......
WELL, LET'S GO HAVE A LOOK.
WAKU (GLEE)
わく
WAKU
わく

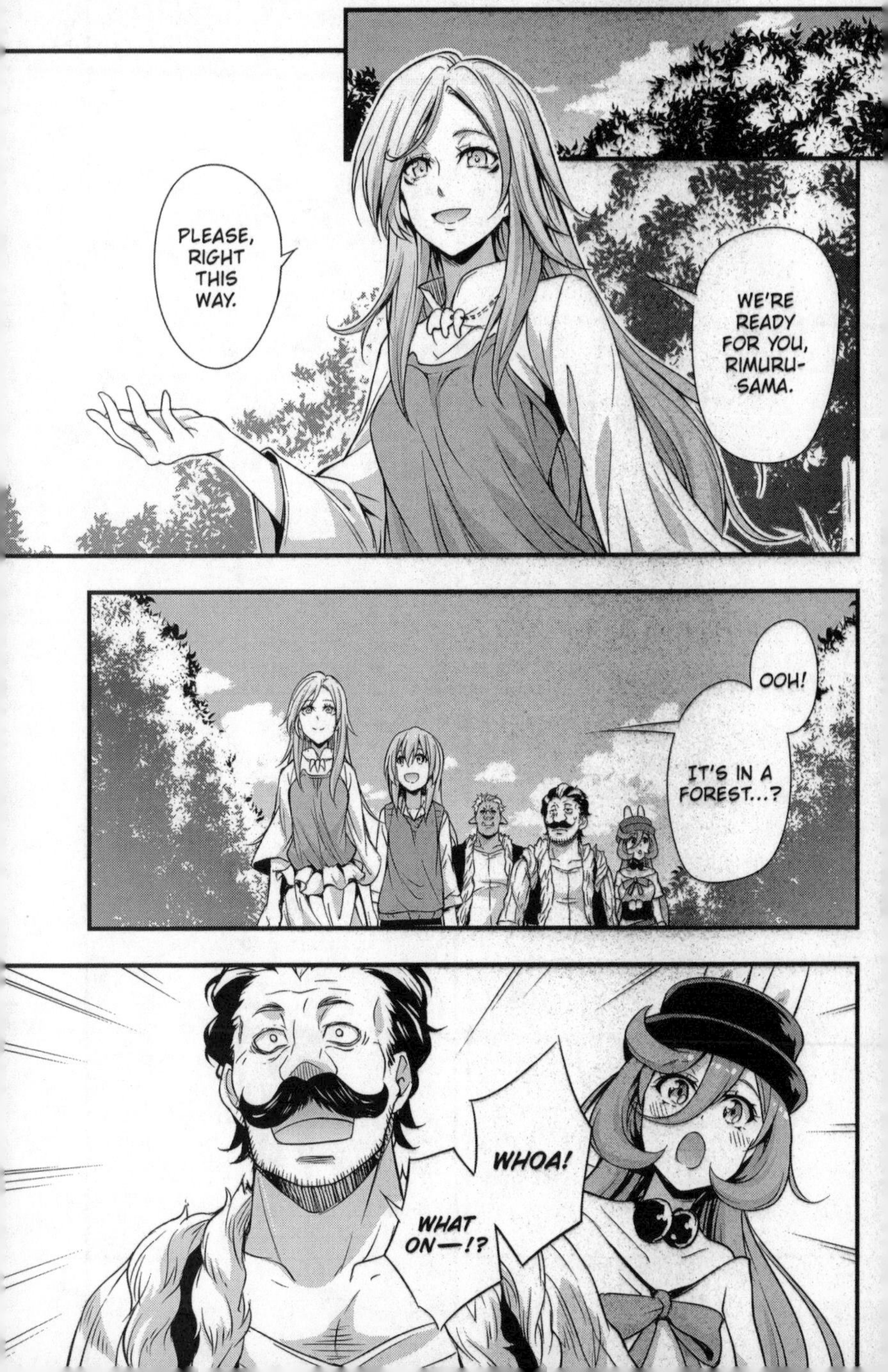
WE'RE READY FOR YOU, RIMURU-SAMA.
PLEASE, RIGHT THIS WAY.
OOH!
IT'S IN A FOREST...?
WHOA!
WHAT ON—!?

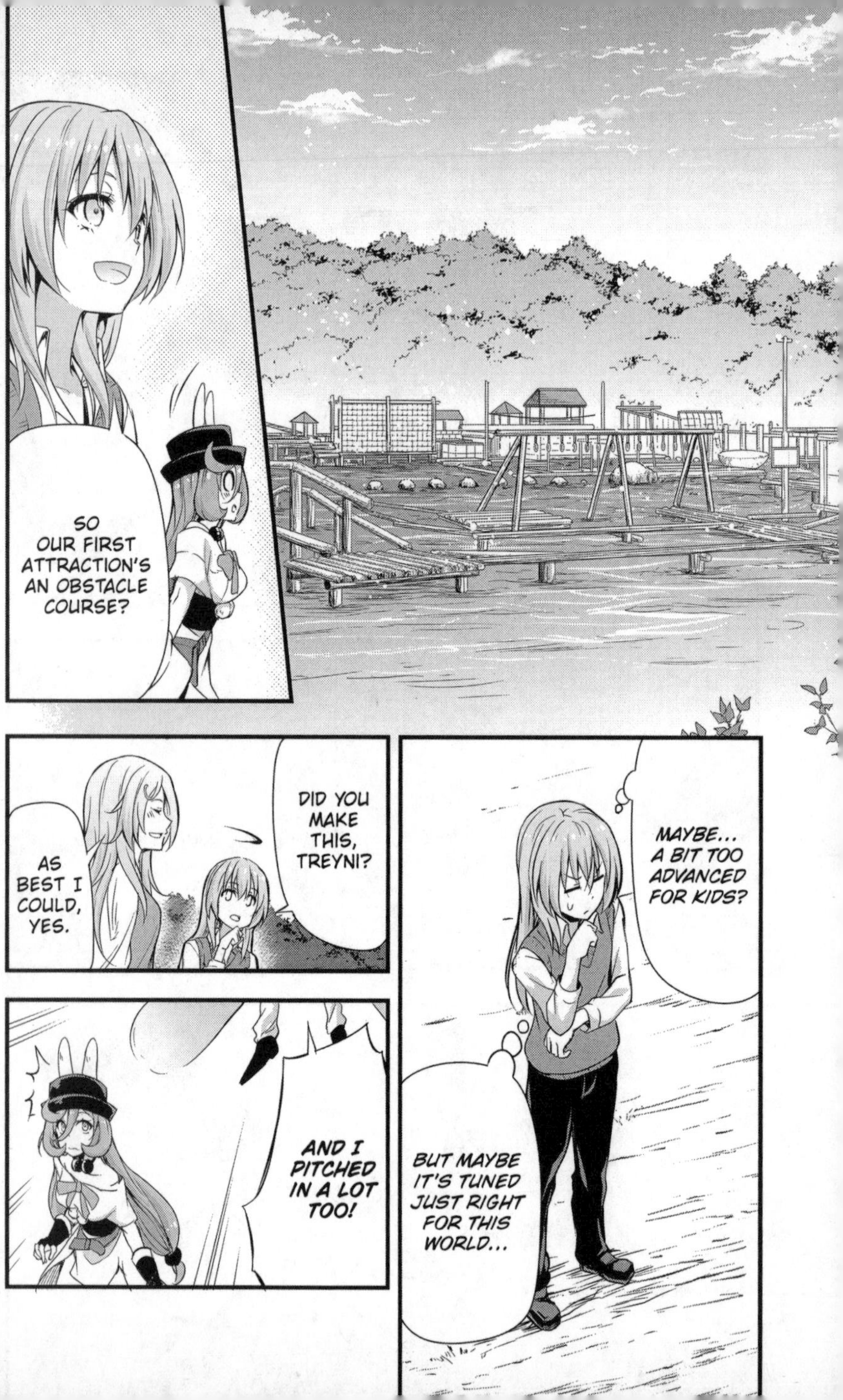
SO OUR FIRST ATTRACTION'S AN OBSTACLE COURSE?
MAYBE… A BIT TOO ADVANCED FOR KIDS?
BUT MAYBE IT'S TUNED JUST RIGHT FOR THIS WORLD…
DID YOU MAKE THIS, TREYNI?
AS BEST I COULD, YES.
AND I PITCHED IN A LOT TOO!

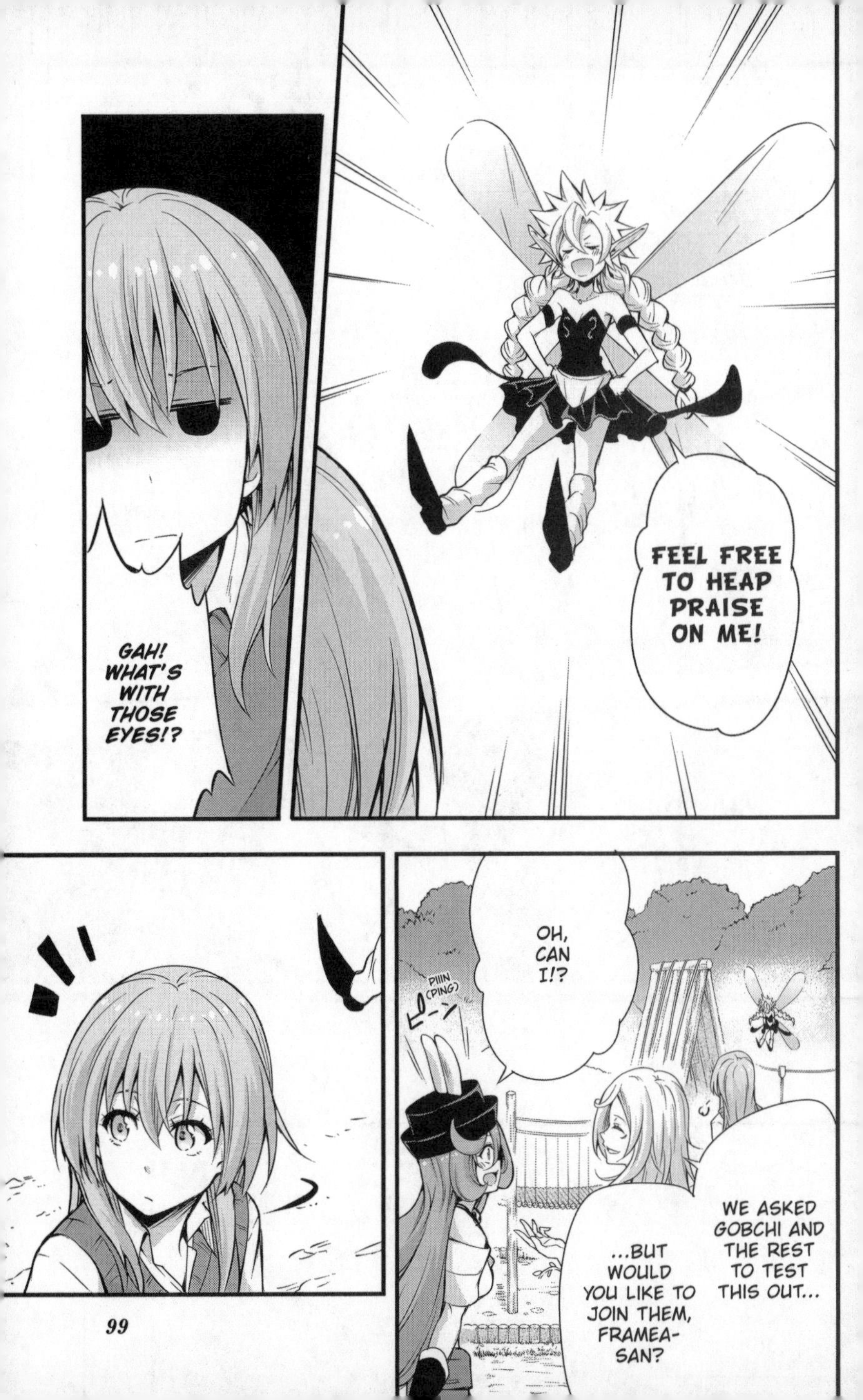
FEEL FREE TO HEAP PRAISE ON ME!
GAH! WHAT'S WITH THOSE EYES!?
WE ASKED GOBCHI AND THE REST TO TEST THIS OUT...
...BUT WOULD YOU LIKE TO JOIN THEM, FRAMEA-SAN?
OH, CAN I!?
PIIN (PING)

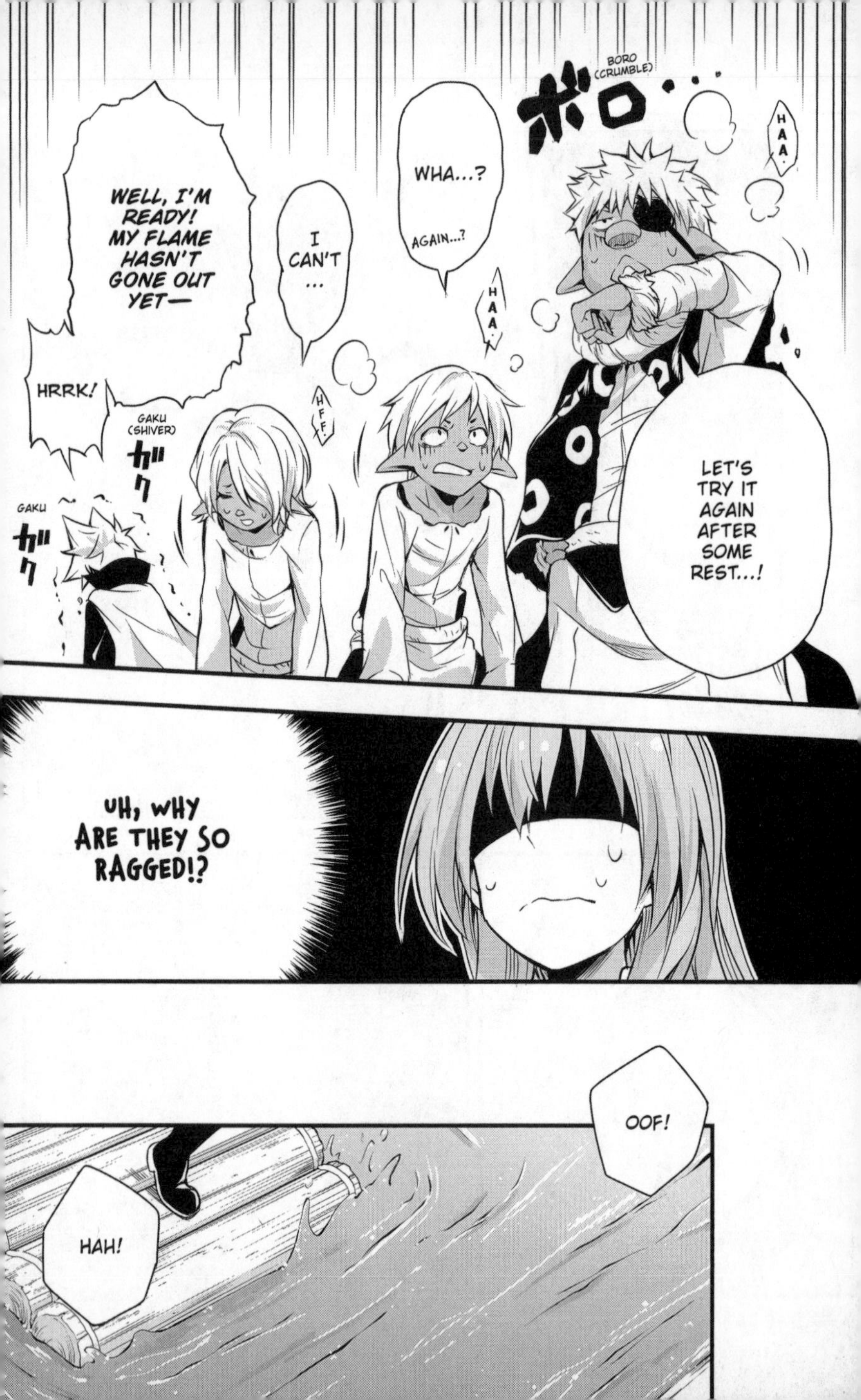
ボロ
BORO (CRUMBLE)
HAA.
LET'S TRY IT AGAIN AFTER SOME REST...!
WHA...?
AGAIN...?
HAA.
I CAN'T ...
HFF.
WELL, I'M READY! MY FLAME HASN'T GONE OUT YET—
HRRK!
ガク
GAKU (SHIVER)
ガク
GAKU
UH, WHY ARE THEY SO RAGGED!?
OOF!
HAH!

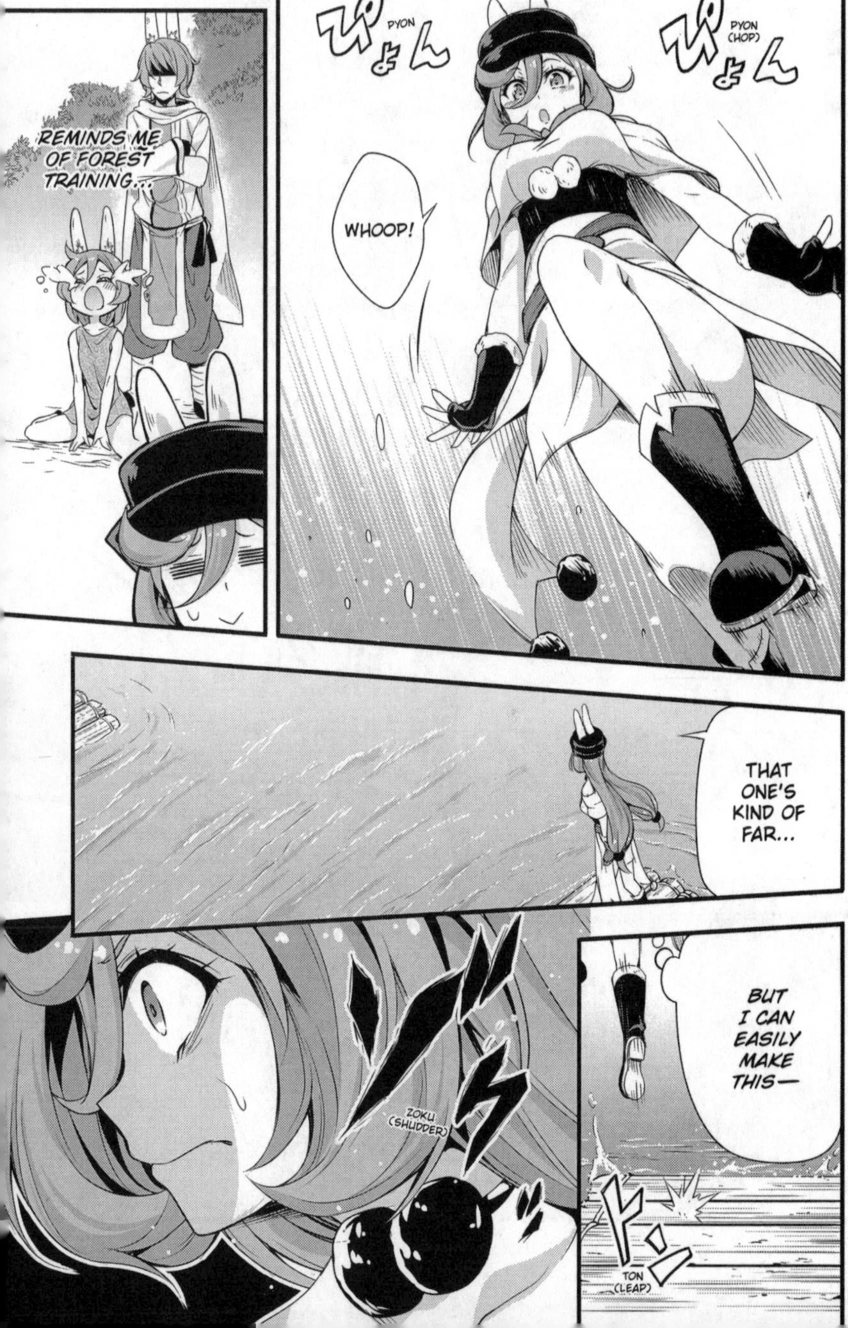

ぴょん
PYON (HOP)
ぴょん
PYON
WHOOP!
REMINDS ME OF FOREST TRAINING...
THAT ONE'S KIND OF FAR...
BUT I CAN EASILY MAKE THIS—
TON (LEAP)
ZOKU (SHUDDER)

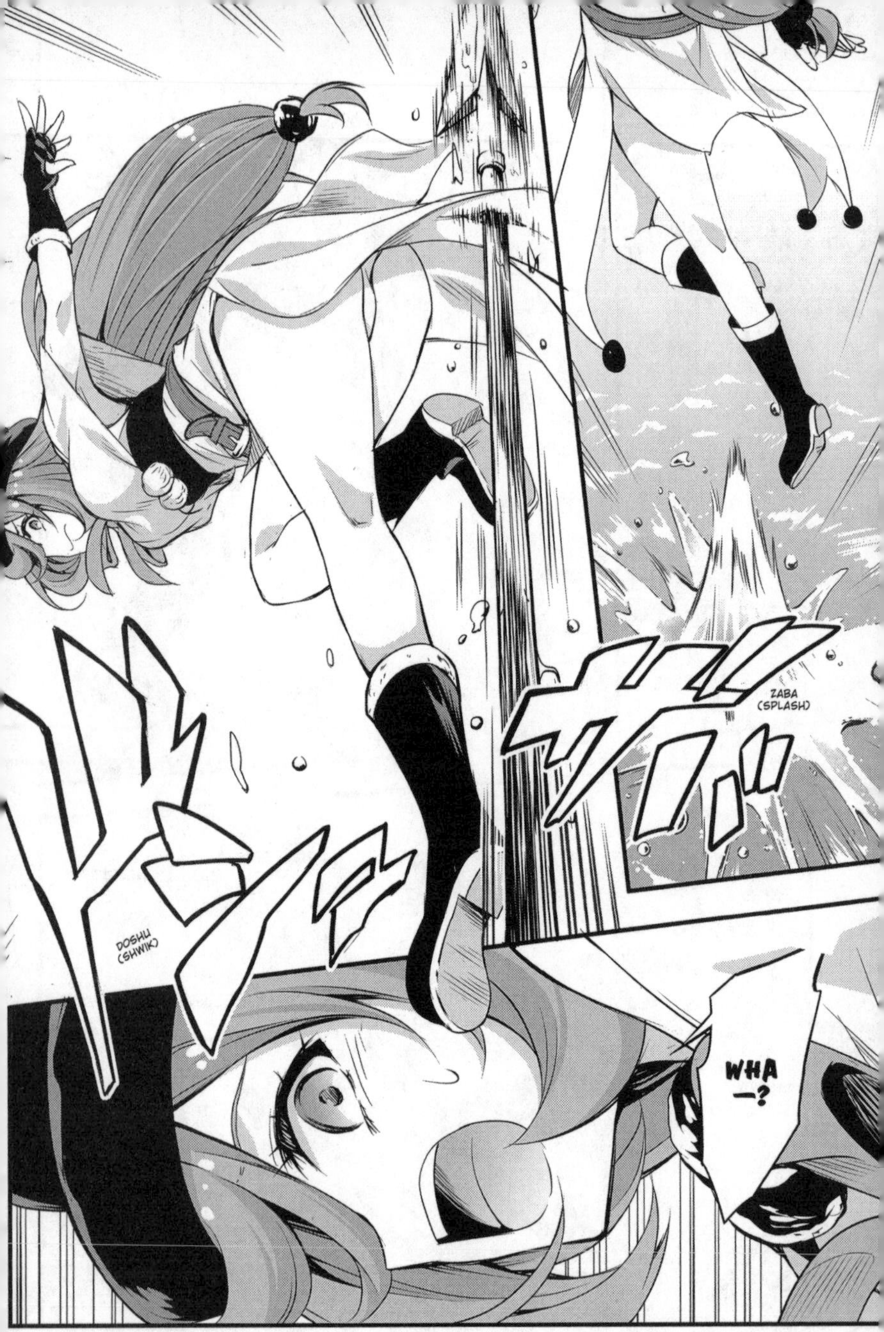
ZABA
(SPLASH)
DOSHU
(SHWIK)
WHA
—?

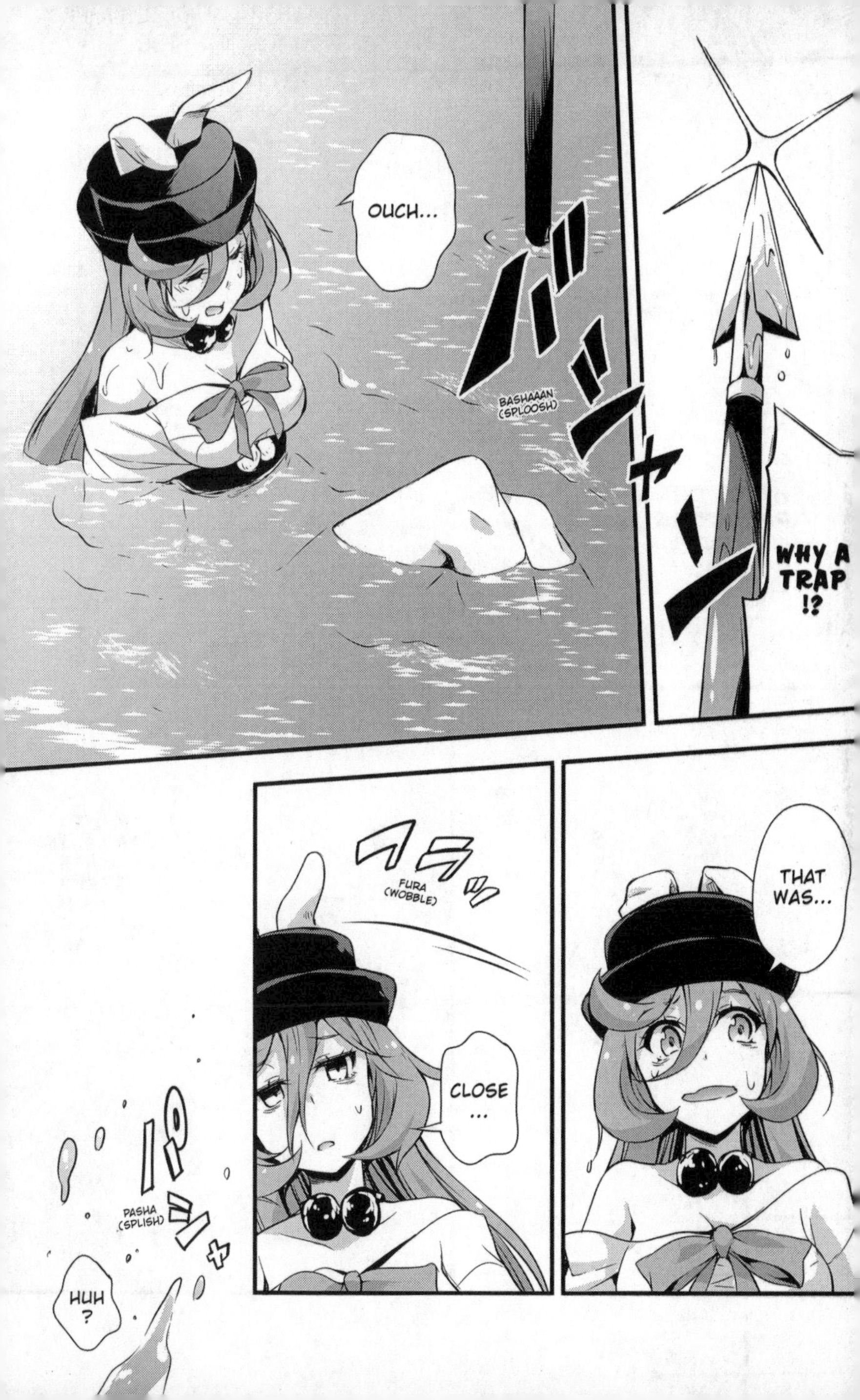
WHY A TRAP !?
OUCH...
BASHAAAN (SPLOOSH)
THAT WAS...
FURA (WOBBLE)
CLOSE ...
PASHA (SPLISH)
HUH ?

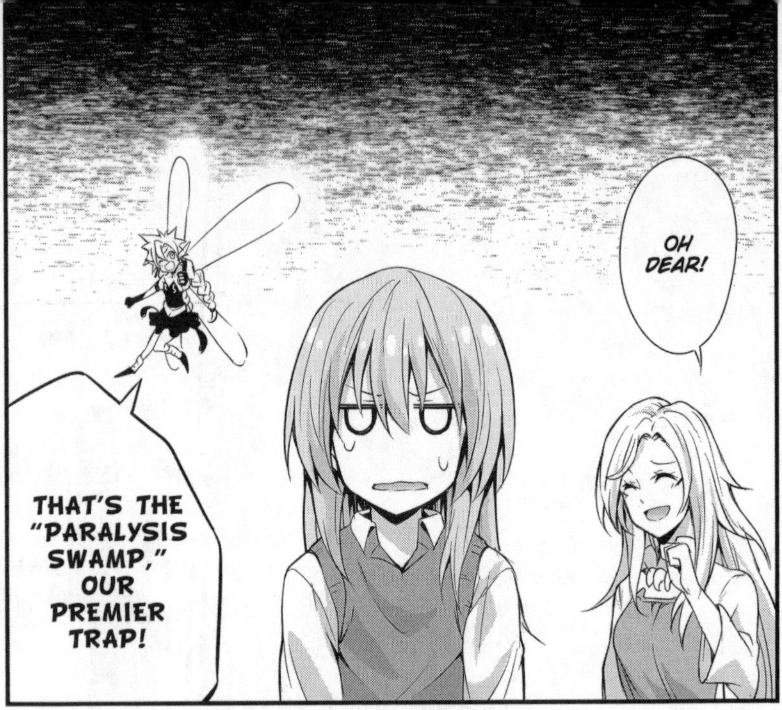
OH DEAR!
THAT'S THE "PARALYSIS SWAMP," OUR PREMIER TRAP!

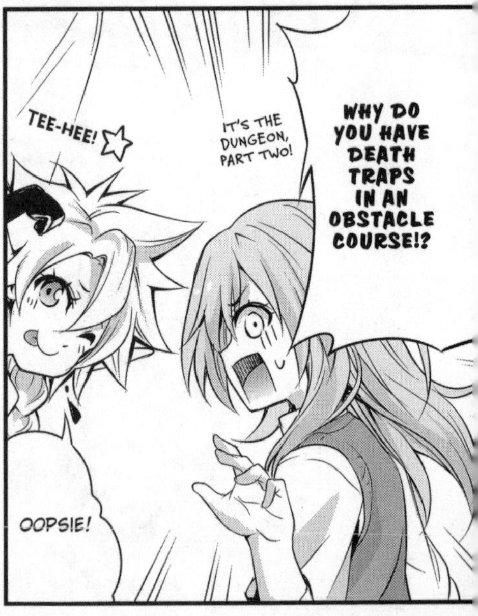
WHY DO YOU HAVE DEATH TRAPS IN AN OBSTACLE COURSE!?
IT'S THE DUNGEON, PART TWO!
TEE-HEE!
OOPSIE!

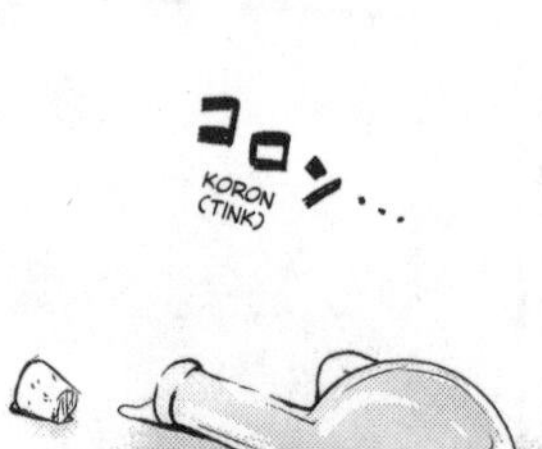
コロン…
KORON (TINK)

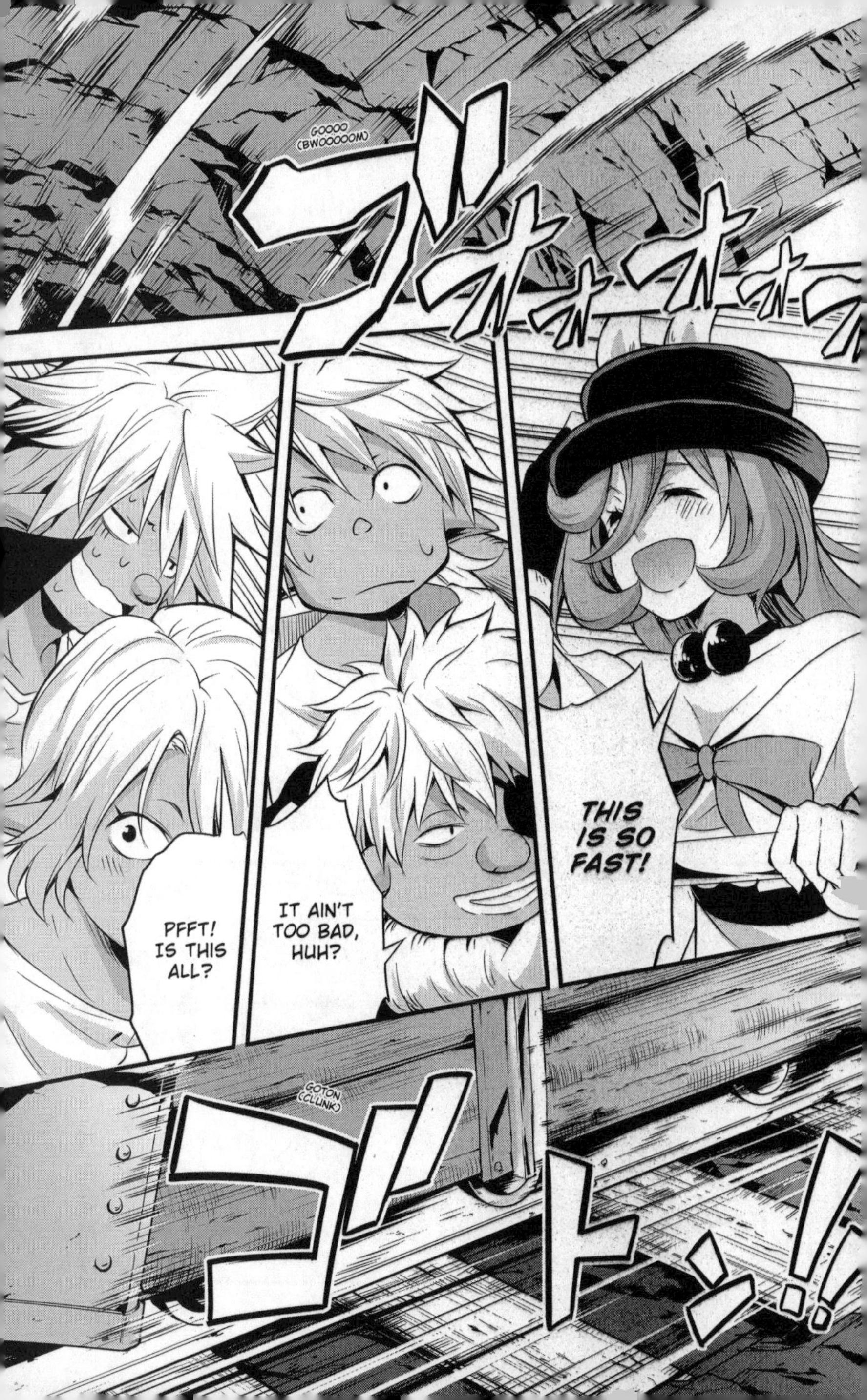
GOOOO (BWOOOOOM)
THIS IS SO FAST!
IT AIN'T TOO BAD, HUH?
PFFT! IS THIS ALL?
GOTON (CLUNK)

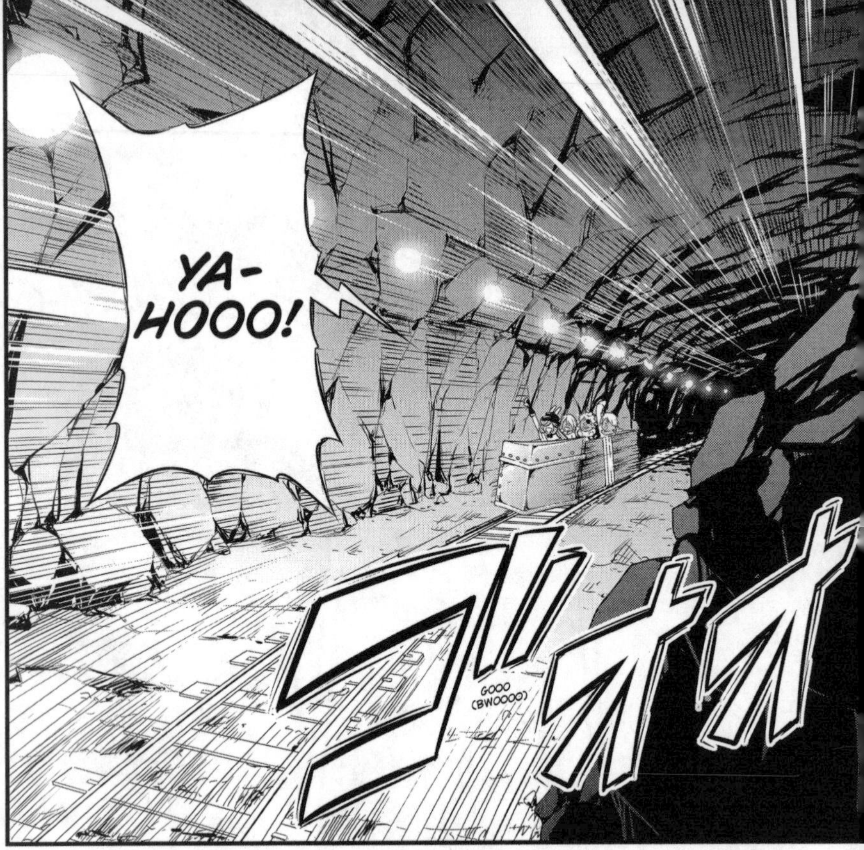
YA-HOOO!
ゴオオ
GOOO (BWOOOO)

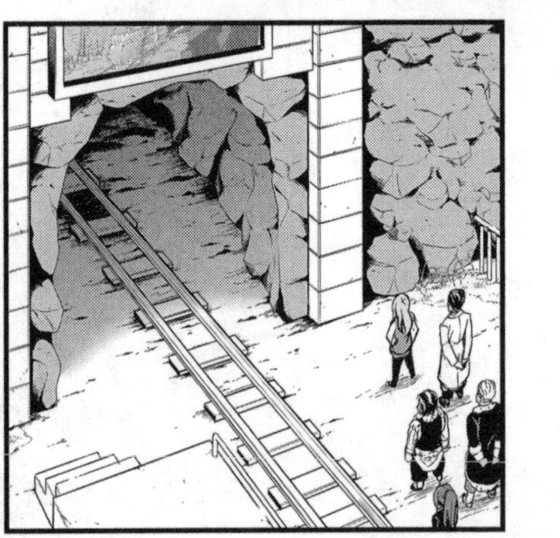

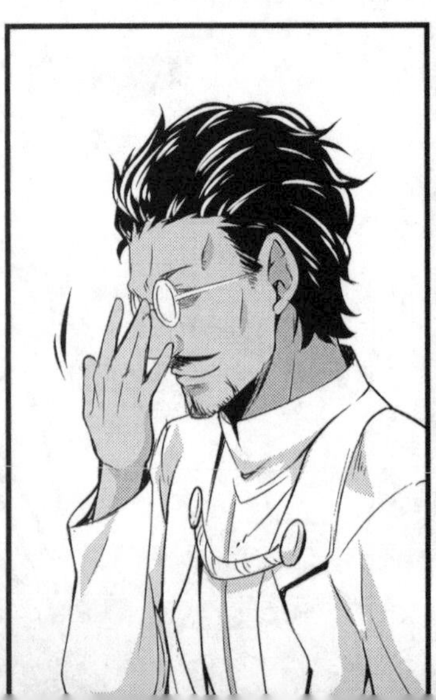

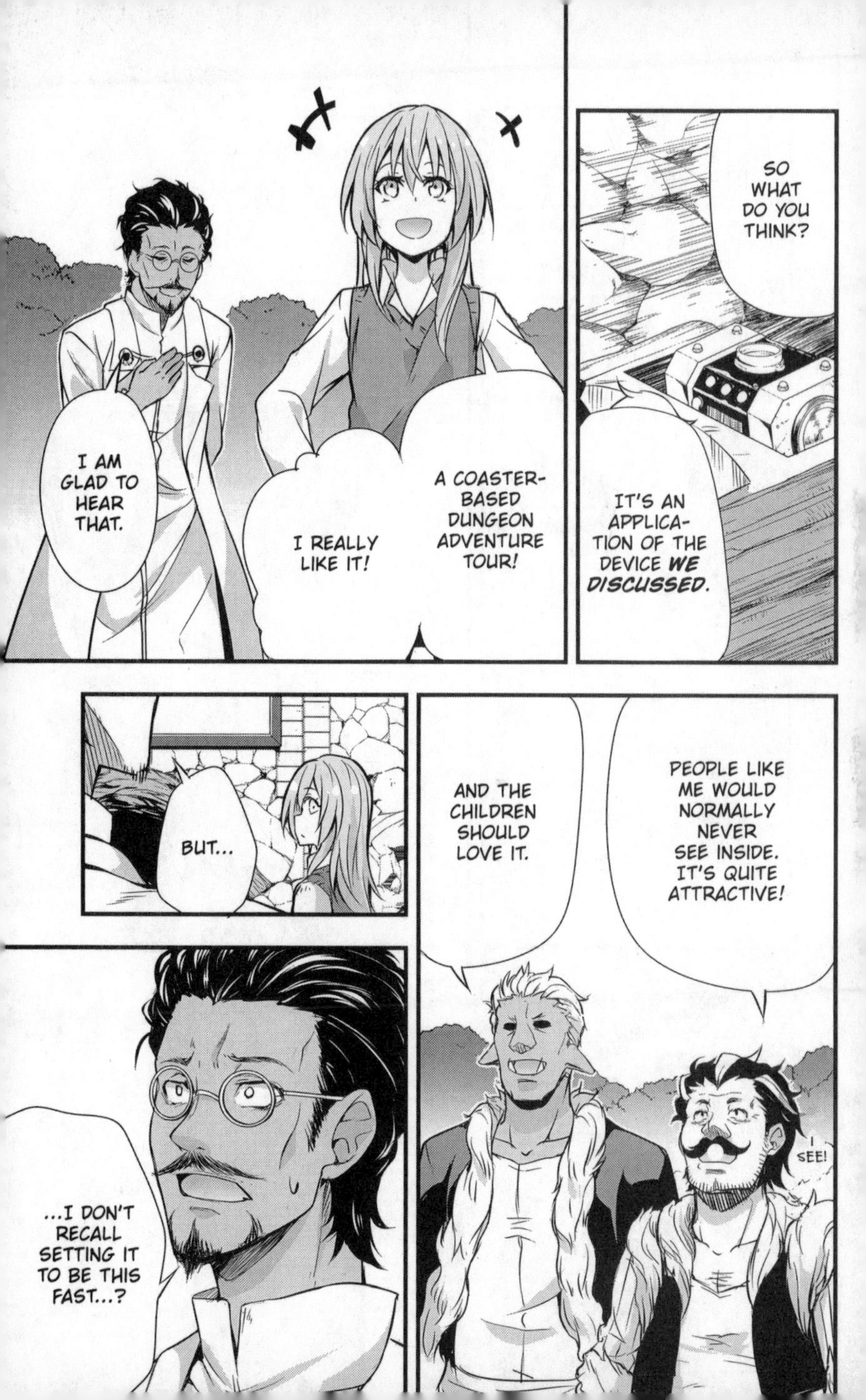
SO WHAT DO YOU THINK?
IT'S AN APPLICATION OF THE DEVICE **WE DISCUSSED**.
A COASTER-BASED DUNGEON ADVENTURE TOUR!
I REALLY LIKE IT!
I AM GLAD TO HEAR THAT.
PEOPLE LIKE ME WOULD NORMALLY NEVER SEE INSIDE. IT'S QUITE ATTRACTIVE!
AND THE CHILDREN SHOULD LOVE IT.
I SEE!
BUT...
...I DON'T RECALL SETTING IT TO BE THIS FAST...?

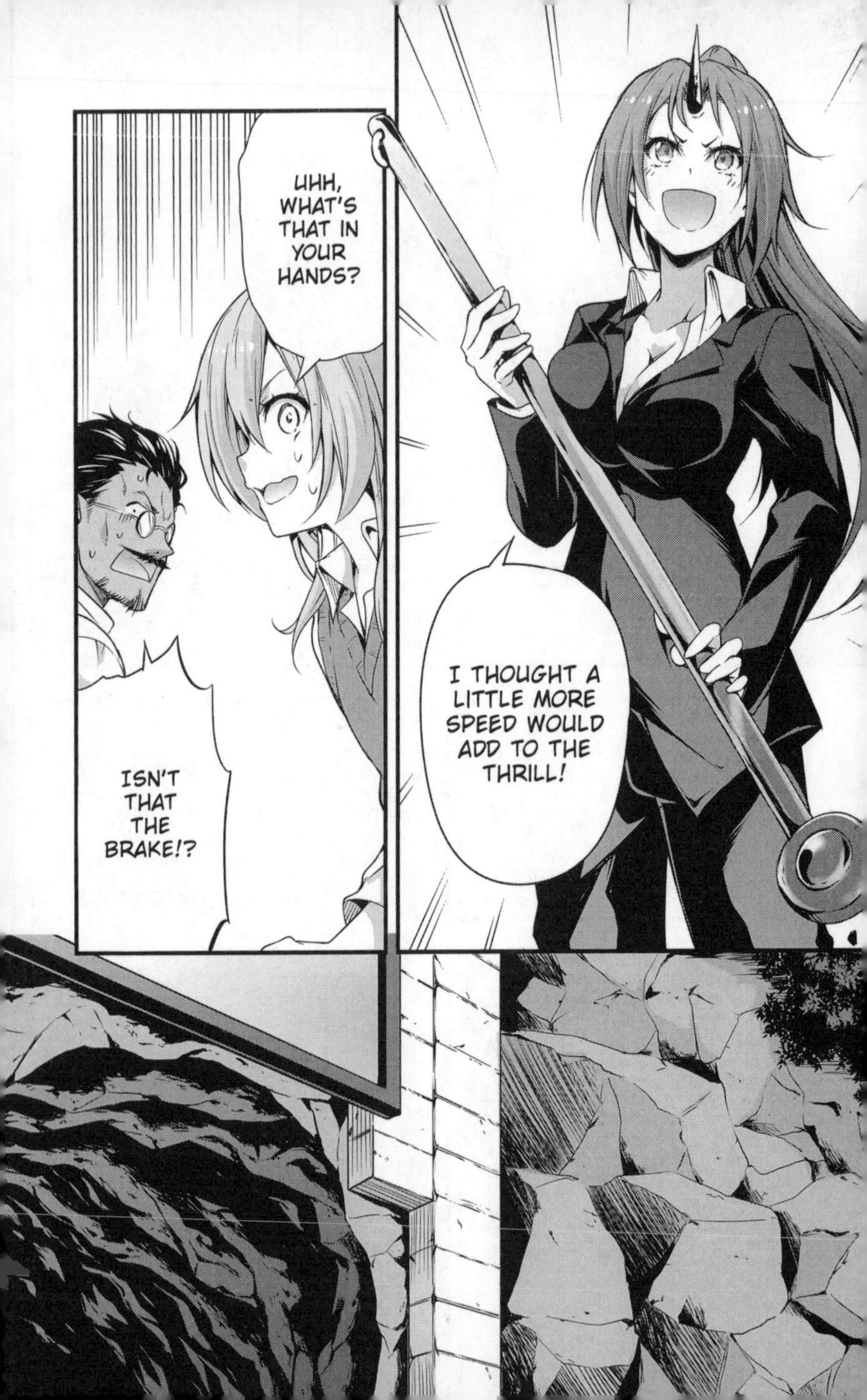
I THOUGHT A LITTLE MORE SPEED WOULD ADD TO THE THRILL!
UHH, WHAT'S THAT IN YOUR HANDS?
ISN'T THAT THE BRAKE!?

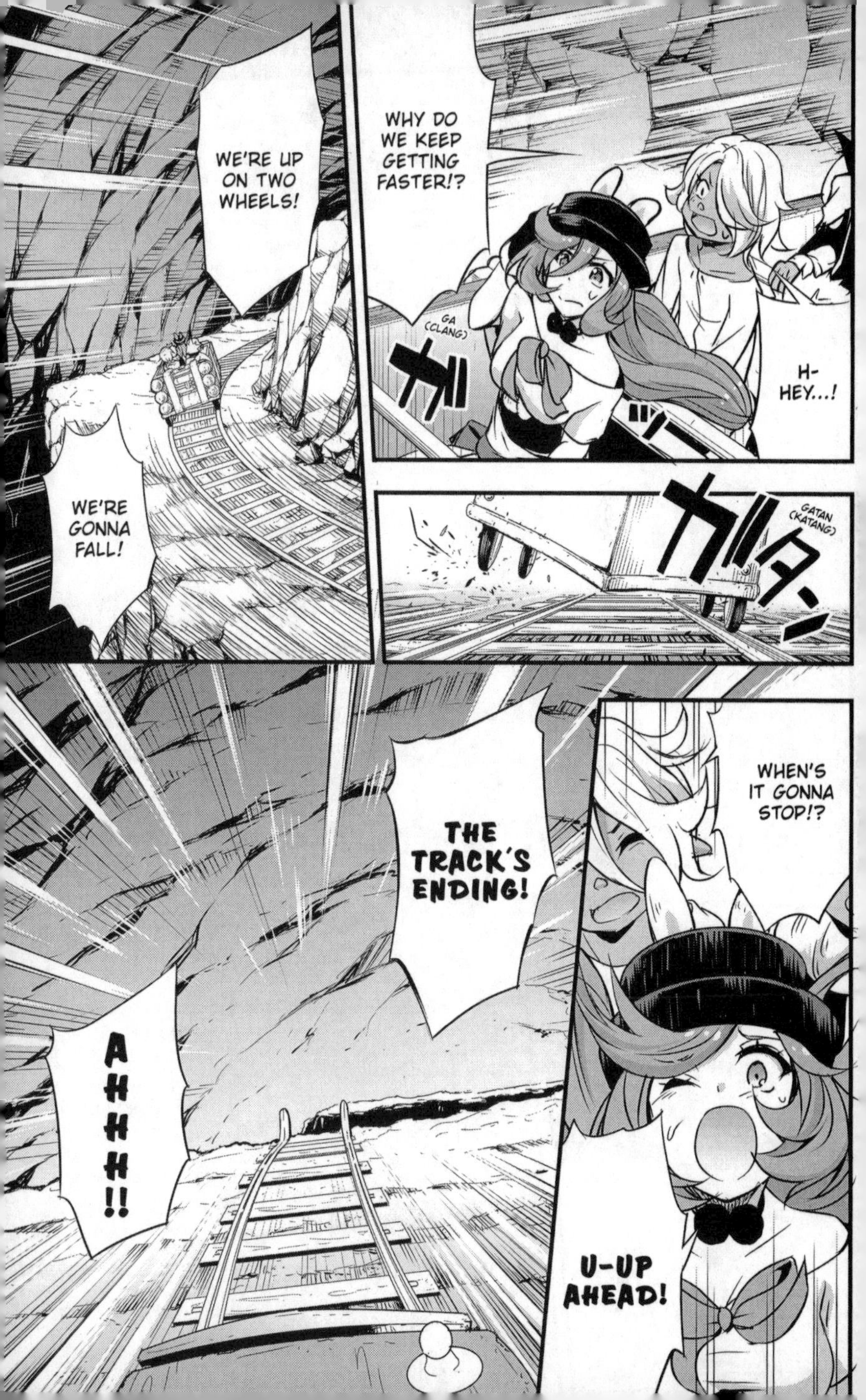
WHY DO WE KEEP GETTING FASTER!?
H-HEY...!
GA (CLANG)
GATAN (KATANG)
WE'RE UP ON TWO WHEELS!
WE'RE GONNA FALL!
WHEN'S IT GONNA STOP!?
U-UP AHEAD!
THE TRACK'S ENDING!
AHHHH!!

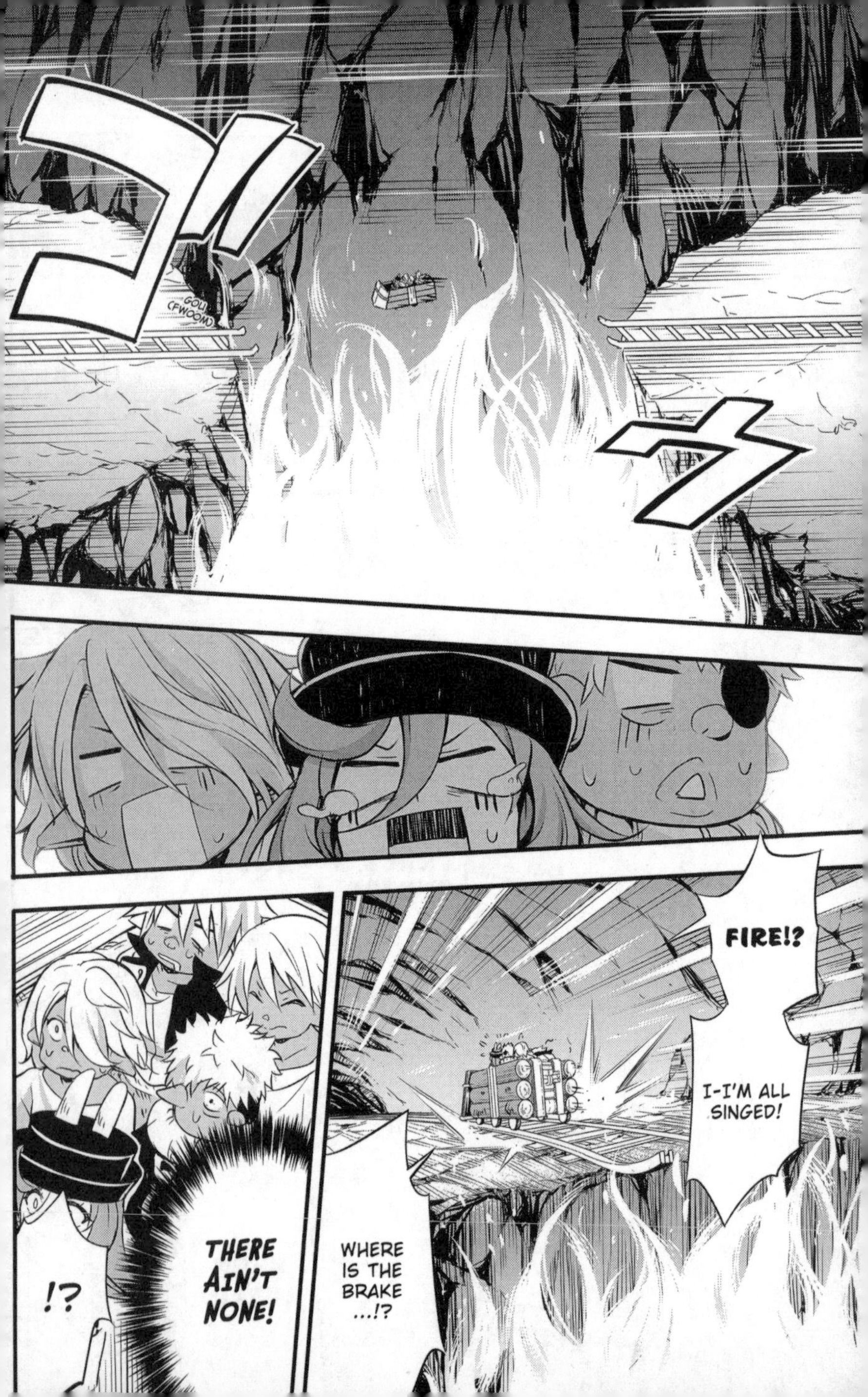
GOU
(FWOOM)
FIRE!?
I-I'M ALL SINGED!
WHERE IS THE BRAKE ...!?
THERE AIN'T NONE!
!?

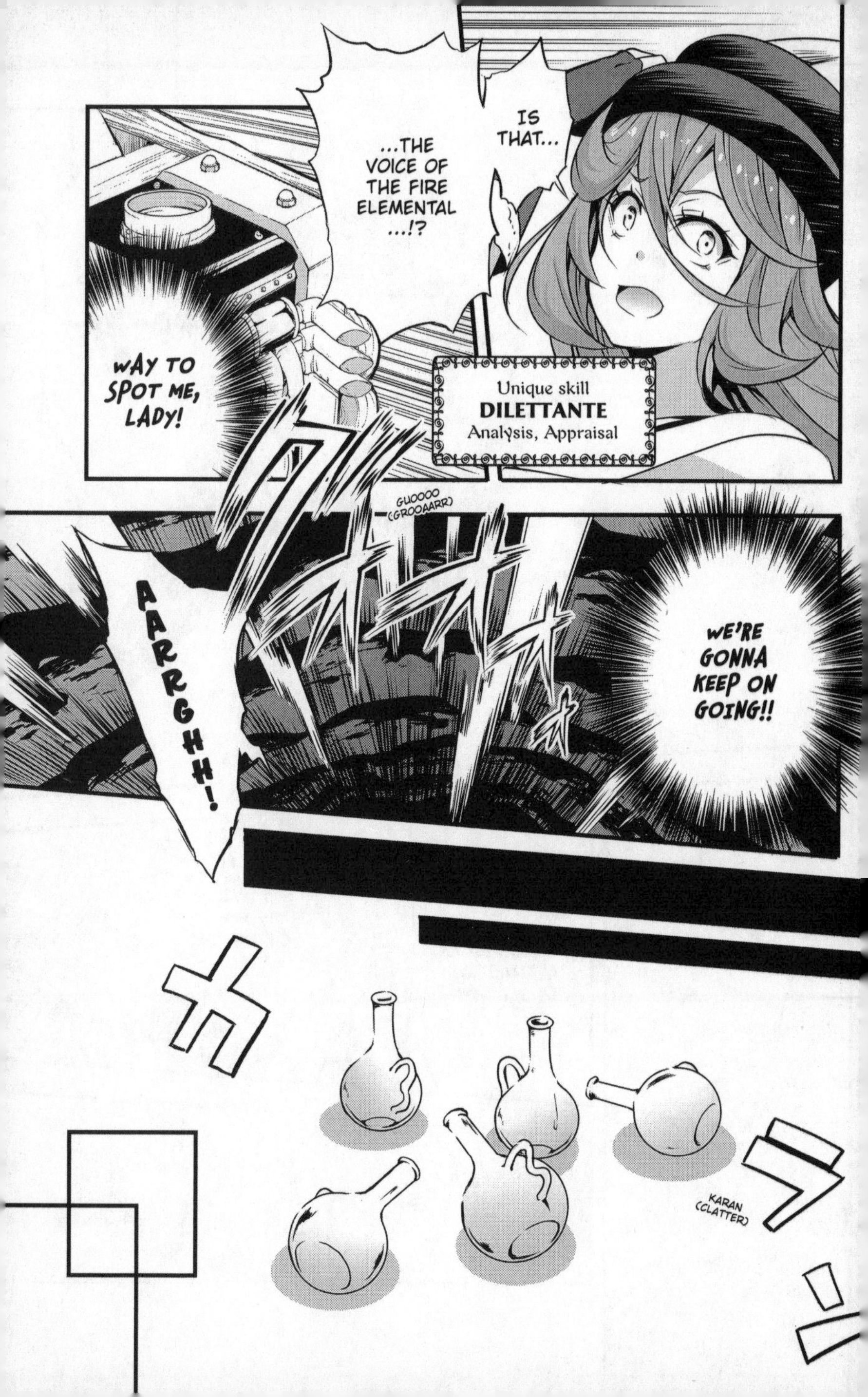
IS THAT...
...THE VOICE OF THE FIRE ELEMENTAL ...!?
Unique skill DILETTANTE Analysis, Appraisal
WAY TO SPOT ME, LADY!
WE'RE GONNA KEEP ON GOING!!
GUOOOO (GROOAARR)
AARRGHH!
KARAN (CLATTER)

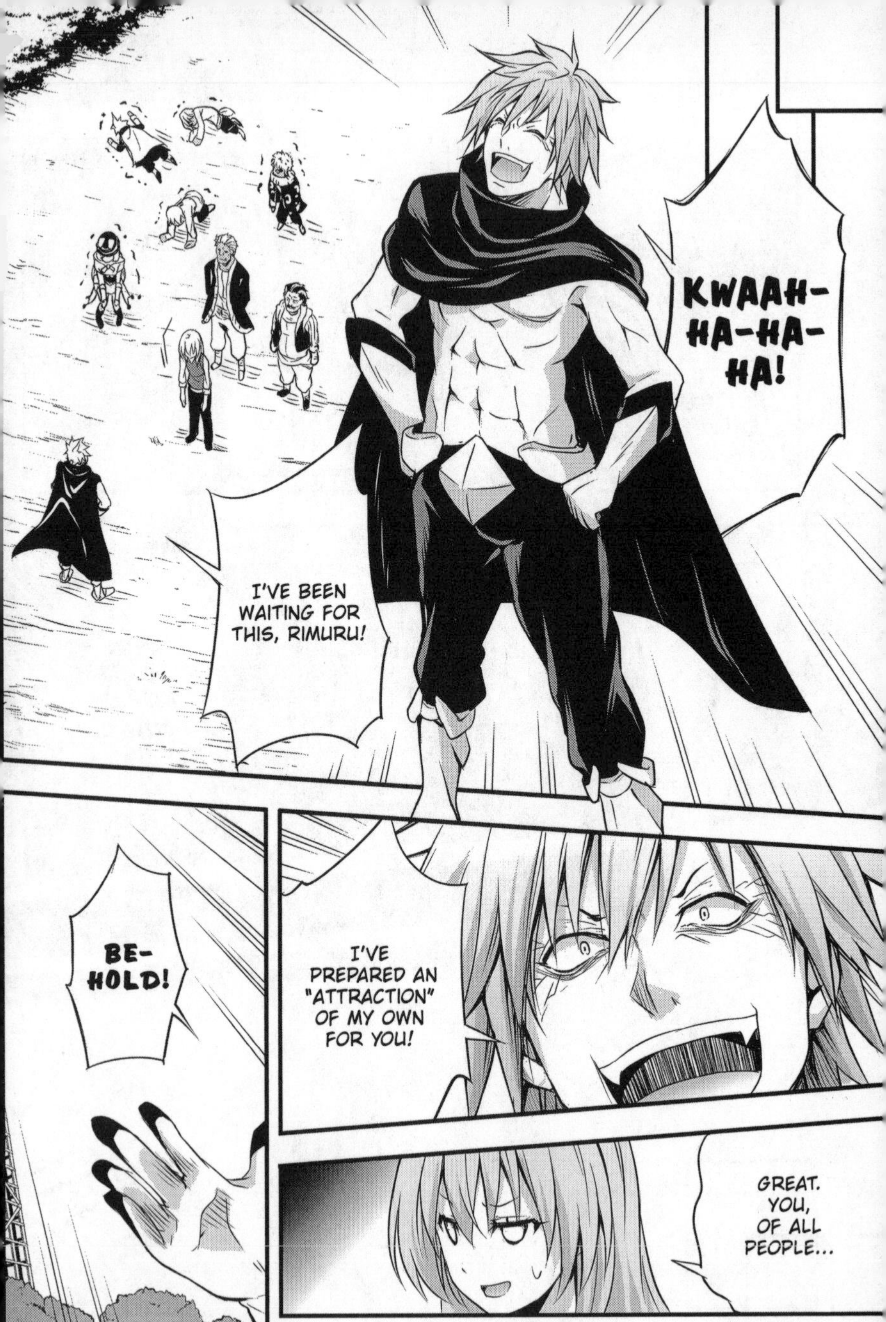
KWAAH-HA-HA-HA!
I'VE BEEN WAITING FOR THIS, RIMURU!
I'VE PREPARED AN "ATTRACTION" OF MY OWN FOR YOU!
GREAT. YOU, OF ALL PEOPLE...
BE-HOLD!

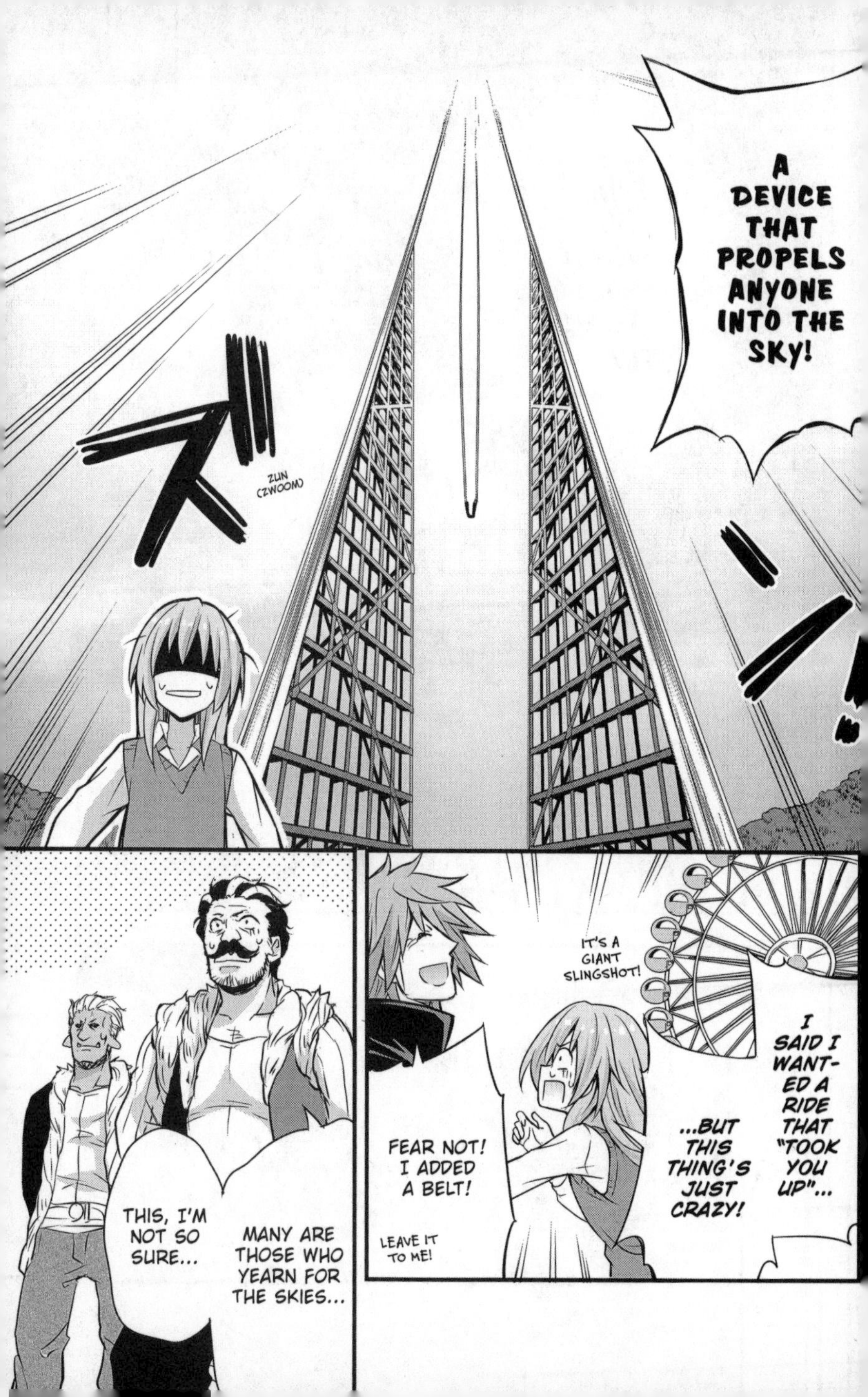
A DEVICE THAT PROPELS ANYONE INTO THE SKY!
ZUN (ZWOOM)
IT'S A GIANT SLINGSHOT!
I SAID I WANT-ED A RIDE THAT "TOOK YOU UP"...
...BUT THIS THING'S JUST CRAZY!
FEAR NOT! I ADDED A BELT!
LEAVE IT TO ME!
MANY ARE THOSE WHO YEARN FOR THE SKIES...
THIS, I'M NOT SO SURE...

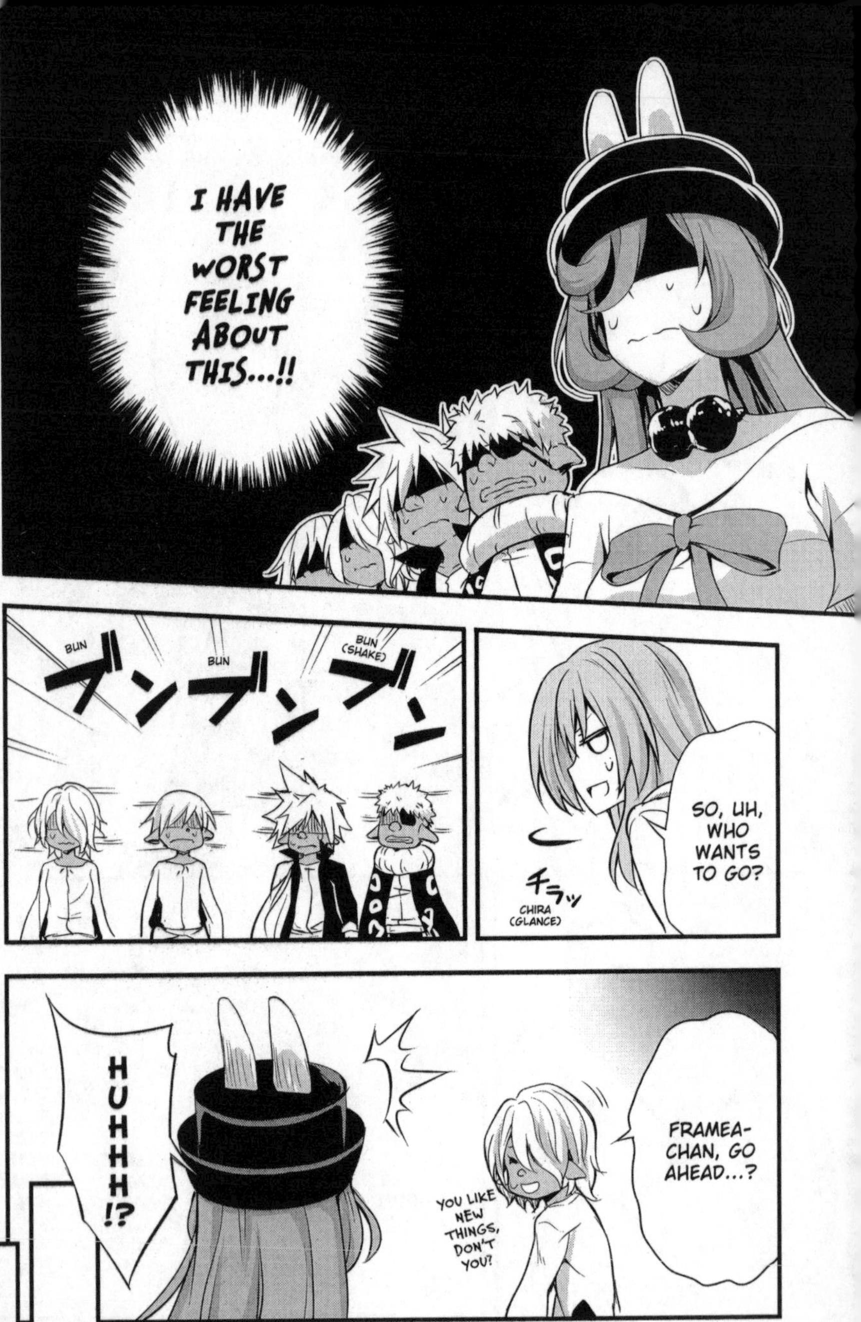
I HAVE THE WORST FEELING ABOUT THIS...!!
SO, UH, WHO WANTS TO GO?
チラッ
CHIRA (GLANCE)
ブンブンブン
BUN
BUN
BUN (SHAKE)
FRAMEA-CHAN, GO AHEAD...?
YOU LIKE NEW THINGS, DON'T YOU?
HUHHHH!?

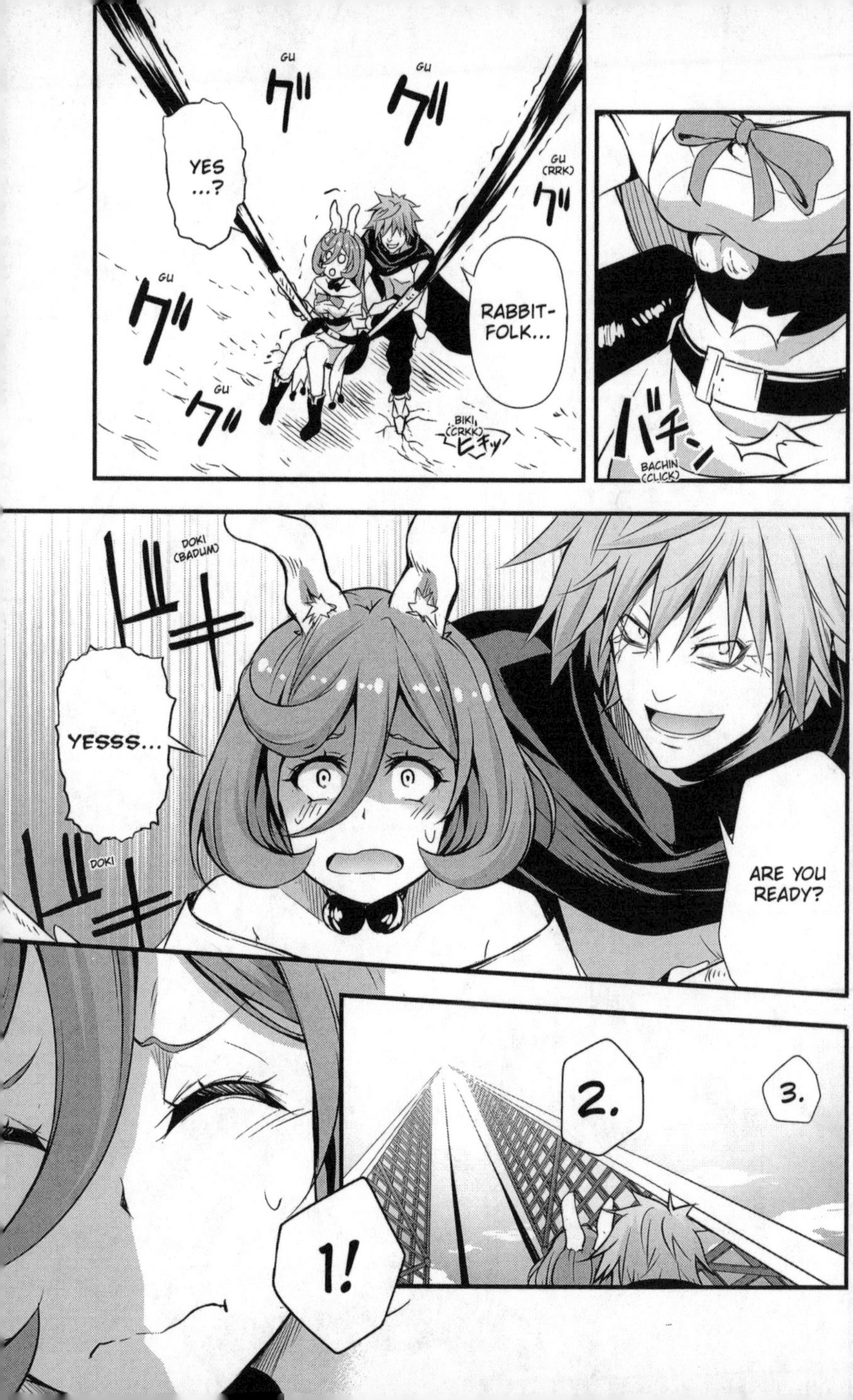

バチン
BACHIN (CLICK)
グ
GU
グ
GU
グ
GU (RRK)
RABBIT-FOLK...
YES ...?
グ
GU
グ
GU
ビキッ
BIKI (CRKK)
ARE YOU READY?
ドキ
DOKI (BADUM)
YESSS...
ドキ
DOKI
3.
2.
1!

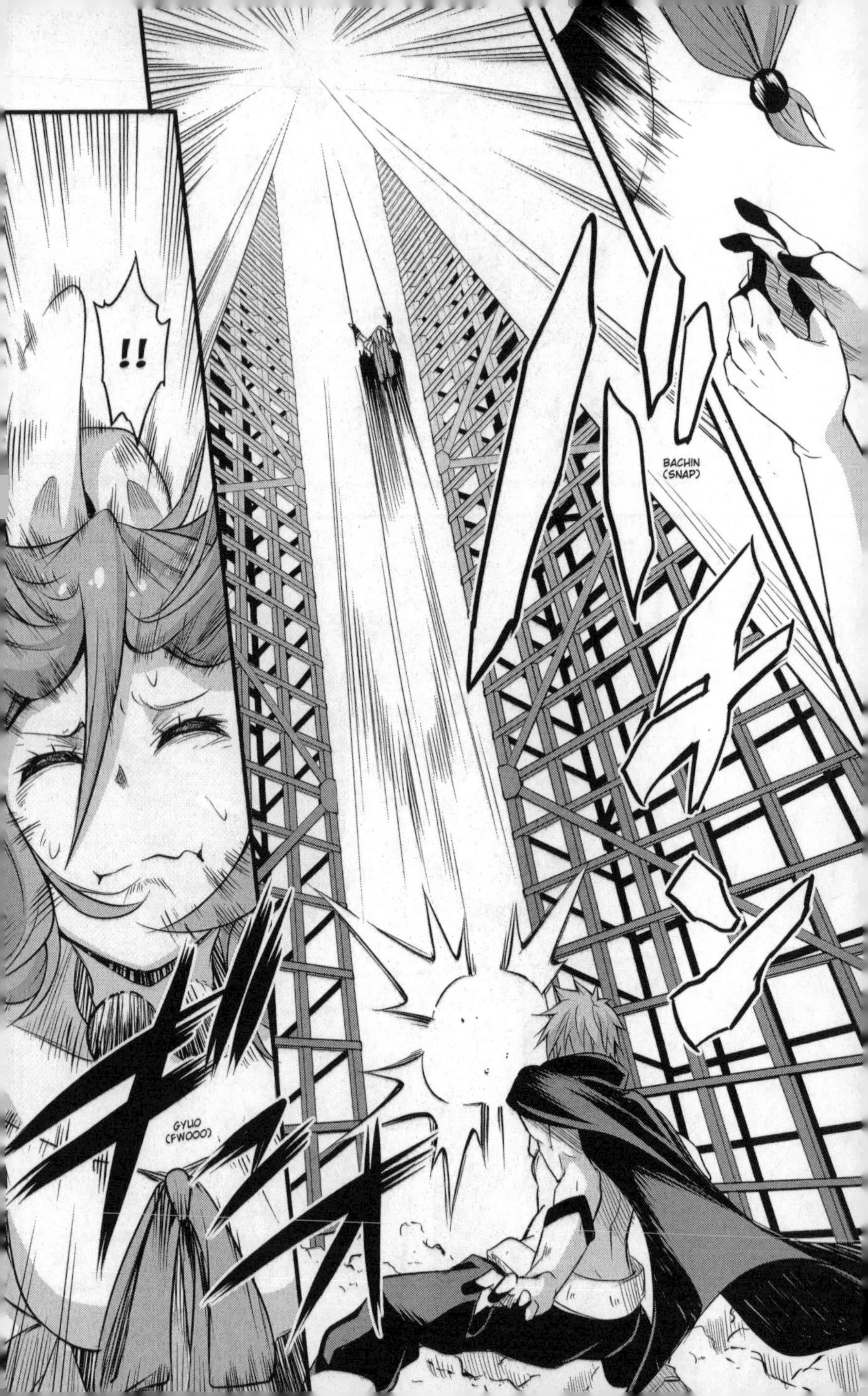
BACHIN
(SNAP)
!!
GYUO
(FWOOO)

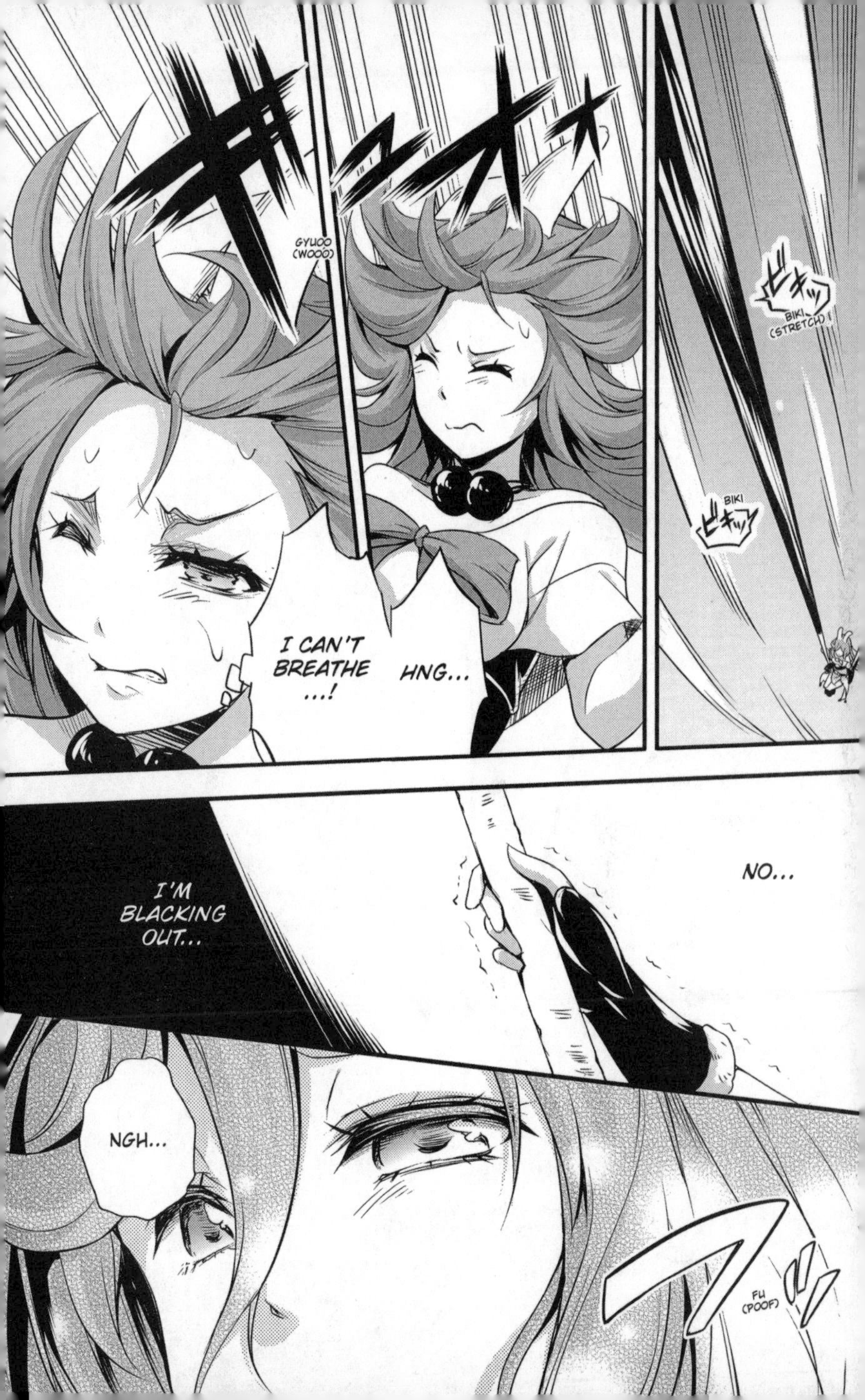
BIKI (STRETCH)!
BIKI
HNG...
GYUOO (WOOO)
I CAN'T BREATHE ...!
NO...
I'M BLACKING OUT...
FU (POOF)
NGH...

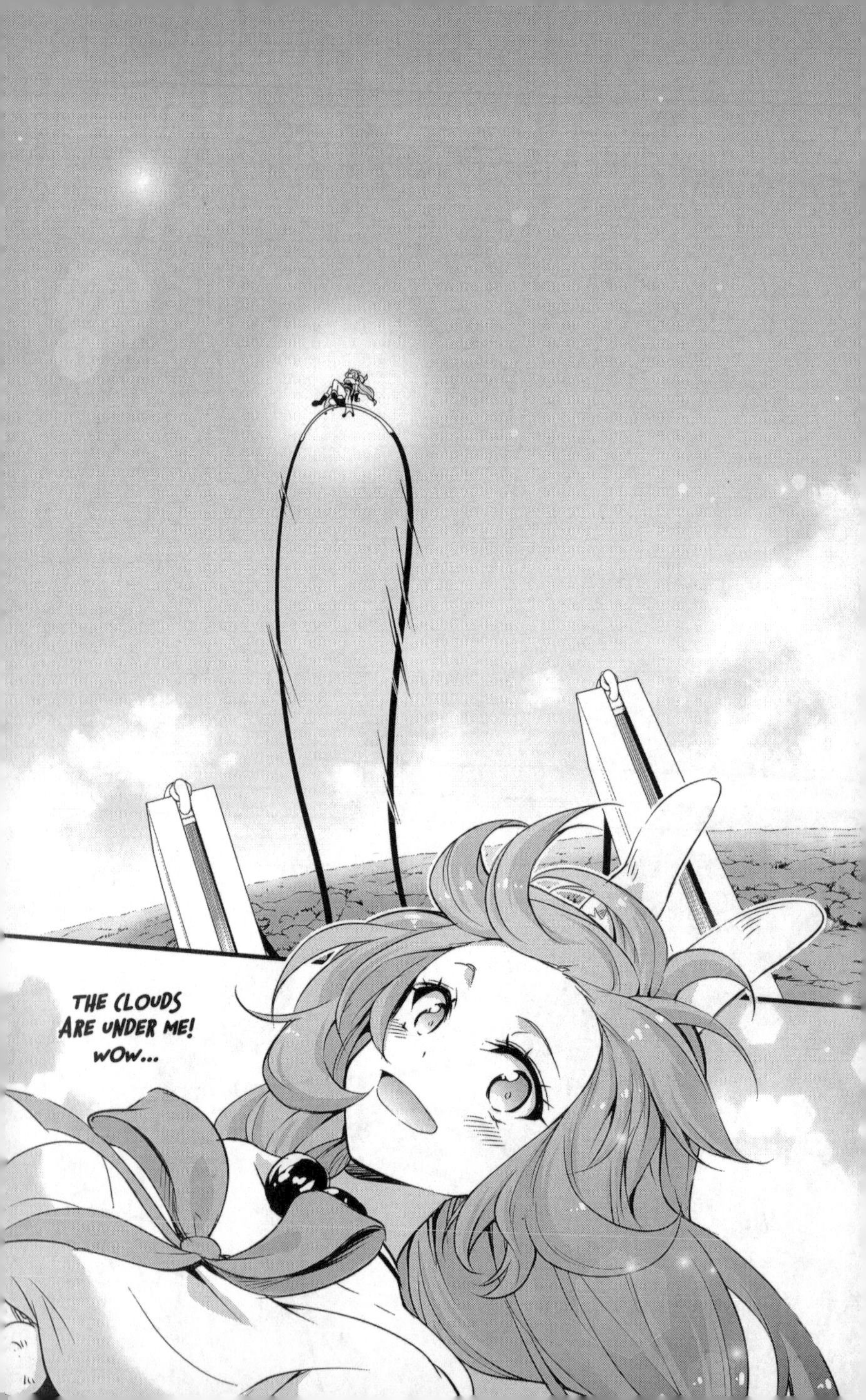
THE CLOUDS ARE UNDER ME! WOW...

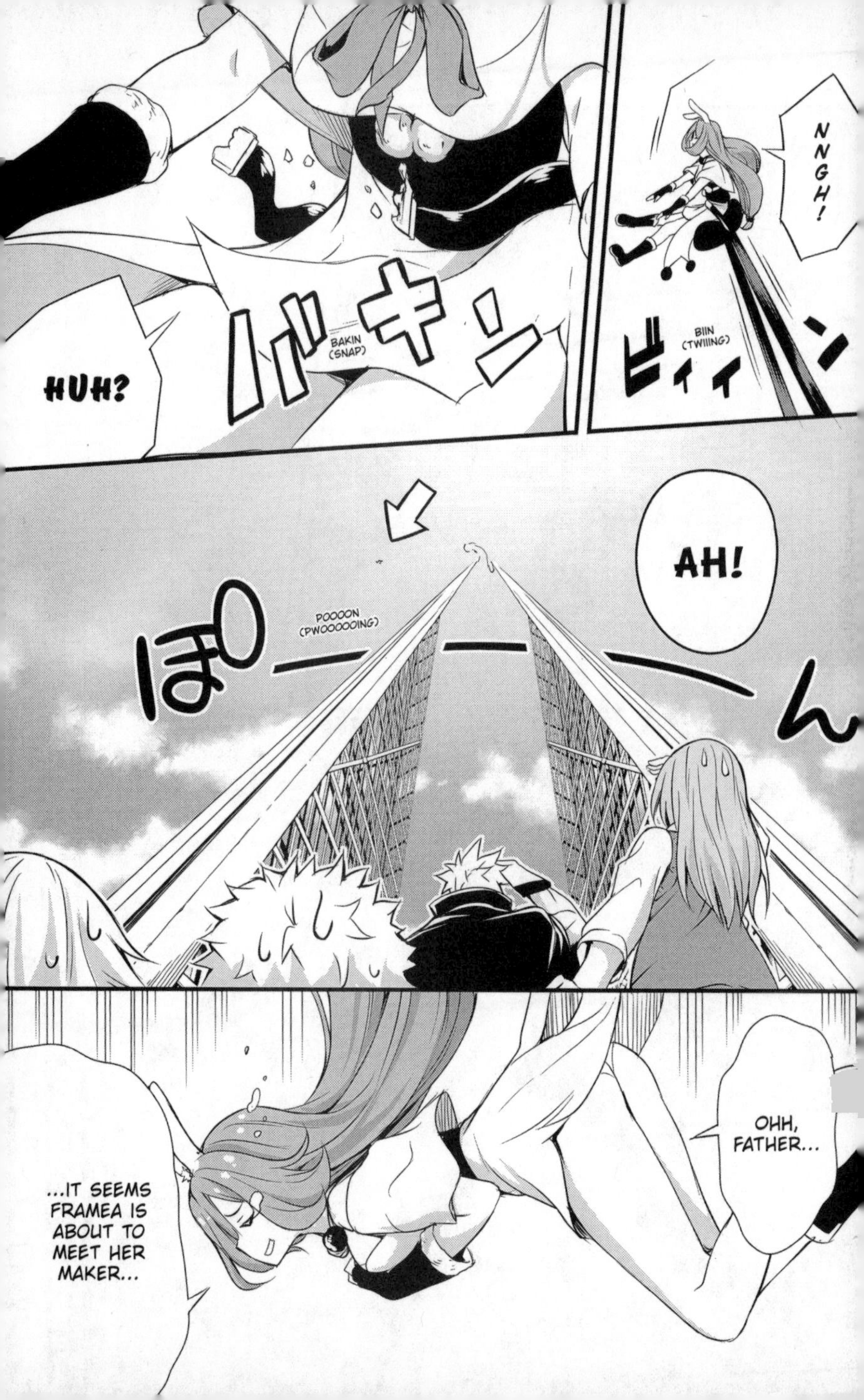
NNGH!
ビィィン
BIIN (TWIIING)
バキン
BAKIN (SNAP)
HUH?
AH!
ぽーーーん
POOOON (PWOOOOOING)
OHH, FATHER...
...IT SEEMS FRAMEA IS ABOUT TO MEET HER MAKER...

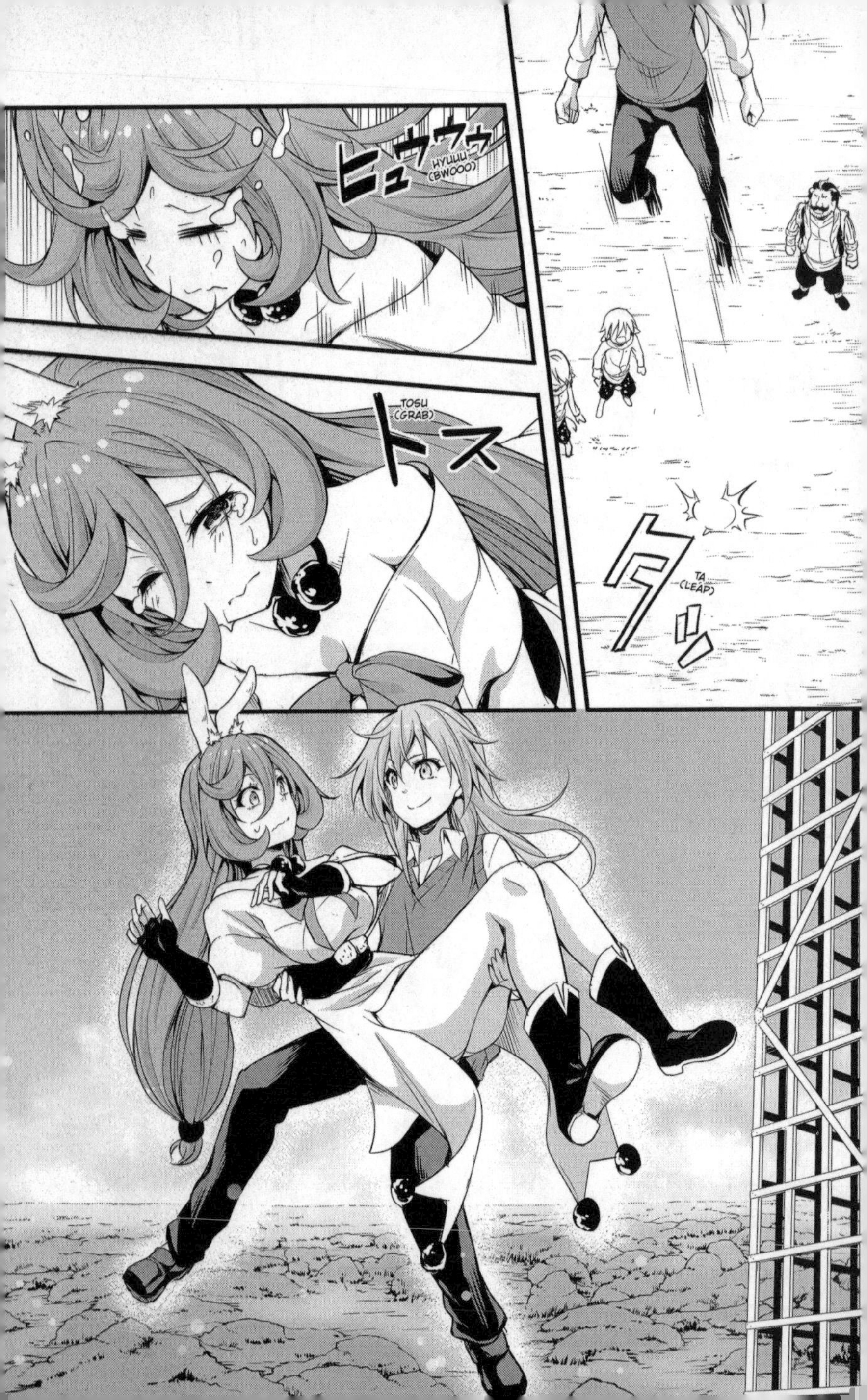
タッ
TA (LEAP)
ヒュウウウ
HYUUU (BWOOO)
トス
TOSU (GRAB)

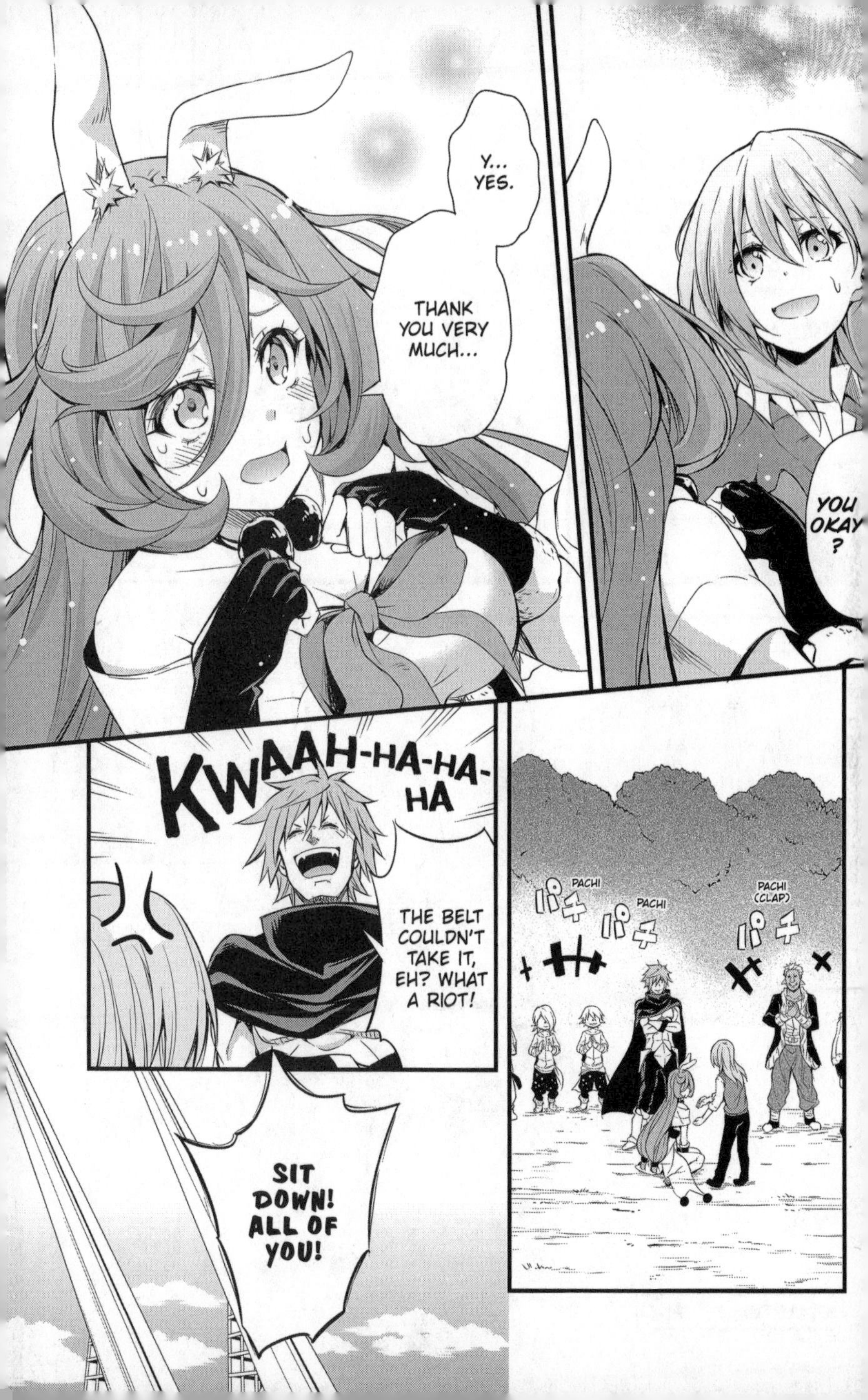
YOU OKAY?
Y... YES.
THANK YOU VERY MUCH...
PACHI
PACHI
PACHI (CLAP)
KWAAH-HA-HA-HA
THE BELT COULDN'T TAKE IT, EH? WHAT A RIOT!
SIT DOWN! ALL OF YOU!

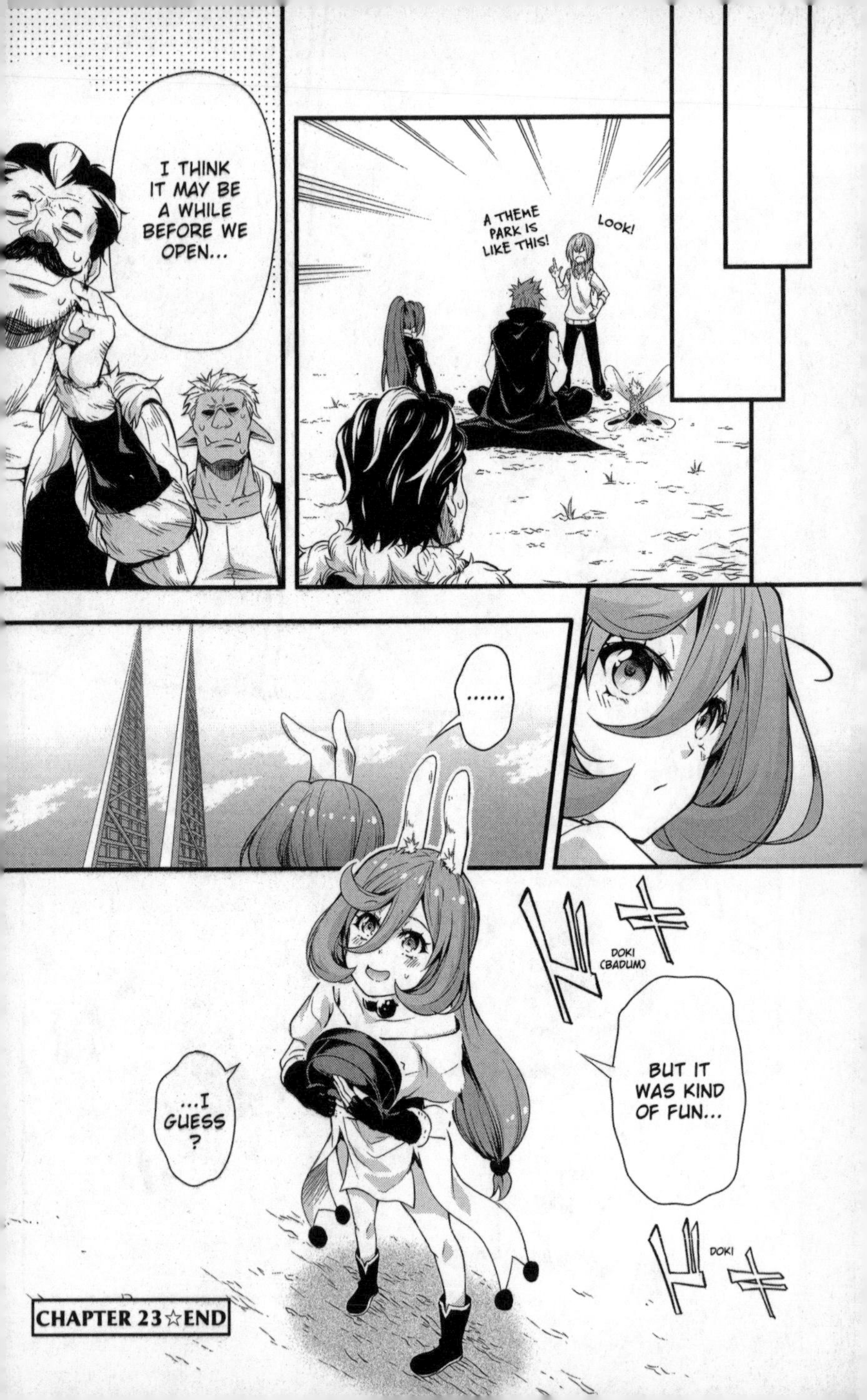
LOOK!
A THEME PARK IS LIKE THIS!
I THINK IT MAY BE A WHILE BEFORE WE OPEN...
......
DOKI (BADUM)
BUT IT WAS KIND OF FUN...
...I GUESS?
DOKI
CHAPTER 23☆END

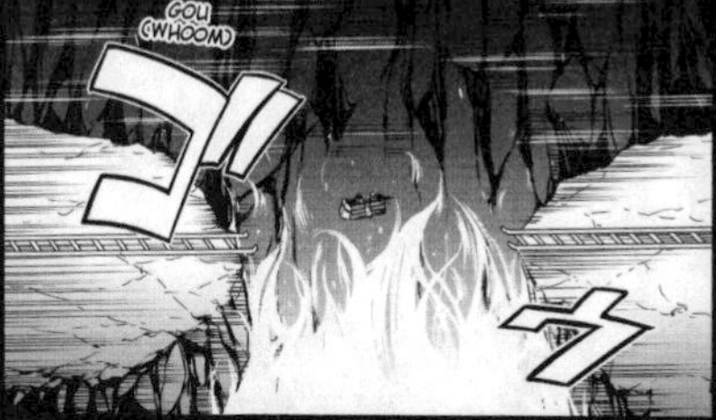
GOU
(WHOOM)
ゴ

That Time I Got Reìncarnated as a SLIME

The Ways of the Monster Nation

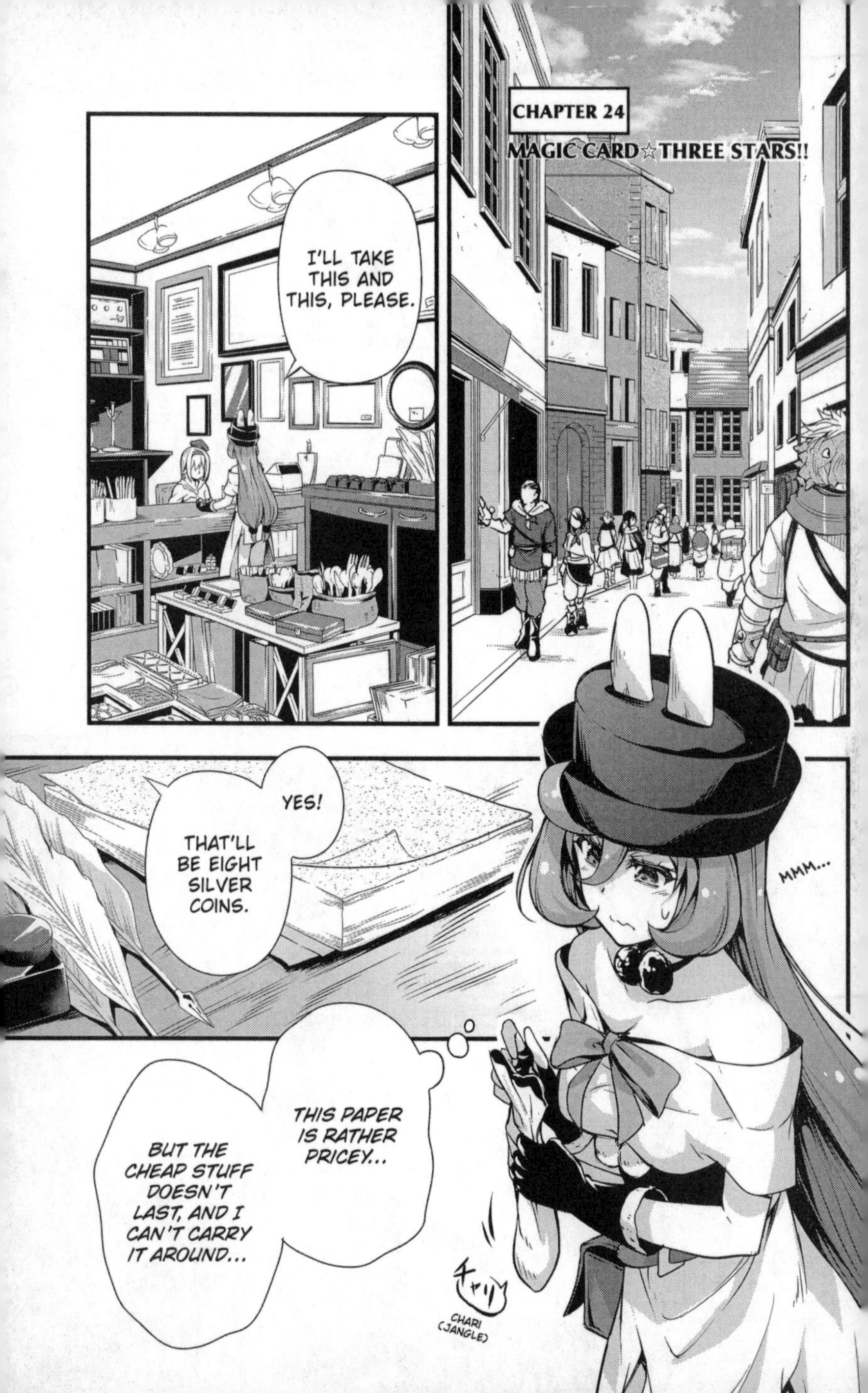
CHAPTER 24
MAGIC CARD☆THREE STARS!!
I'LL TAKE THIS AND THIS, PLEASE.
MMM...
YES!
THAT'LL BE EIGHT SILVER COINS.
THIS PAPER IS RATHER PRICEY...
BUT THE CHEAP STUFF DOESN'T LAST, AND I CAN'T CARRY IT AROUND...
CHARI (JANGLE)

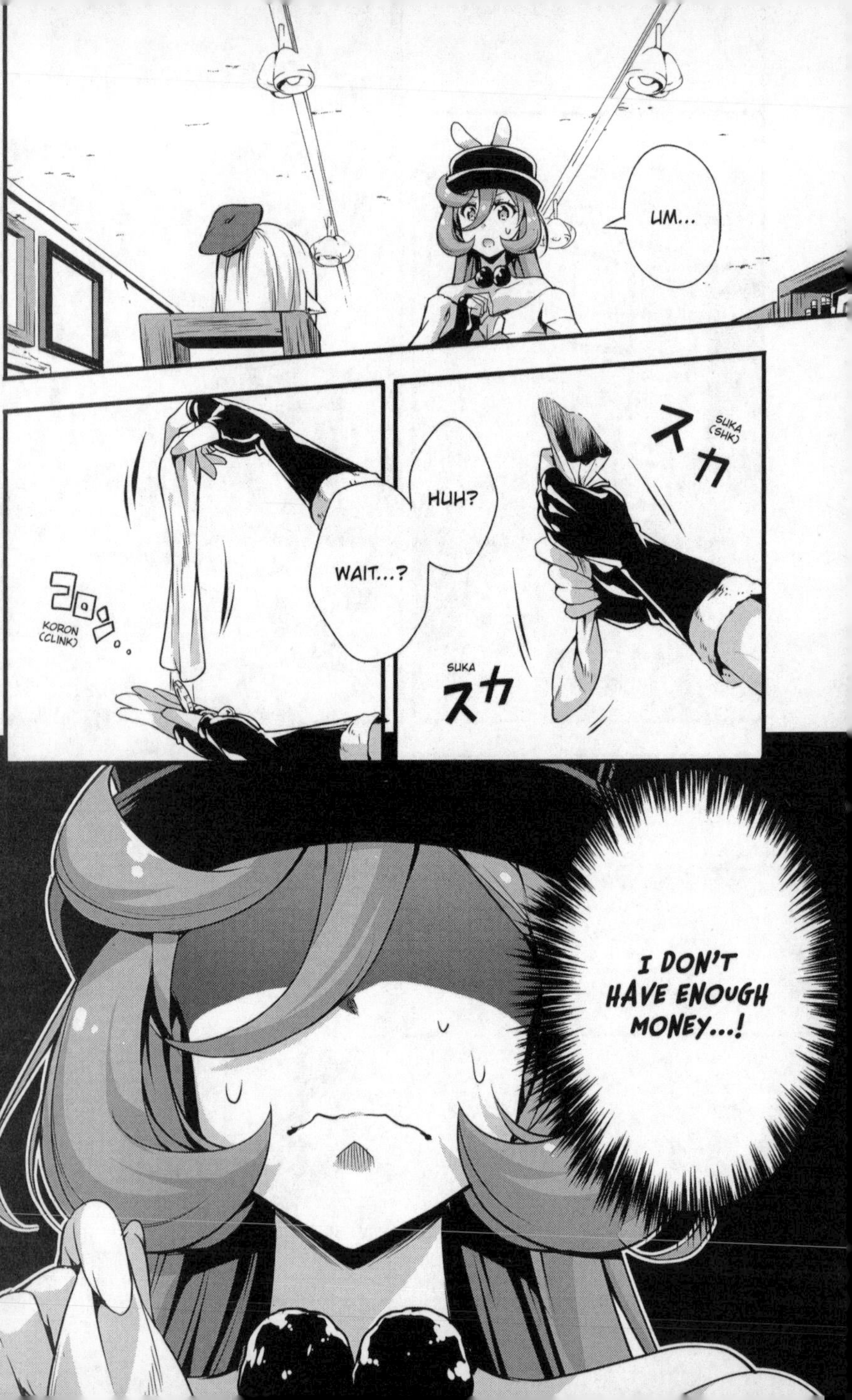
UM...
スカ
SUKA (SHK)
SUKA
スカ
HUH?
WAIT...?
コロン
KORON (CLINK)
I DON'T HAVE ENOUGH MONEY...!

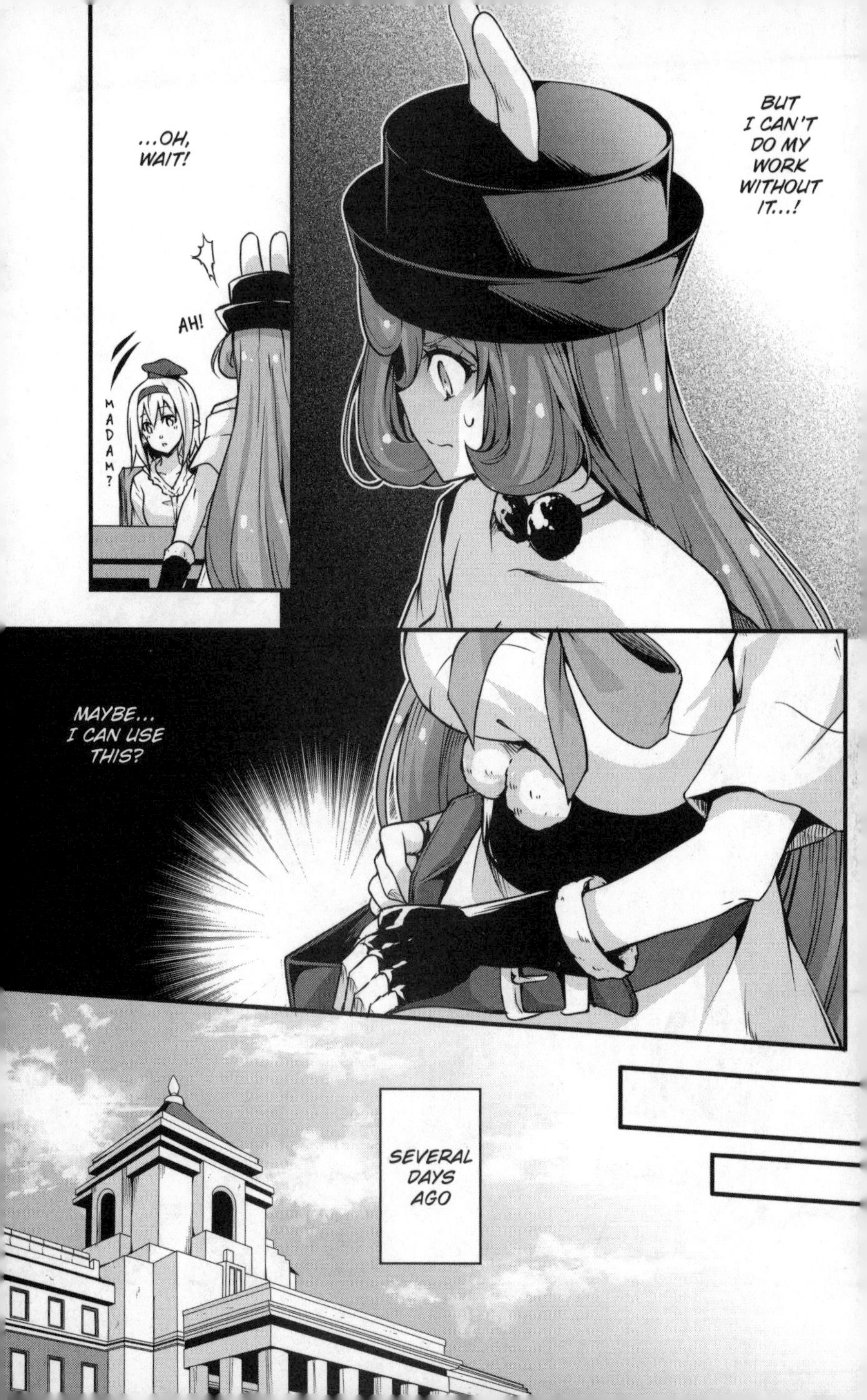
BUT I CAN'T DO MY WORK WITHOUT IT...!
...OH, WAIT!
AH!
MADAM?
MAYBE... I CAN USE THIS?
SEVERAL DAYS AGO

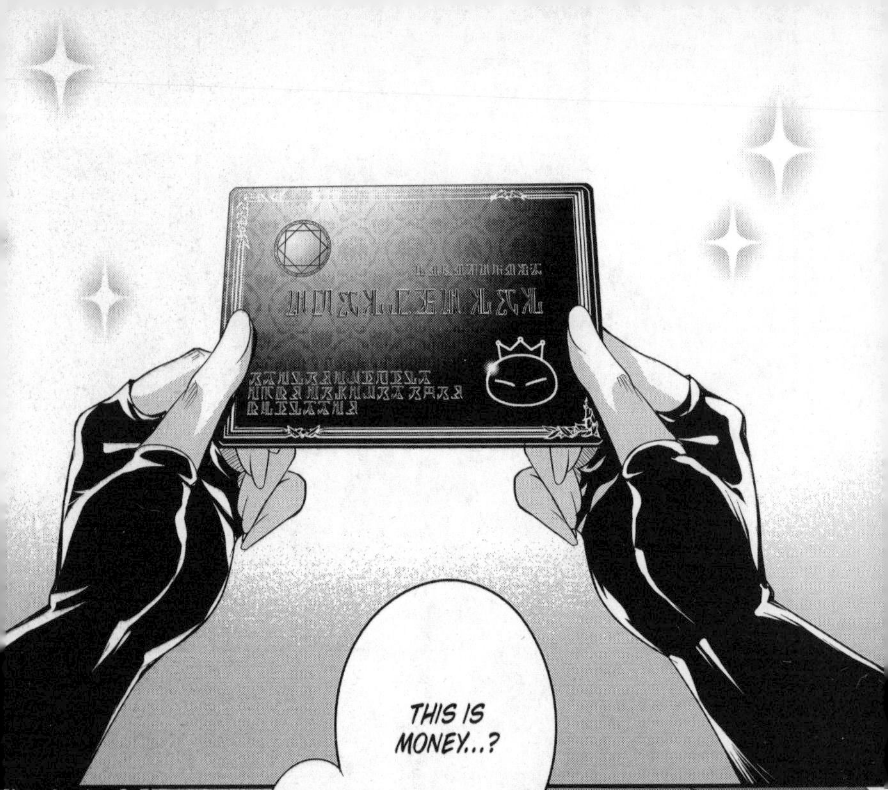
THIS IS MONEY...?
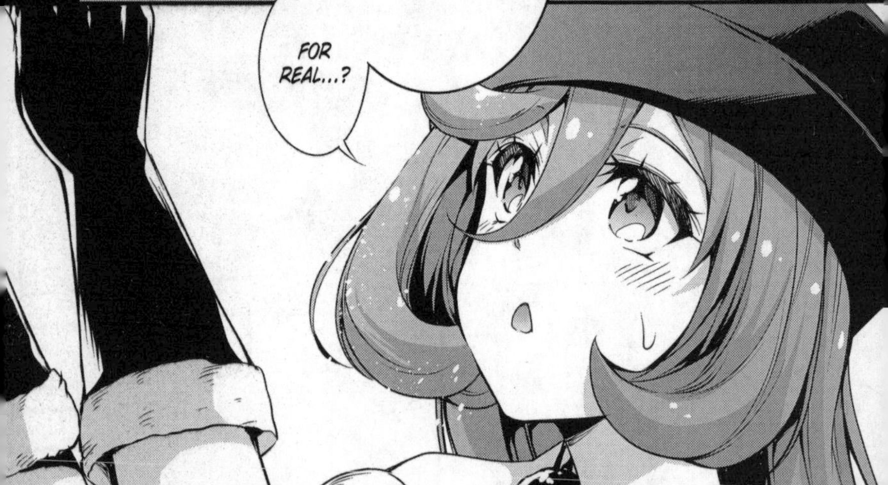
FOR REAL...?

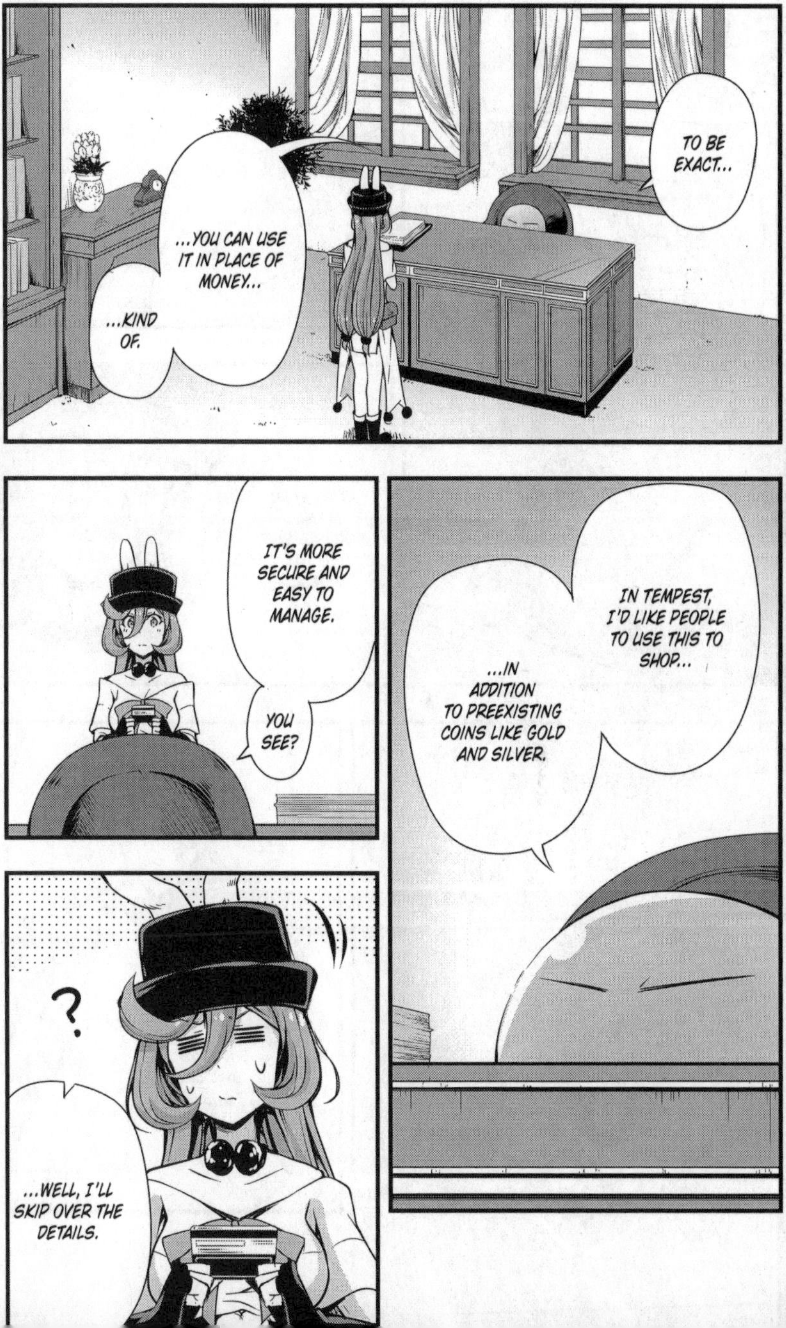
TO BE EXACT...
...YOU CAN USE IT IN PLACE OF MONEY...
...KIND OF.
IN TEMPEST, I'D LIKE PEOPLE TO USE THIS TO SHOP...
...IN ADDITION TO PREEXISTING COINS LIKE GOLD AND SILVER.
IT'S MORE SECURE AND EASY TO MANAGE.
YOU SEE?
?
...WELL, I'LL SKIP OVER THE DETAILS.

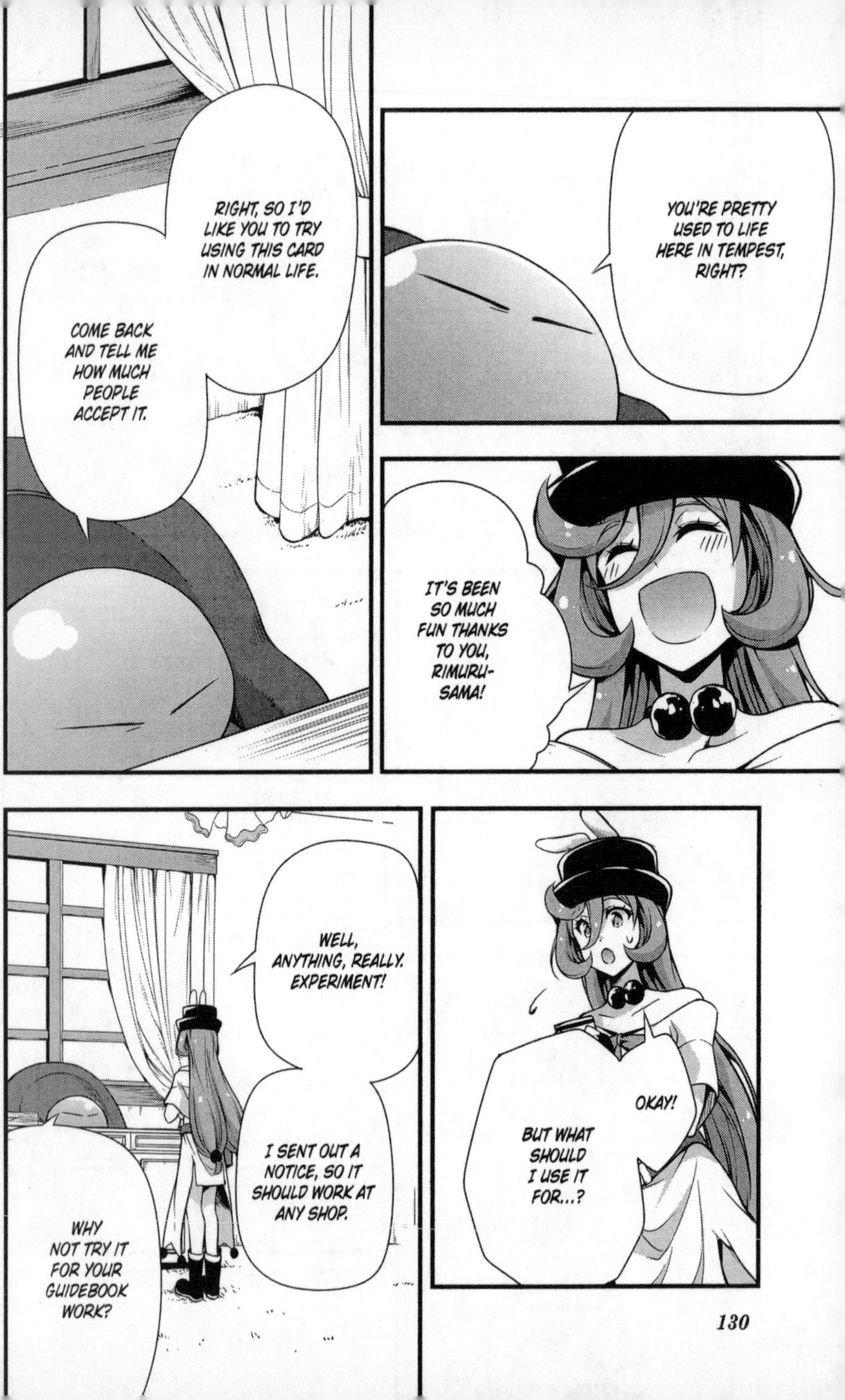
YOU'RE PRETTY USED TO LIFE HERE IN TEMPEST, RIGHT?
IT'S BEEN SO MUCH FUN THANKS TO YOU, RIMURU-SAMA!
RIGHT, SO I'D LIKE YOU TO TRY USING THIS CARD IN NORMAL LIFE.
COME BACK AND TELL ME HOW MUCH PEOPLE ACCEPT IT.
OKAY!
BUT WHAT SHOULD I USE IT FOR...?
WELL, ANYTHING, REALLY. EXPERIMENT!
I SENT OUT A NOTICE, SO IT SHOULD WORK AT ANY SHOP.
WHY NOT TRY IT FOR YOUR GUIDEBOOK WORK?

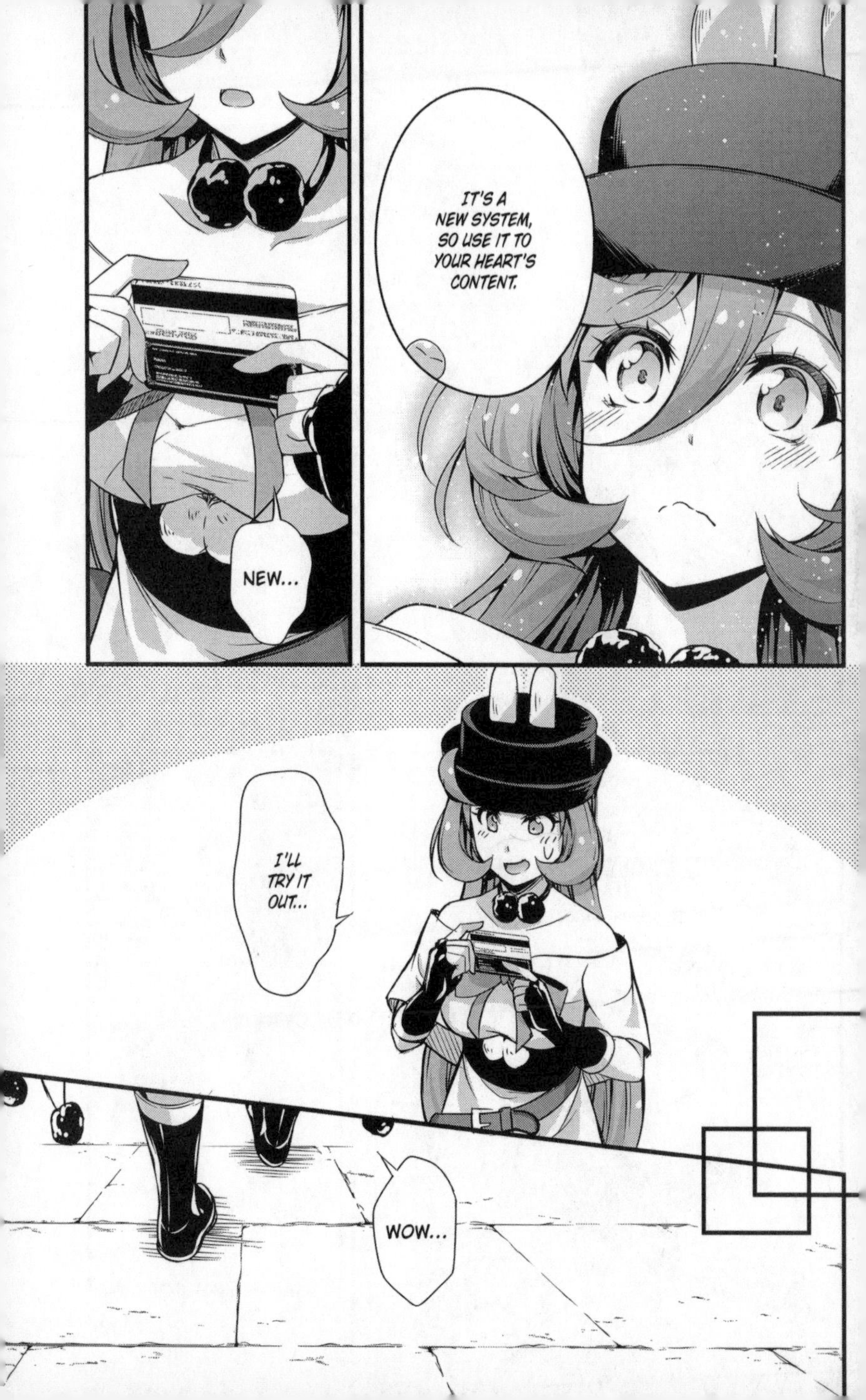
IT'S A NEW SYSTEM, SO USE IT TO YOUR HEART'S CONTENT.
NEW...
I'LL TRY IT OUT...
WOW...

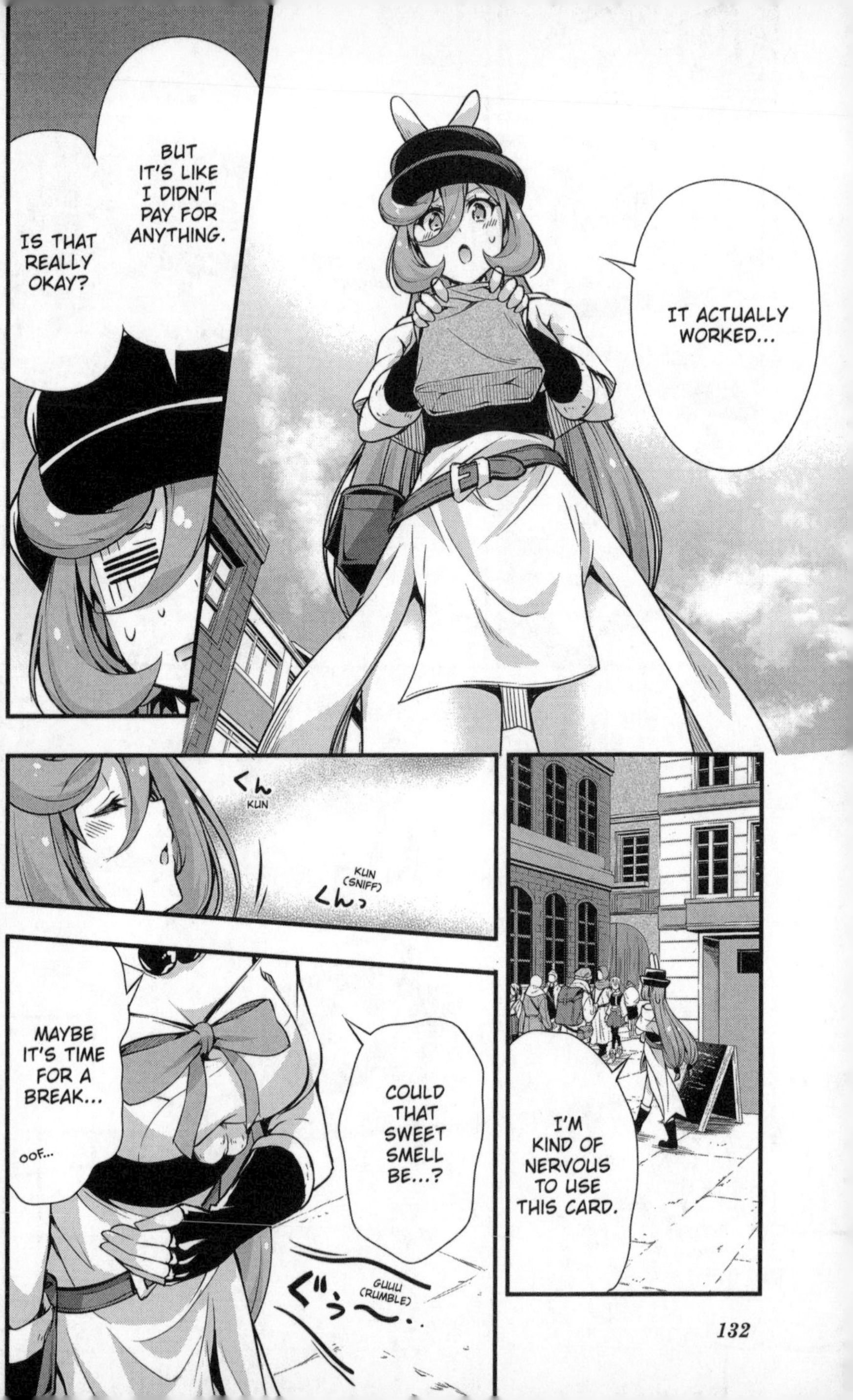
IT ACTUALLY WORKED...
BUT IT'S LIKE I DIDN'T PAY FOR ANYTHING.
IS THAT REALLY OKAY?
I'M KIND OF NERVOUS TO USE THIS CARD.
くん
KUN
KUN (SNIFF)
くんっ
COULD THAT SWEET SMELL BE...?
MAYBE IT'S TIME FOR A BREAK...
OOF...
GUUU (RUMBLE)
ぐぅ〜.

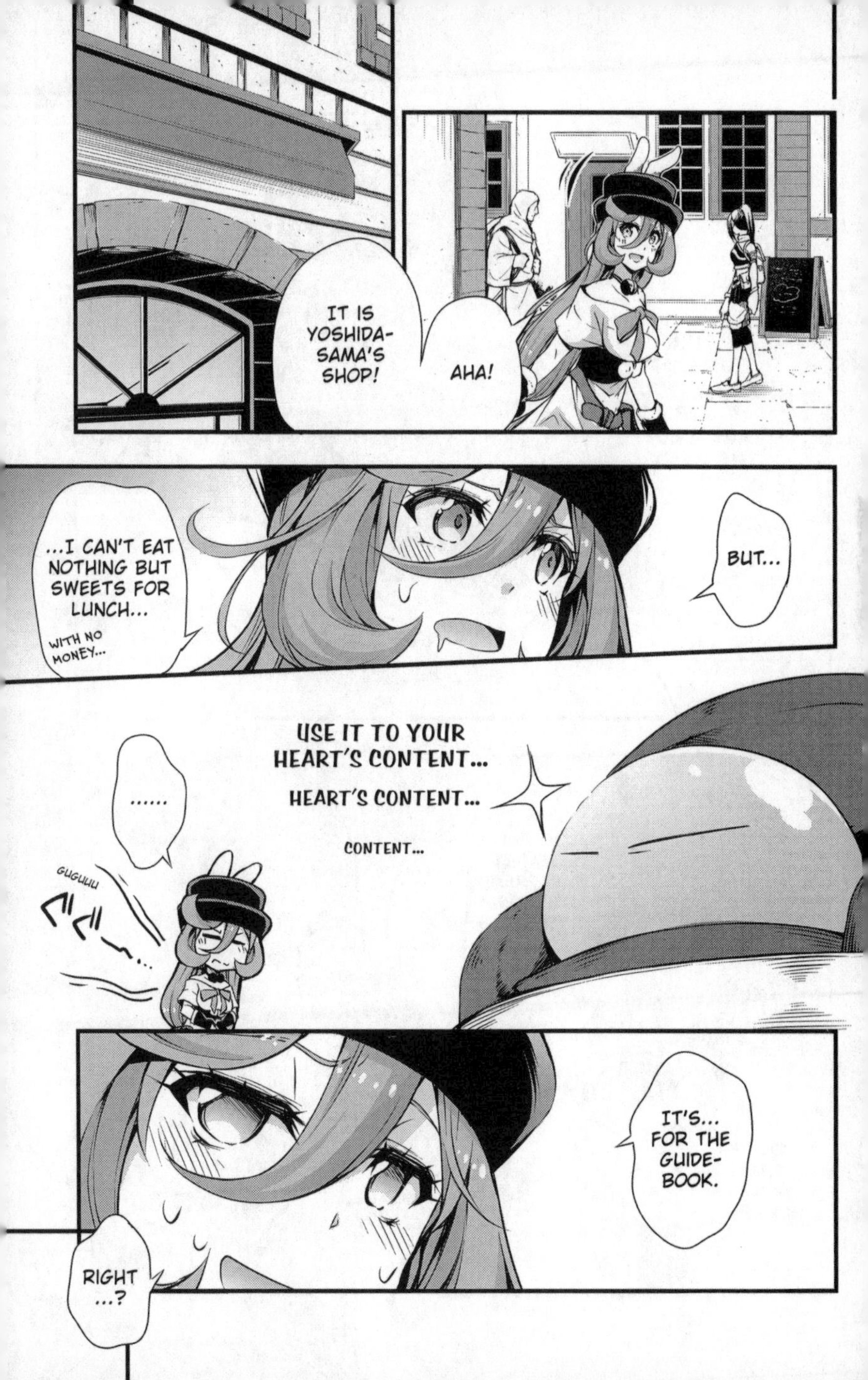
AHA!
IT IS YOSHIDA-SAMA'S SHOP!
BUT...
...I CAN'T EAT NOTHING BUT SWEETS FOR LUNCH...
WITH NO MONEY...
USE IT TO YOUR HEART'S CONTENT...
HEART'S CONTENT...
CONTENT...
......
GUGUUU
IT'S... FOR THE GUIDE-BOOK.
RIGHT ...?

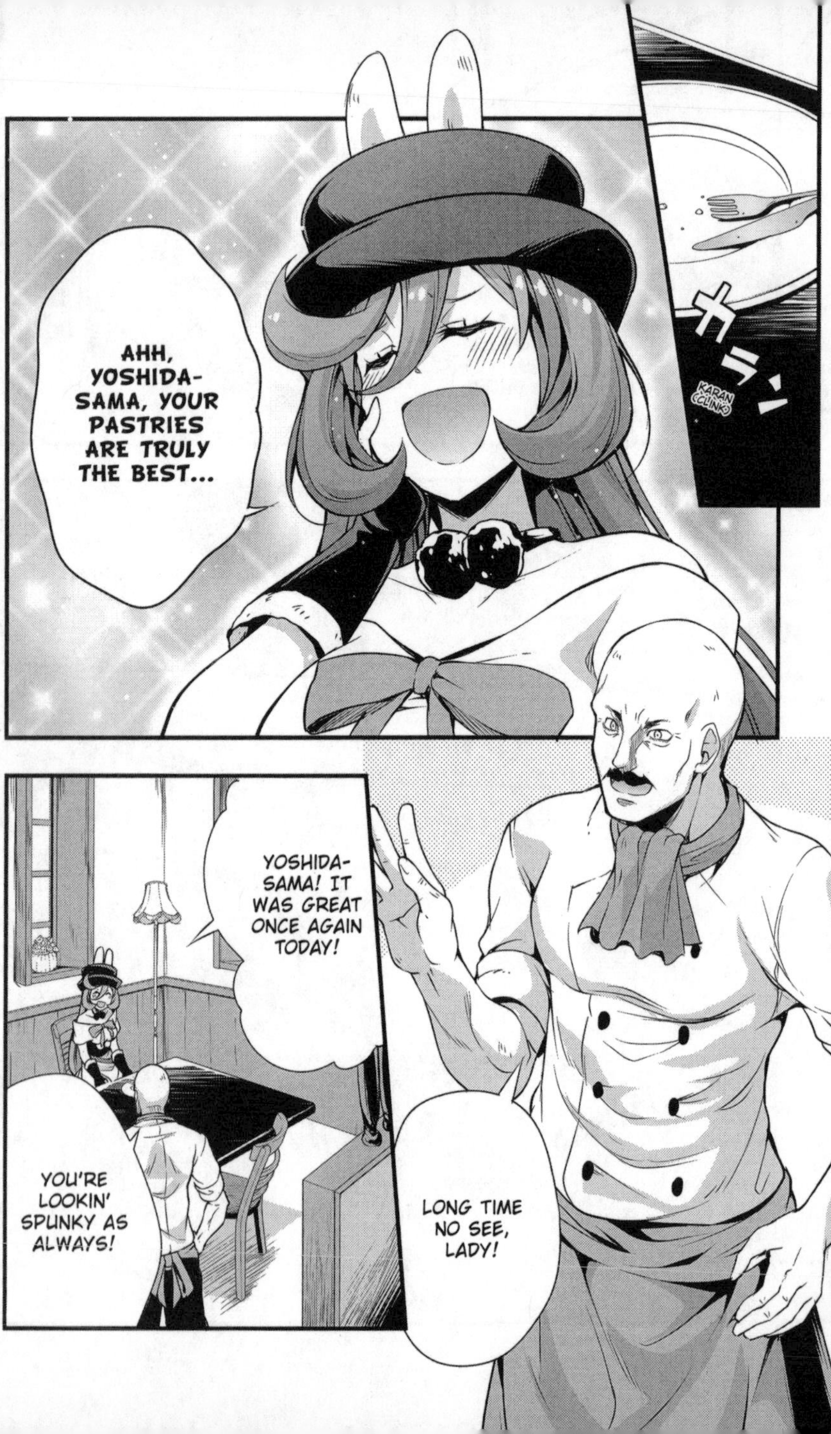
カラン
KARAN (CLINK)
AHH, YOSHIDA-SAMA, YOUR PASTRIES ARE TRULY THE BEST...
YOSHIDA-SAMA! IT WAS GREAT ONCE AGAIN TODAY!
LONG TIME NO SEE, LADY!
YOU'RE LOOKIN' SPUNKY AS ALWAYS!

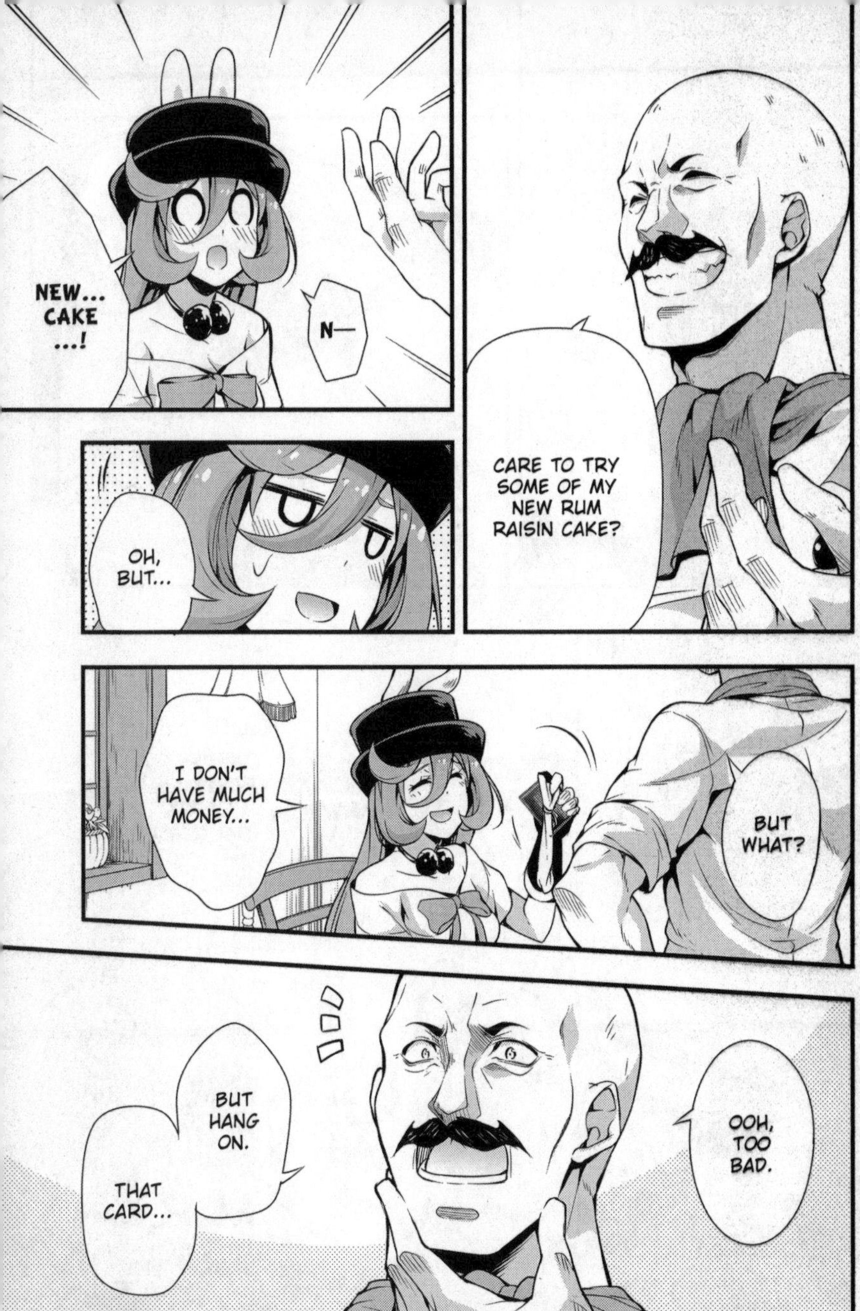

CARE TO TRY SOME OF MY NEW RUM RAISIN CAKE?
N—
NEW... CAKE ...!
OH, BUT...
BUT WHAT?
I DON'T HAVE MUCH MONEY...
OOH, TOO BAD.
BUT HANG ON.
THAT CARD...

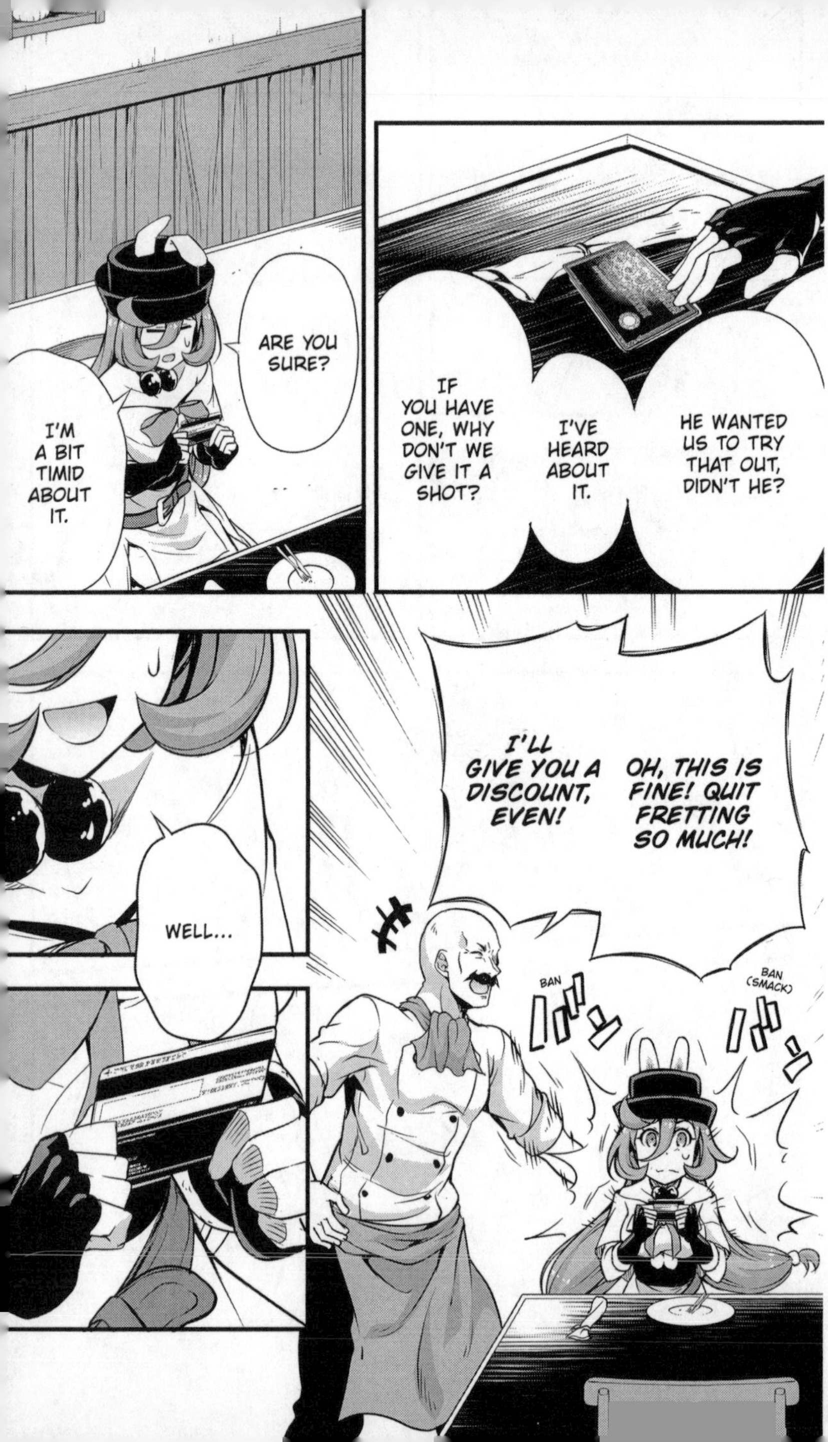
HE WANTED US TO TRY THAT OUT, DIDN'T HE?
I'VE HEARD ABOUT IT.
IF YOU HAVE ONE, WHY DON'T WE GIVE IT A SHOT?
ARE YOU SURE?
I'M A BIT TIMID ABOUT IT.
OH, THIS IS FINE! QUIT FRETTING SO MUCH!
I'LL GIVE YOU A DISCOUNT, EVEN!
BAN (SMACK)
BAN
WELL...

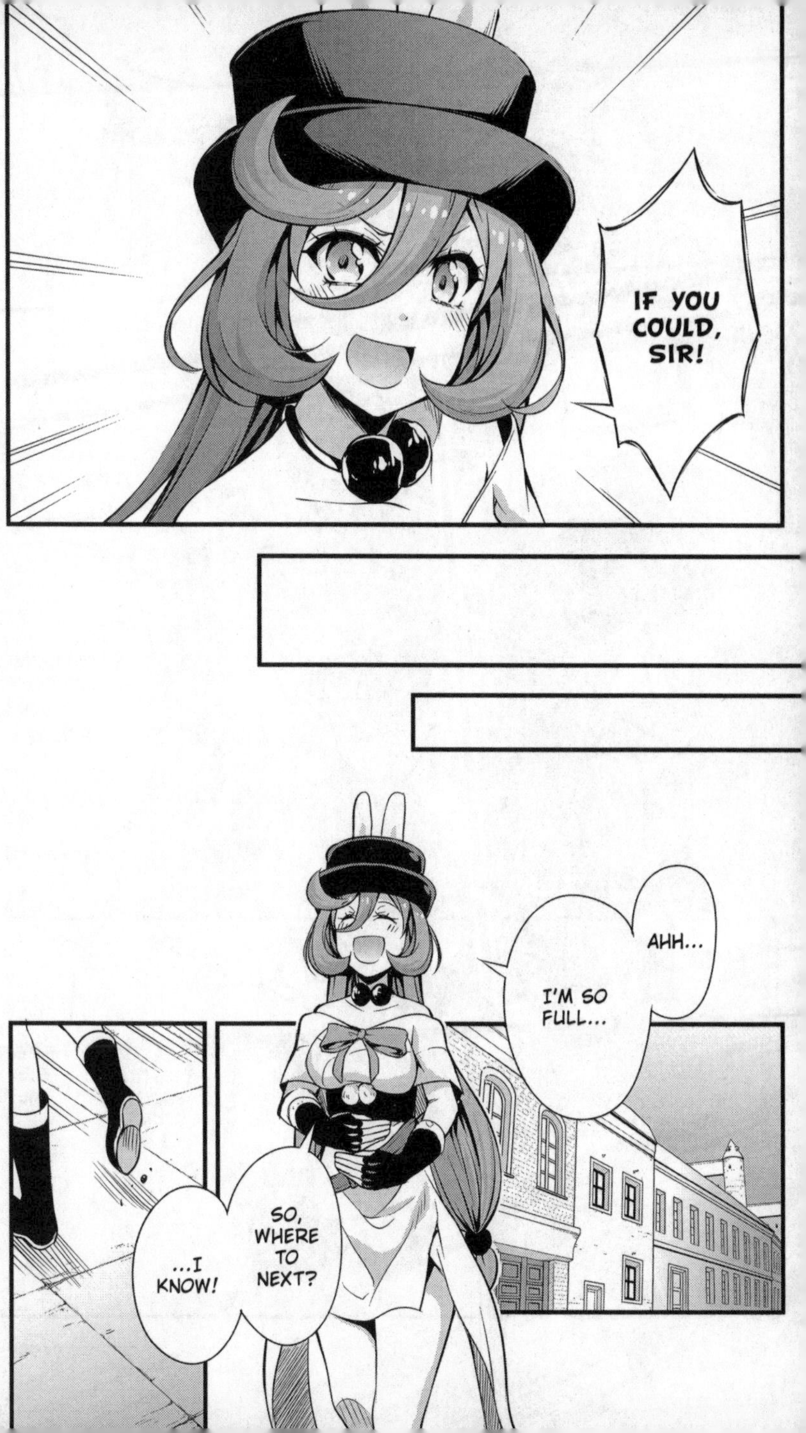
IF YOU COULD, SIR!
AHH...
I'M SO FULL...
SO, WHERE TO NEXT?
...I KNOW!

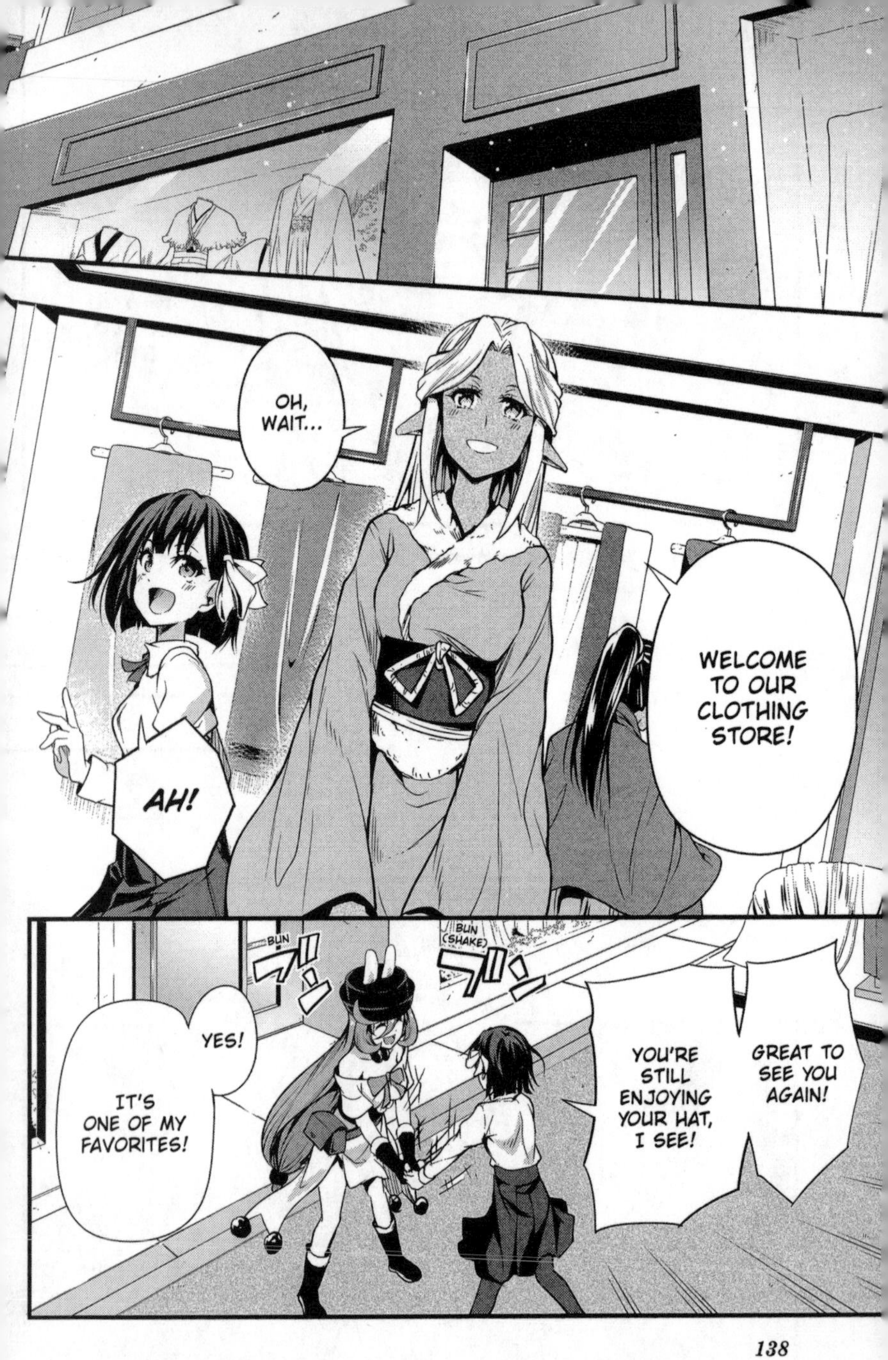
WELCOME TO OUR CLOTHING STORE!
OH, WAIT...
AH!
ブン
BUN (SHAKE)
ブン
BUN
GREAT TO SEE YOU AGAIN!
YOU'RE STILL ENJOYING YOUR HAT, I SEE!
YES!
IT'S ONE OF MY FAVORITES!

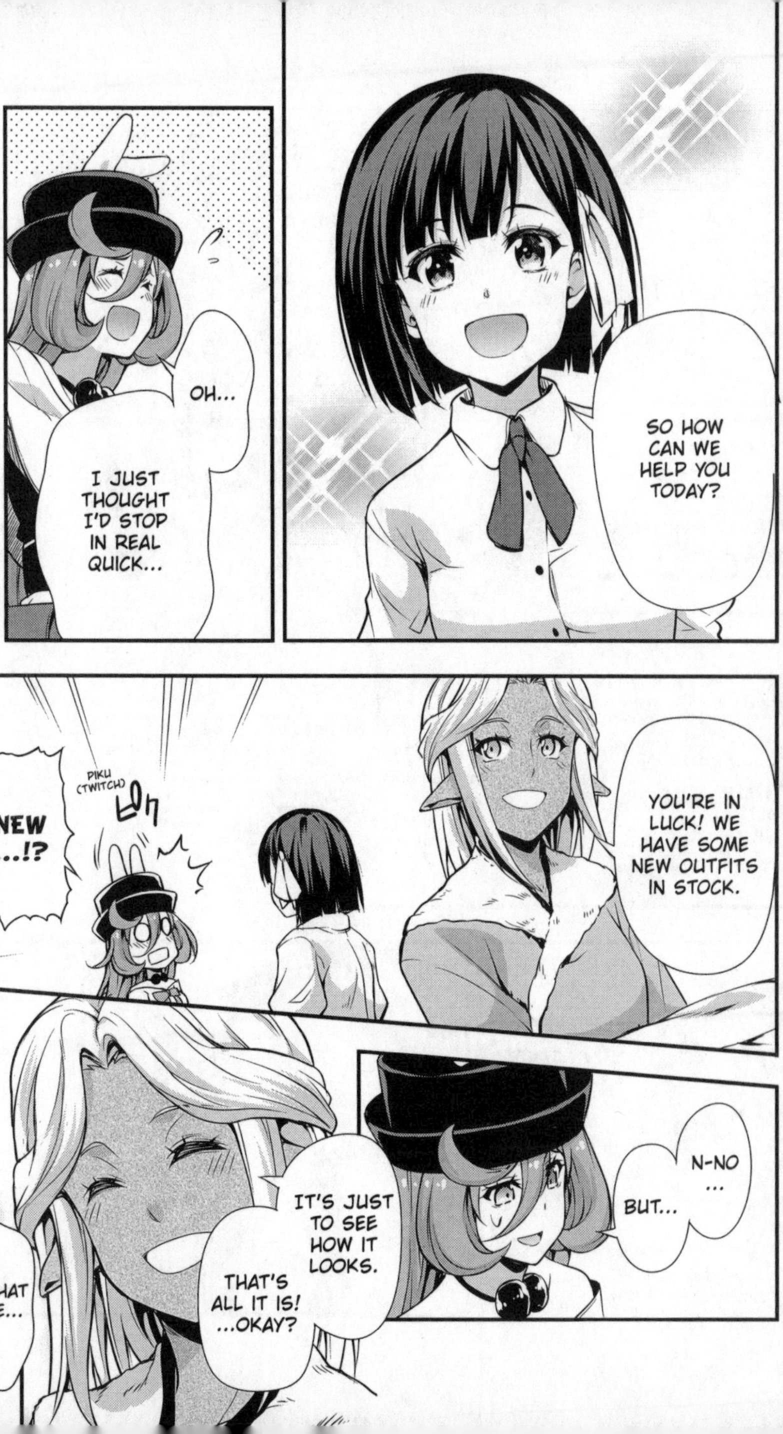
SO HOW CAN WE HELP YOU TODAY?
OH...
I JUST THOUGHT I'D STOP IN REAL QUICK...
YOU'RE IN LUCK! WE HAVE SOME NEW OUTFITS IN STOCK.
PIKU (TWITCH)
NEW ...!?
N-NO ...
BUT...
IT'S JUST TO SEE HOW IT LOOKS.
THAT'S ALL IT IS! ...OKAY?
IN THAT CASE...

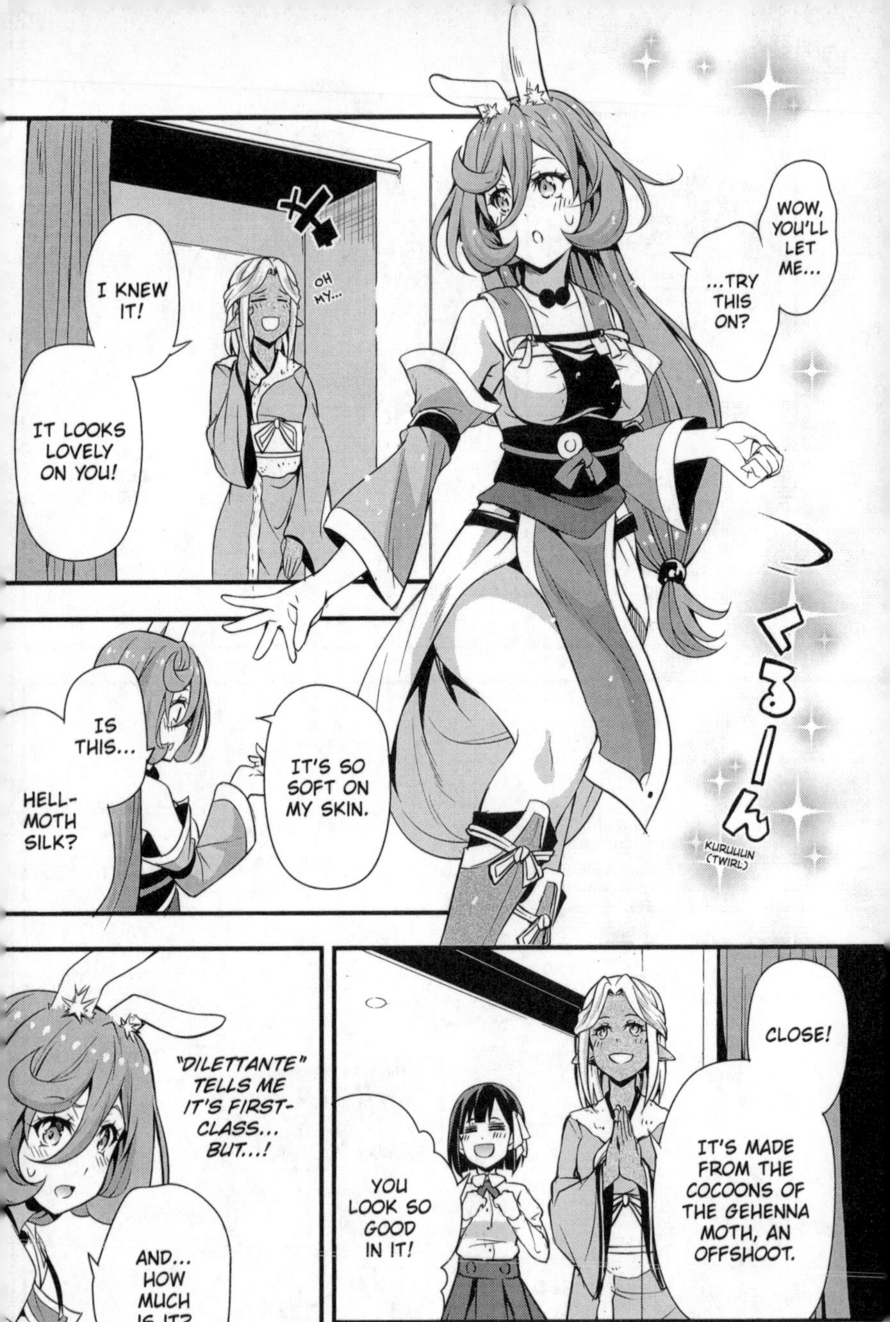
WOW, YOU'LL LET ME...
...TRY THIS ON?
KURUUUN (TWIRL)
OH MY...
I KNEW IT!
IT LOOKS LOVELY ON YOU!
IT'S SO SOFT ON MY SKIN.
IS THIS...
HELL-MOTH SILK?
CLOSE!
IT'S MADE FROM THE COCOONS OF THE GEHENNA MOTH, AN OFFSHOOT.
YOU LOOK SO GOOD IN IT!
"DILETTANTE" TELLS ME IT'S FIRST-CLASS... BUT...!
AND... HOW MUCH IS IT?

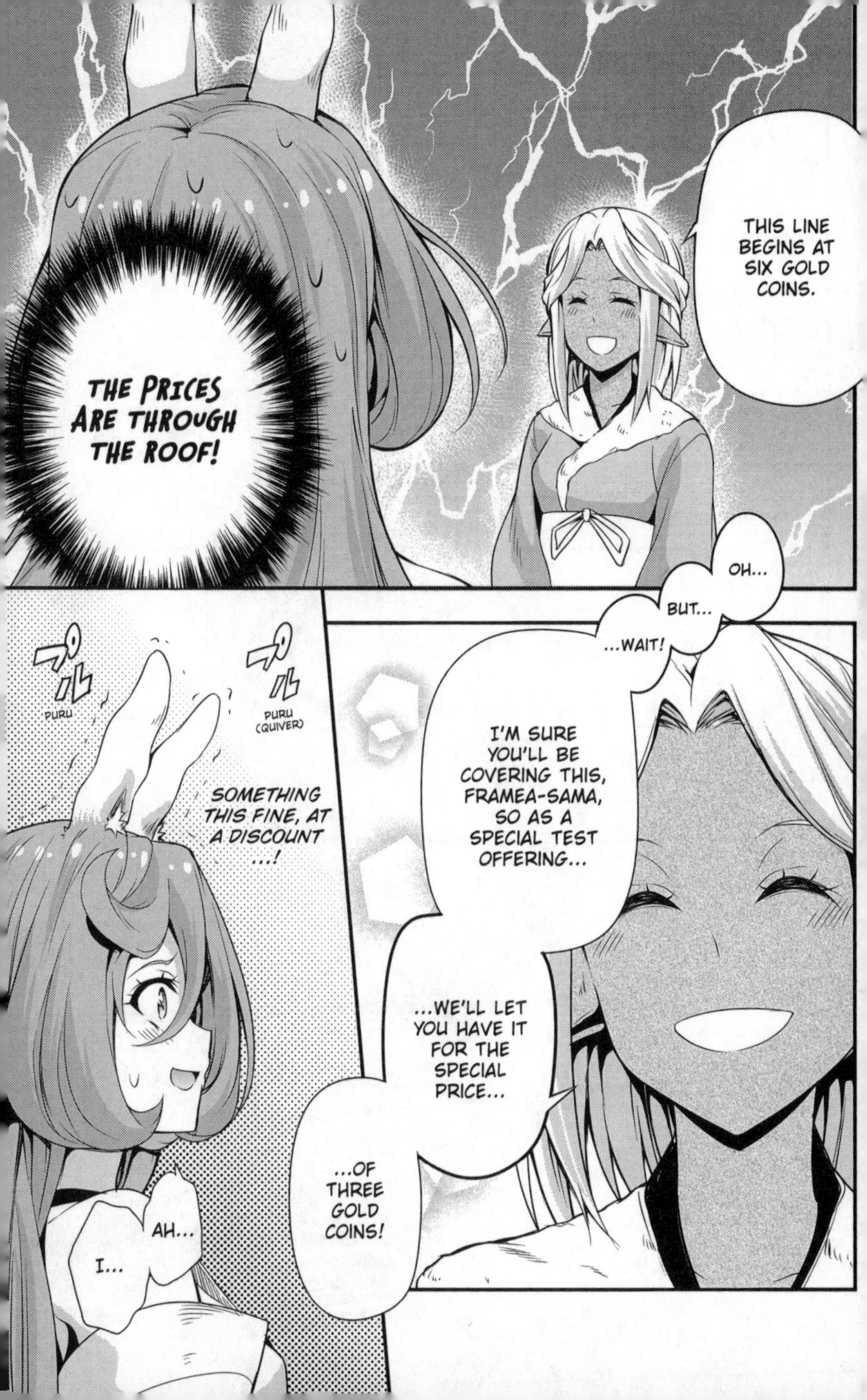
THIS LINE BEGINS AT SIX GOLD COINS.
THE PRICES ARE THROUGH THE ROOF!
OH...
BUT...
...WAIT!
I'M SURE YOU'LL BE COVERING THIS, FRAMEA-SAMA, SO AS A SPECIAL TEST OFFERING...
...WE'LL LET YOU HAVE IT FOR THE SPECIAL PRICE...
...OF THREE GOLD COINS!
PURU (QUIVER)
PURU
SOMETHING THIS FINE, AT A DISCOUNT ...!
AH...
I...

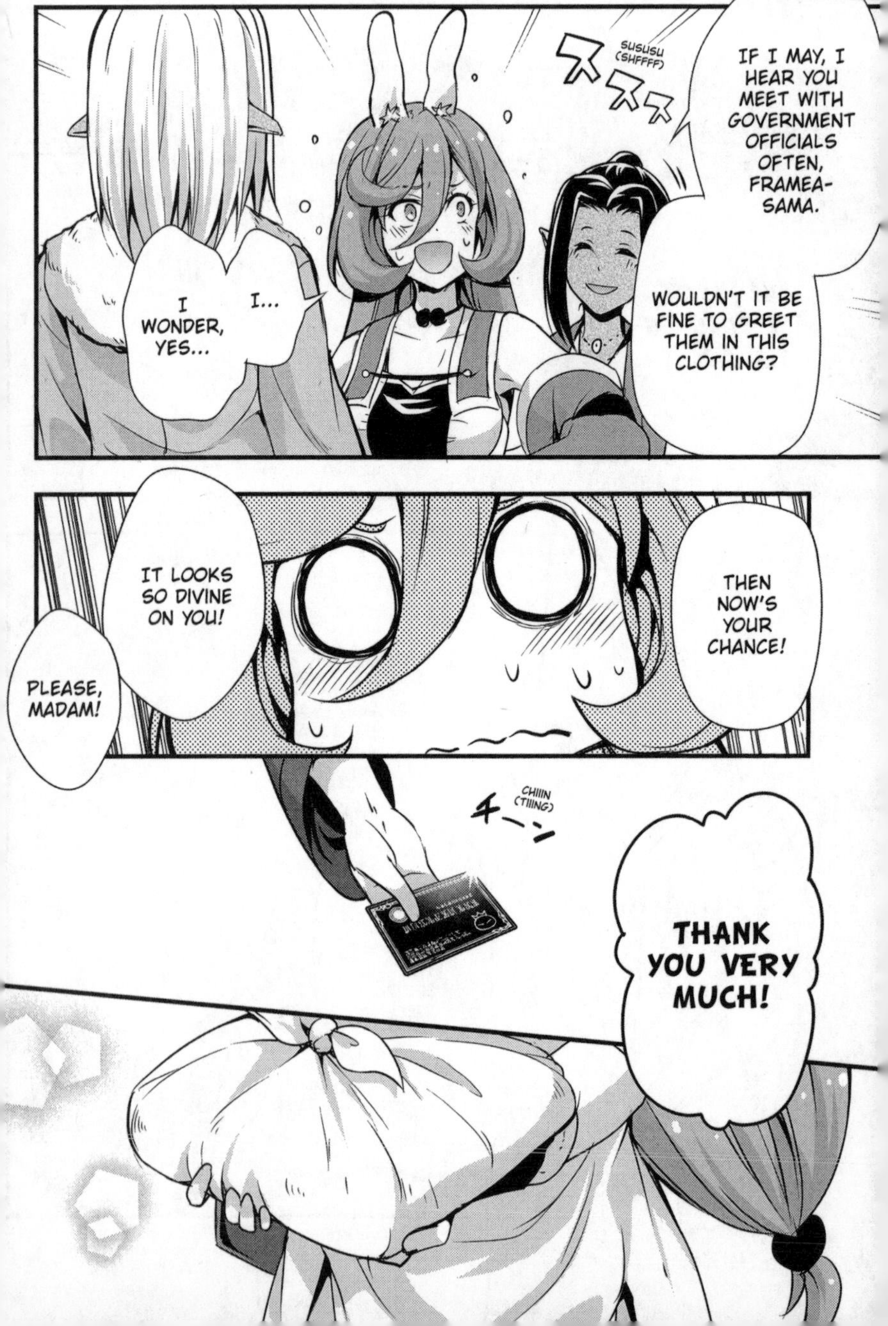
IF I MAY, I HEAR YOU MEET WITH GOVERNMENT OFFICIALS OFTEN, FRAMEA-SAMA.
WOULDN'T IT BE FINE TO GREET THEM IN THIS CLOTHING?
SUSUSU (SHFFFF)
I...
I WONDER, YES...
THEN NOW'S YOUR CHANCE!
IT LOOKS SO DIVINE ON YOU!
PLEASE, MADAM!
CHIIIN (TIIING)
THANK YOU VERY MUCH!

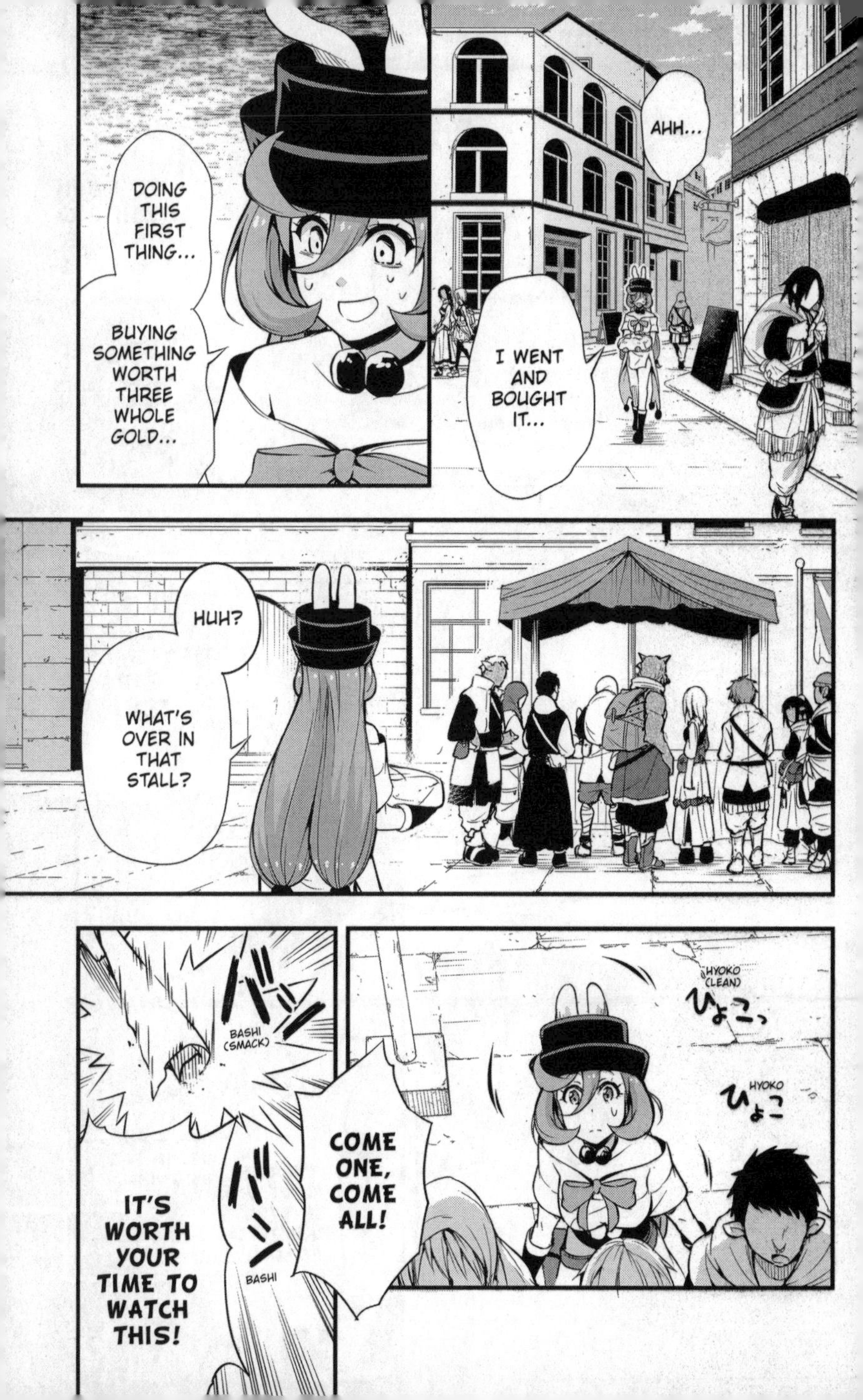
AHH...
I WENT AND BOUGHT IT...
DOING THIS FIRST THING...
BUYING SOMETHING WORTH THREE WHOLE GOLD...
HUH?
WHAT'S OVER IN THAT STALL?
HYOKO (CLEAN)
ひょこっ
HYOKO
ひょこ
BASHI (SMACK)
COME ONE, COME ALL!
IT'S WORTH YOUR TIME TO WATCH THIS!
BASHI

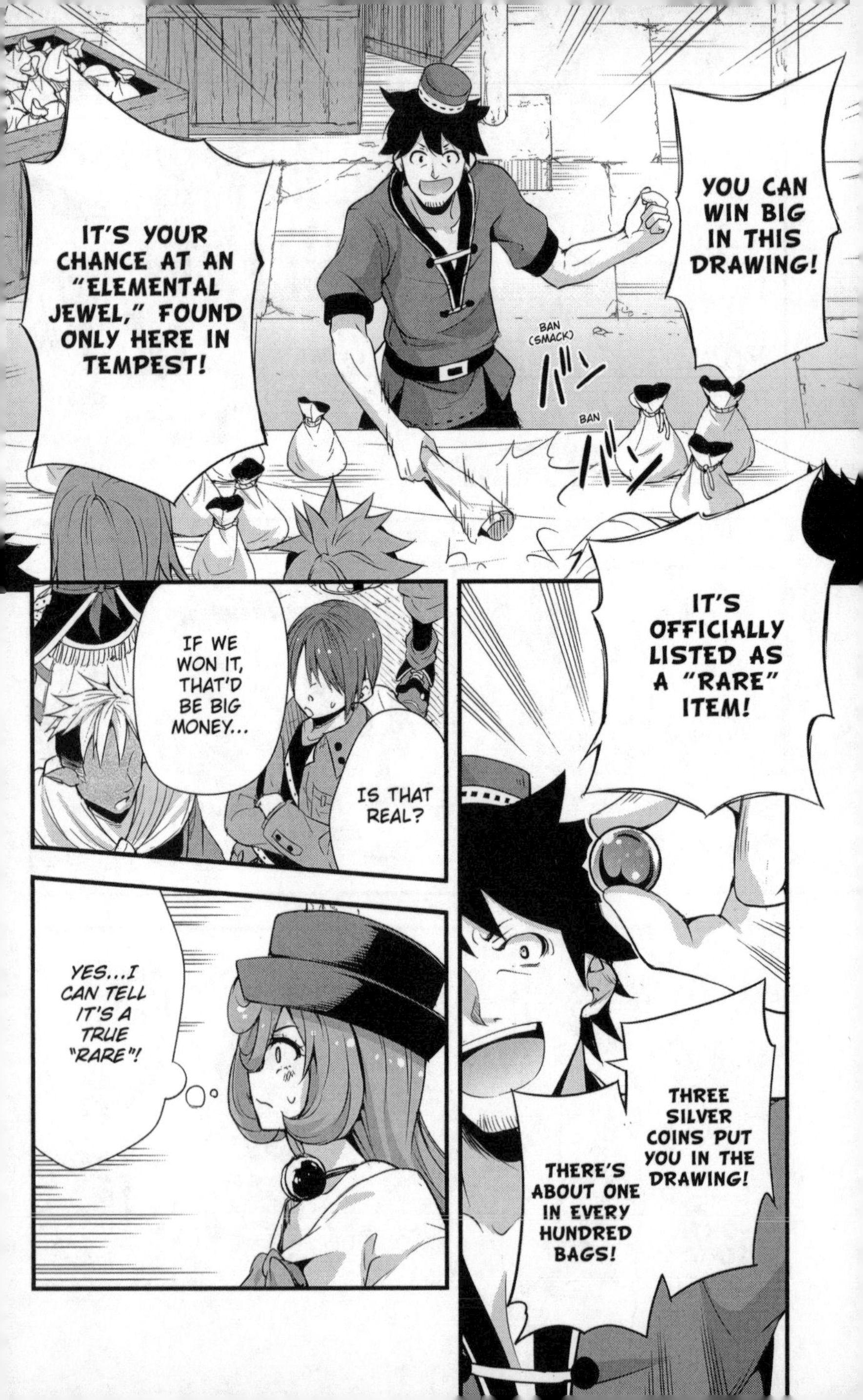
YOU CAN WIN BIG IN THIS DRAWING!
BAN (SMACK)
BAN
IT'S YOUR CHANCE AT AN "ELEMENTAL JEWEL," FOUND ONLY HERE IN TEMPEST!
IT'S OFFICIALLY LISTED AS A "RARE" ITEM!
THREE SILVER COINS PUT YOU IN THE DRAWING!
THERE'S ABOUT ONE IN EVERY HUNDRED BAGS!
IS THAT REAL?
IF WE WON IT, THAT'D BE BIG MONEY...
YES...I CAN TELL IT'S A TRUE "RARE"!

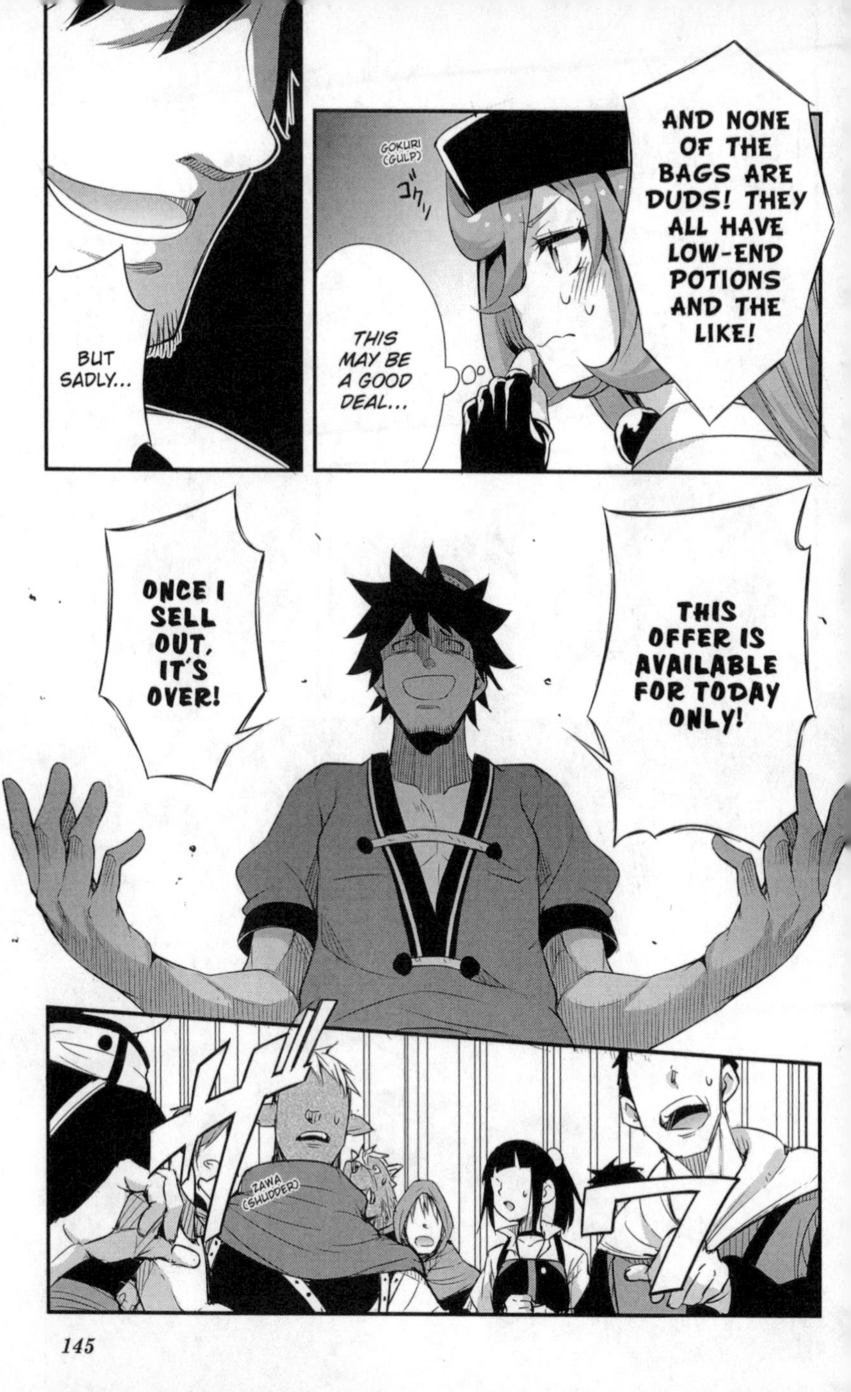
AND NONE OF THE BAGS ARE DUDS! THEY ALL HAVE LOW-END POTIONS AND THE LIKE!
GOKURI (GULP)
ゴクッ
THIS MAY BE A GOOD DEAL...
BUT SADLY...
THIS OFFER IS AVAILABLE FOR TODAY ONLY!
ONCE I SELL OUT, IT'S OVER!
ZAWA (SHUDDER)

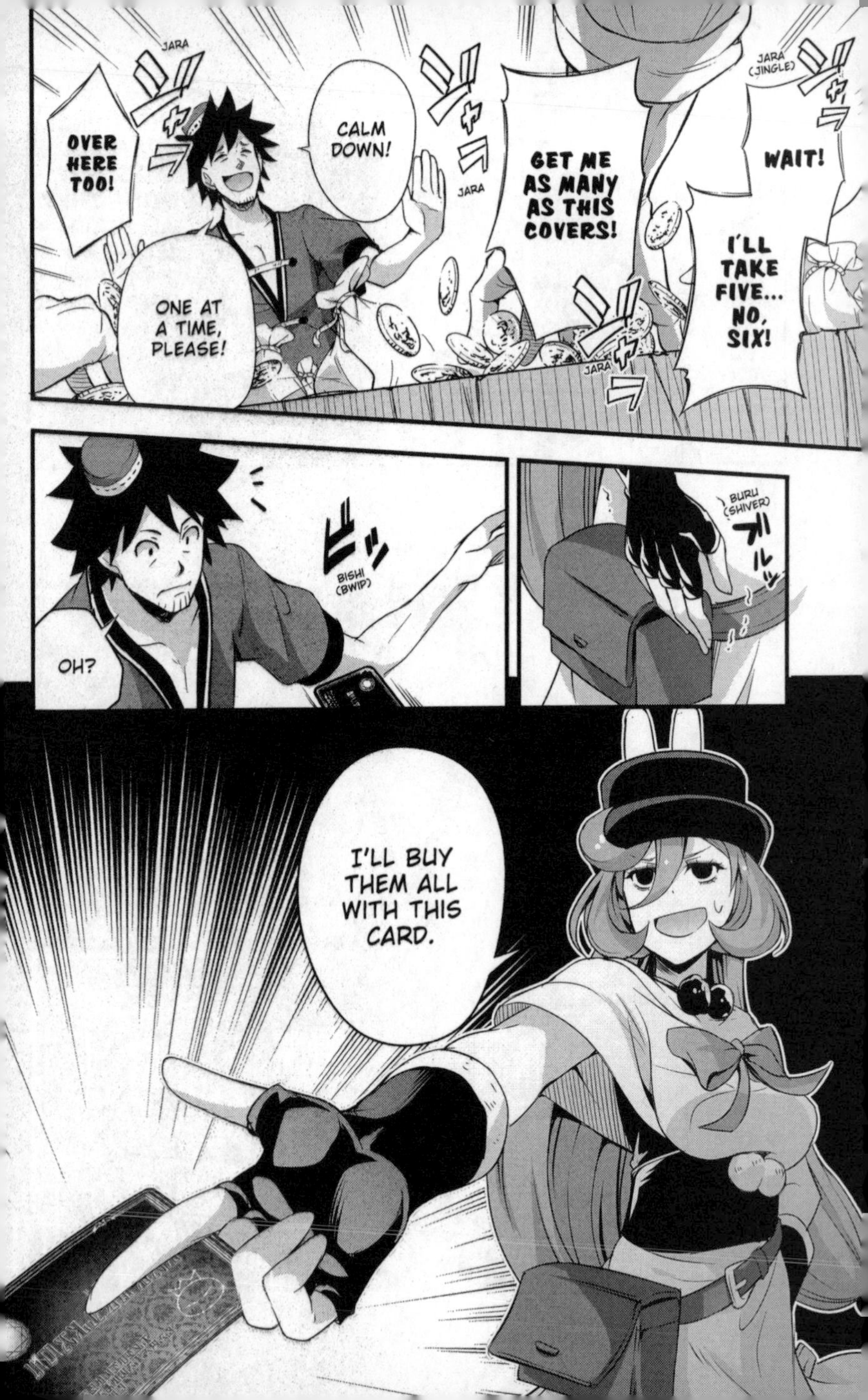
JARA (JINGLE)
WAIT!
I'LL TAKE FIVE... NO, SIX!
JARA
GET ME AS MANY AS THIS COVERS!
JARA
CALM DOWN!
JARA
OVER HERE TOO!
ONE AT A TIME, PLEASE!
BURU (SHIVER)
BISHI (BWIP)
OH?
I'LL BUY THEM ALL WITH THIS CARD.

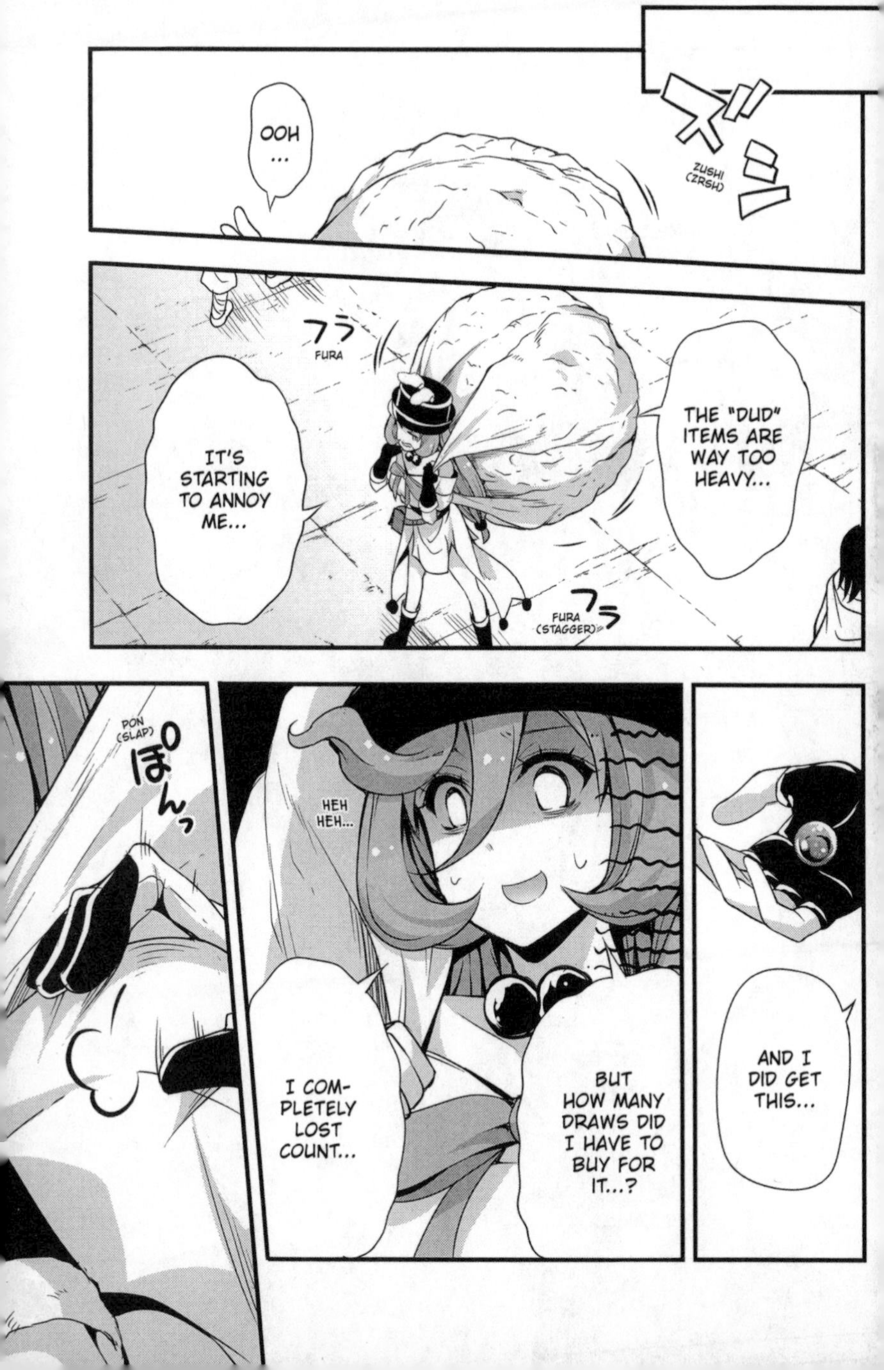
ZUSHI (ZRSH)
OOH ...
THE "DUD" ITEMS ARE WAY TOO HEAVY...
FURA (STAGGER)
FURA
IT'S STARTING TO ANNOY ME...
AND I DID GET THIS...
BUT HOW MANY DRAWS DID I HAVE TO BUY FOR IT...?
I COM-PLETELY LOST COUNT...
HEH HEH...
PON (SLAP)

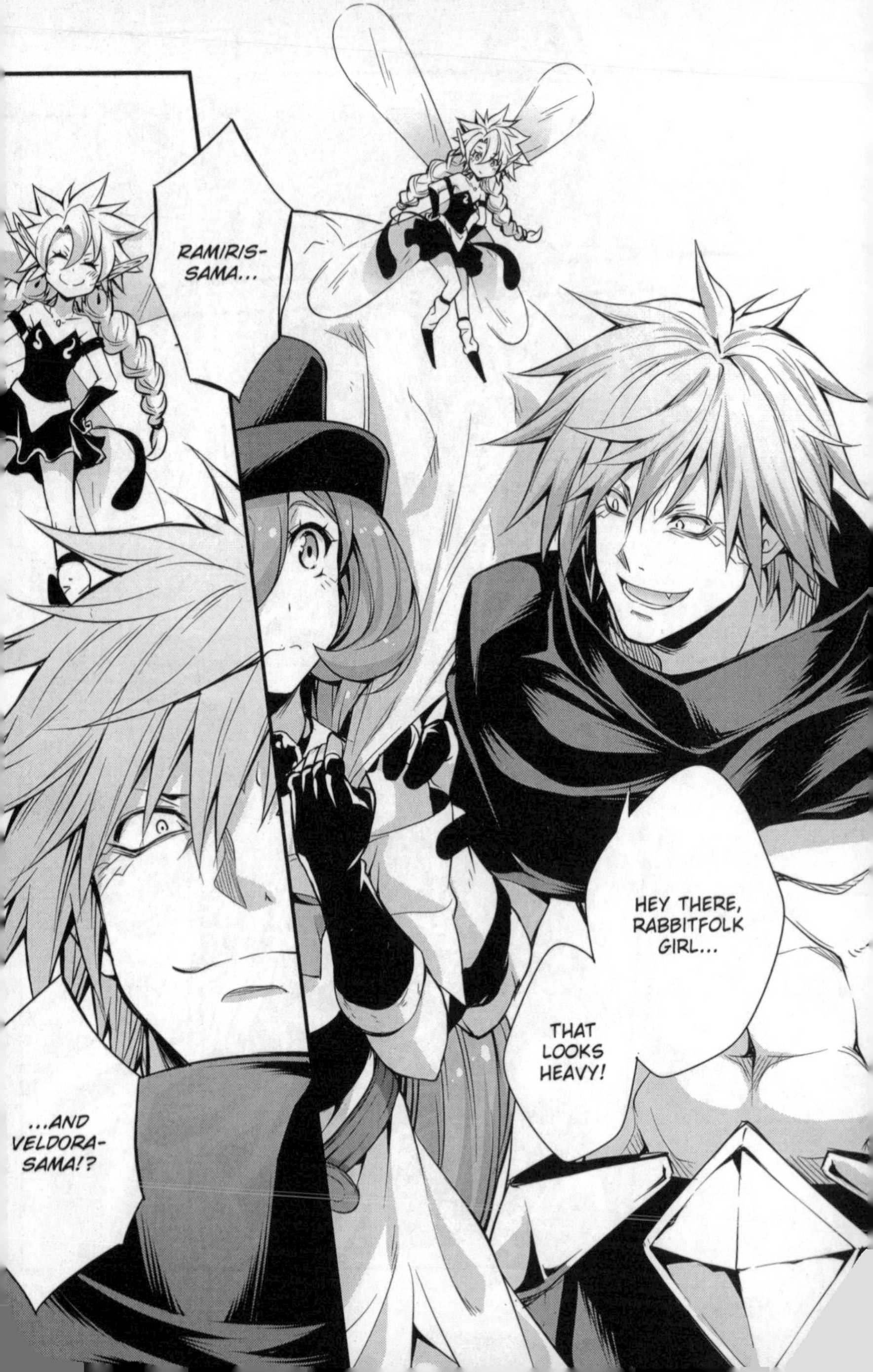
HEY THERE, RABBITFOLK GIRL...
THAT LOOKS HEAVY!
RAMIRIS-SAMA...
...AND VELDORA-SAMA!?

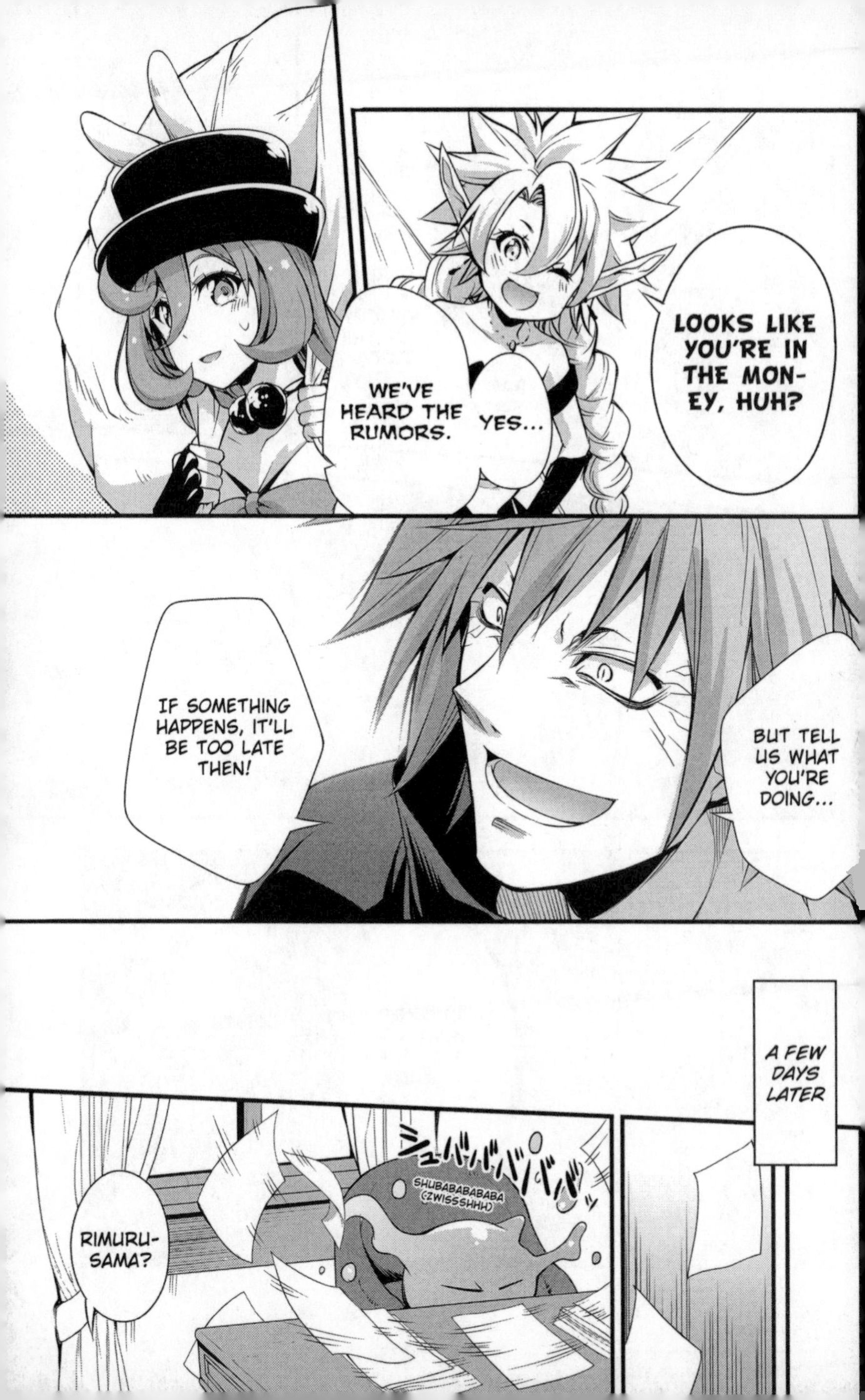
LOOKS LIKE YOU'RE IN THE MON-EY, HUH?
YES...
WE'VE HEARD THE RUMORS.
BUT TELL US WHAT YOU'RE DOING...
IF SOMETHING HAPPENS, IT'LL BE TOO LATE THEN!
A FEW DAYS LATER
シュバババババッ
SHUBABABABABA (ZWISSSHHH)
RIMURU-SAMA?

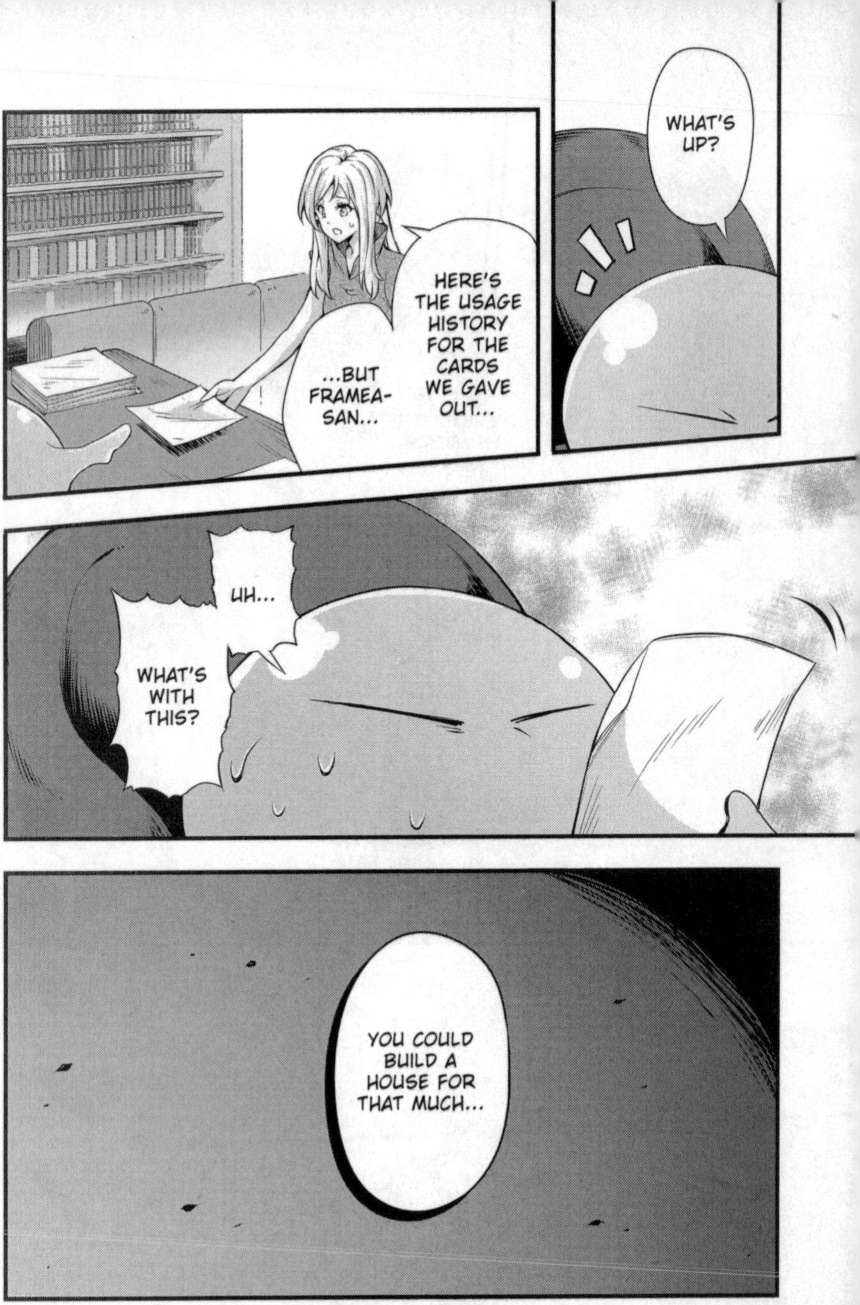
WHAT'S UP?
HERE'S THE USAGE HISTORY FOR THE CARDS WE GAVE OUT...
...BUT FRAMEA-SAN...
UH...
WHAT'S WITH THIS?
YOU COULD BUILD A HOUSE FOR THAT MUCH...

CHAPTER 24☆END

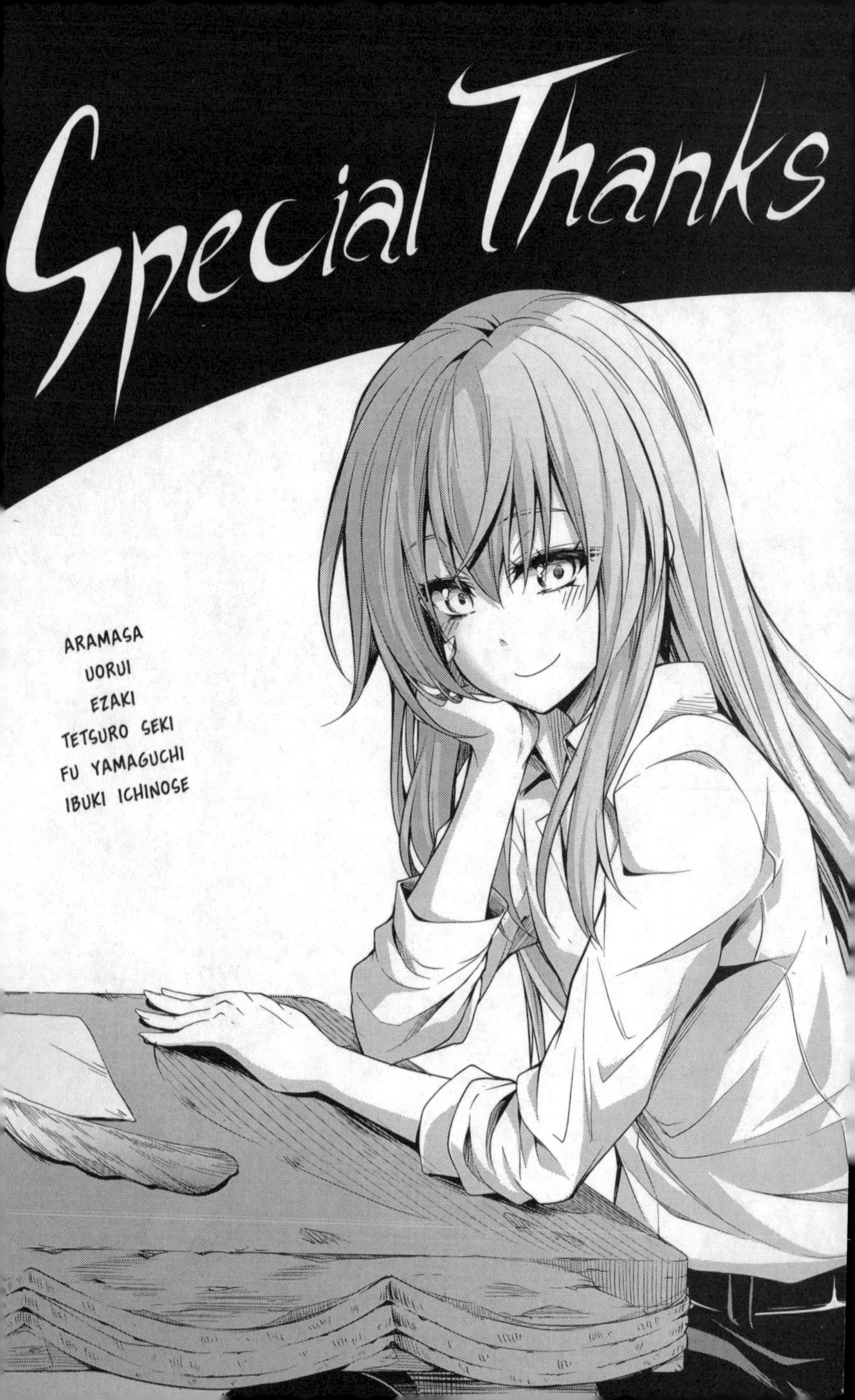
Special Thanks
ARAMASA
UORUI
EZAKI
TETSURO SEKI
FU YAMAGUCHI
IBUKI ICHINOSE

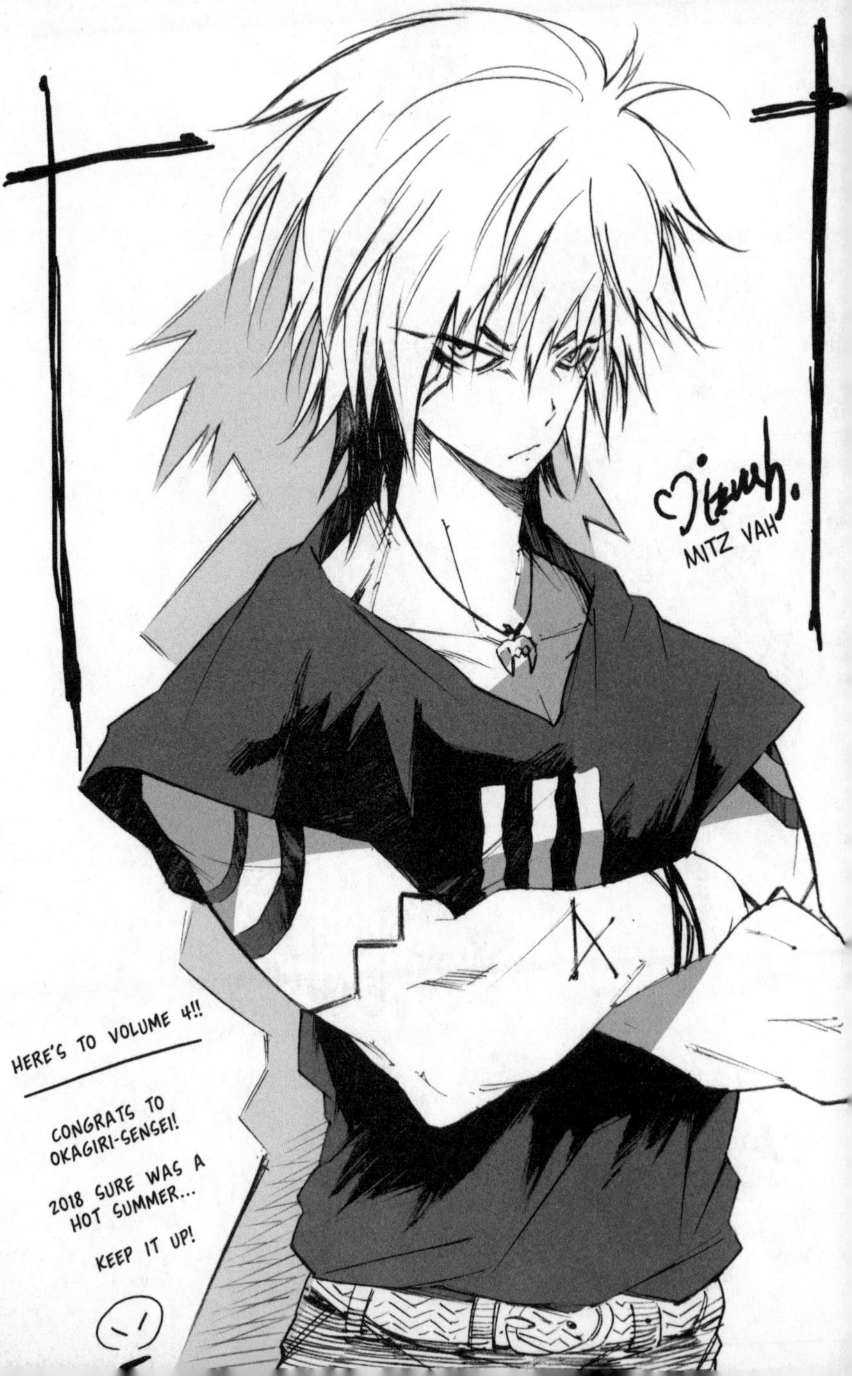
MITZ VAH
HERE'S TO VOLUME 4!!
CONGRATS TO OKAGIRI-SENSEI!
2018 SURE WAS A HOT SUMMER...
KEEP IT UP!

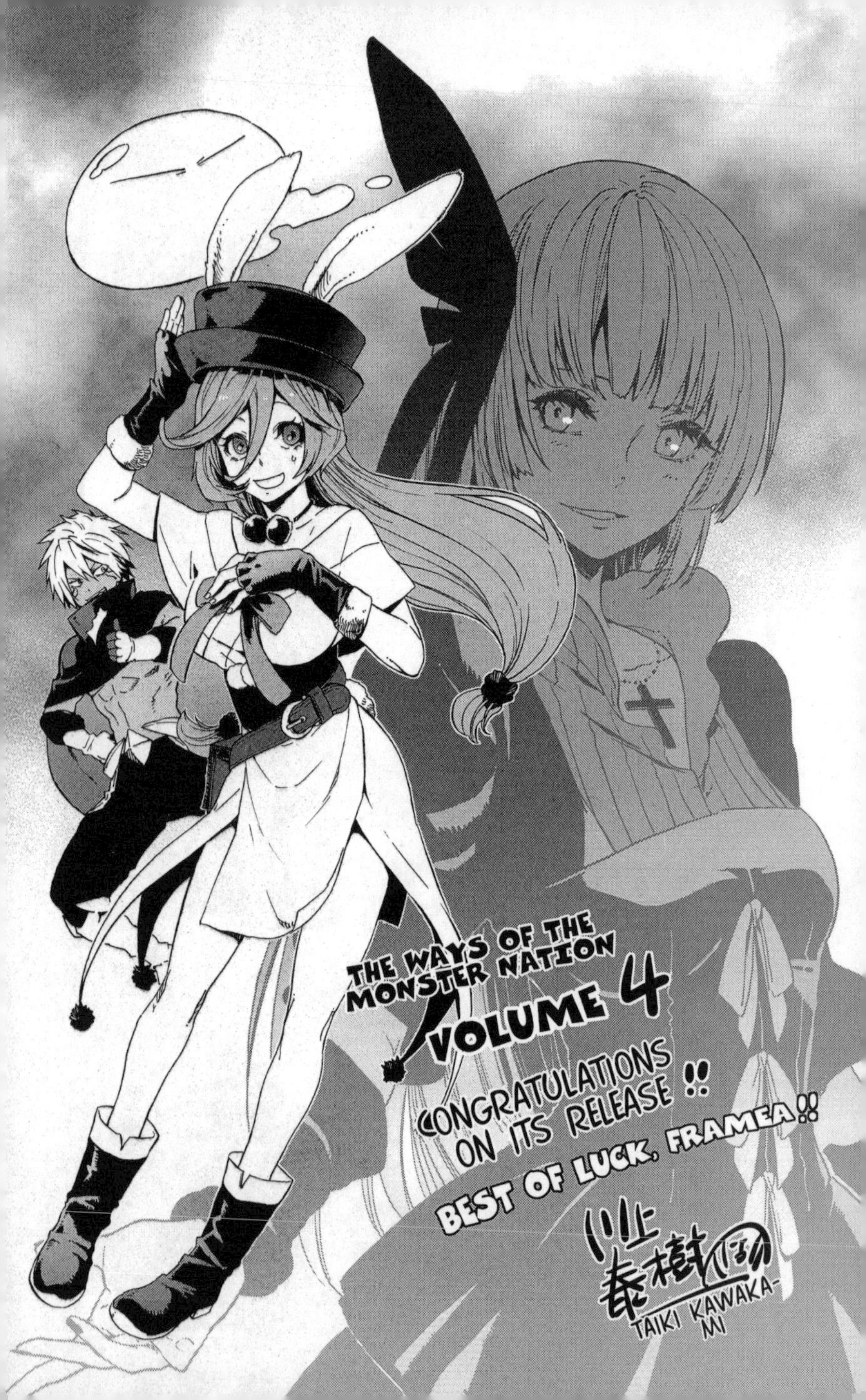

THE WAYS OF THE MONSTER NATION
VOLUME 4
CONGRATULATIONS ON ITS RELEASE !!
BEST OF LUCK, FRAMEA!!
川上春樹
TAIKI KAWAKAMI

THE WAYS OF THE MONSTER NATION
I LOVE BEING GUIDED THROUGH THE MONSTER NATION!!
CONGRATS, OKAGIRI-SENSEI!
2018 SHIBA
HOORAY
VOLUME 4!!

That
Time I Got
Reincarnated
as a
Slime

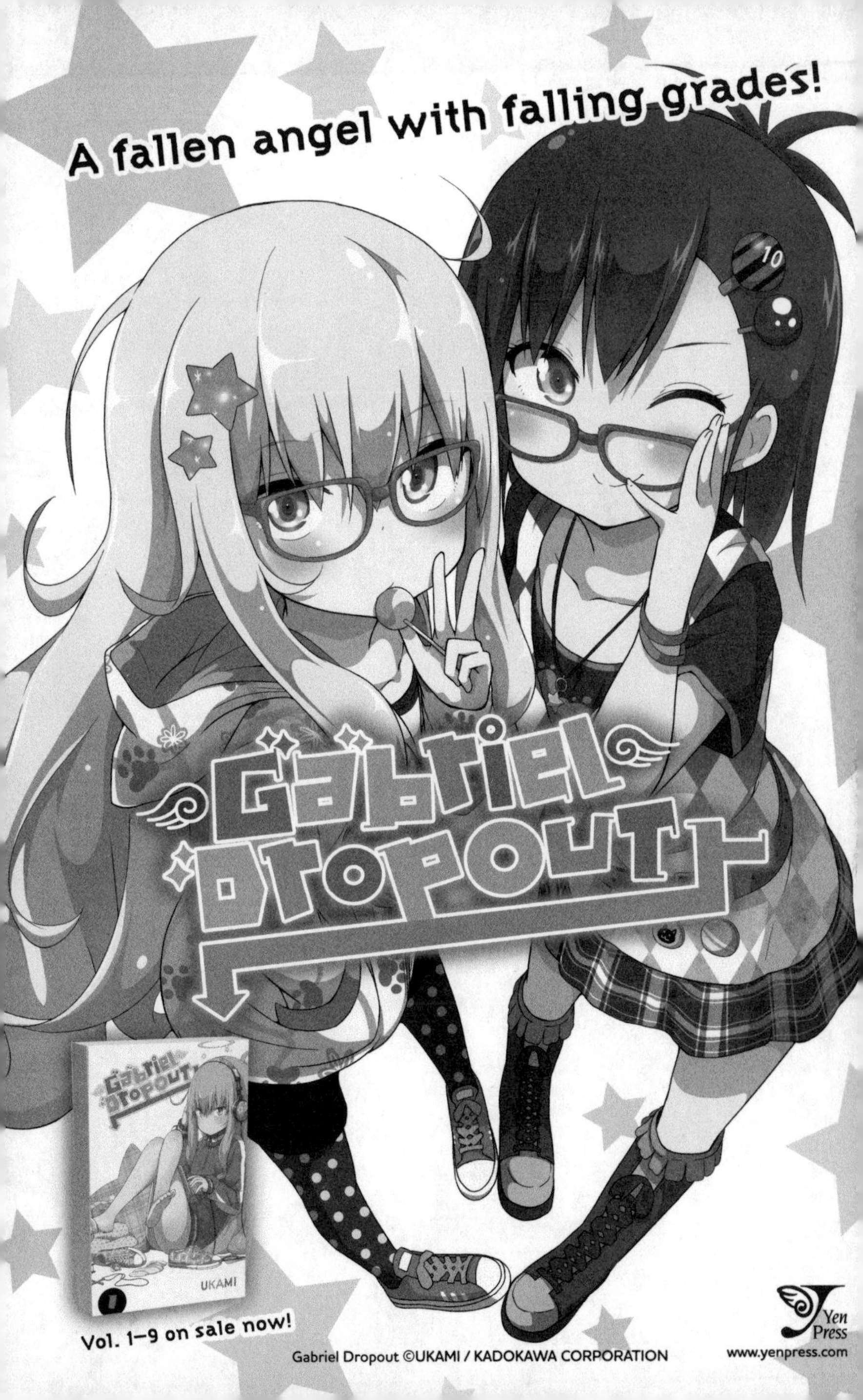

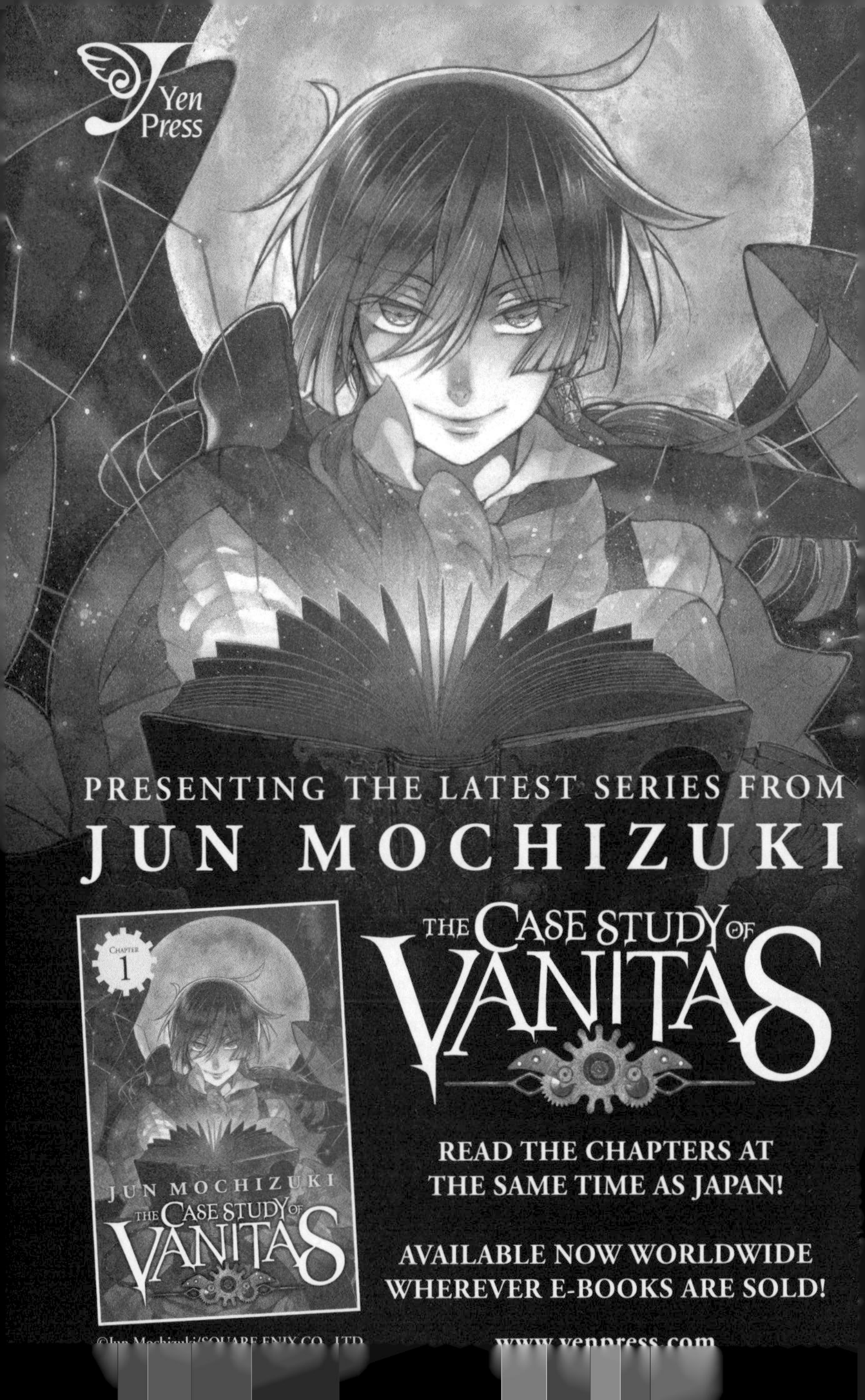

Yen Press
PRESENTING THE LATEST SERIES FROM
JUN MOCHIZUKI
CHAPTER 1
JUN MOCHIZUKI
THE CASE STUDY OF VANITAS
THE CASE STUDY OF VANITAS
READ THE CHAPTERS AT THE SAME TIME AS JAPAN!
AVAILABLE NOW WORLDWIDE WHEREVER E-BOOKS ARE SOLD!
©Jun Mochizuki/SQUARE ENIX CO., LTD.
www.yenpress.com

That Time I Got Reincarnated as a SLIME
The Ways of the Monster Nation
4

Translation: Kevin Gifford • Lettering: Barri Shrager

This book is a work of fiction. Names, characters, places, and
incidents are the product of the author's imagination or are used fictitiously.
Any resemblance to actual events, locales, or persons, living or dead, is coincidental.

TENSEI SHITARA SURAIMU DATTA KEN ~MAMONO NO KUNI NO ARUKIKATA~ Vol. 4
©Fuse 2018
©Sho Okagiri, Mitz Vah 2018
First published in Japan in 2018 by MICRO MAGAZINE, INC.
English translation rights arranged with MICRO MAGAZINE, INC.
through Tuttle-Mori Agency, Inc., Tokyo.

English translation © 2021 by Yen Press, LLC

Yen Press
150 West 30th Street, 19th Floor
New York, NY 10001

Visit us at yenpress.com
facebook.com/yenpress
twitter.com/yenpress
yenpress.tumblr.com
instagram.com/yenpress

First Yen Press Edition: March 2021

Yen Press is an imprint of Yen Press, LLC.
The Yen Press name and logo are trademarks of Yen Press, LLC.

The publisher is not responsible for websites (or their content) that are
not owned by the publisher.

Library of Congress Control Number: 2020936422

ISBNs: 978-1-9753-1360-9 (paperback)
978-1-9753-1359-3 (ebook)

10 9 8 7 6 5 4 3 2 1

BVG

Printed in the United States of America